The Death-Ego
and the Vital Self

The Death-Ego and the Vital Self

Romances of Desire in Literature and Psychoanalysis

Gavriel Reisner (Ben-Ephraim)

Madison • Teaneck
Fairleigh Dickinson University Press
London: Associated University Presses

Associated University Presses
2010 Eastpark Boulevard
Cranbury, NJ 08512

Associated University Presses
Unit 304, The Chandlery
50 Westminster Bridge Road
London SE1 7QY, England

Associated University Presses
P.O. Box 338, Port Credit
Mississauga, Ontario
Canada L5G 4L8

The paper used in this publication meets the requirements of the American National Standard for Permanence of Paper for Printed Library Materials Z39.48-1984.

Library of Congress Cataloging-in-Publication Data

Reisner, Gavriel
The death-ego and the vital self : romances of desire in literature and psychoanalysis / Gavriel Reisner (Ben-Ephraim).
p. cm.
Includes bibliographical references and index.
ISBN 0-8386-3921-6 (alk. paper)
1. English literature—19th century—History and criticism. 2. Psychoanalysis and literature—Great Britain. 3. Lawrence, D. H. (David Herbert), 1885–1930 Sons and lovers. 4. Freud, Sigmund, 1856–1939. Jenseits des Lustprinzips. 5. Psychology in literature. 6. Desire in literature. 7. Death in literature. 8. Self in literature. I. Title.
PR468.P68R45 2003
820.9′355—dc21 2002151740

PRINTED IN THE UNITED STATES OF AMERICA

For Ruth
mixed equally, it will not die

"[Freud surmises that] the deepest satisfactions of literature . . . come from a release of tensions in the psyche. That Freud has found, as almost always, either part of the truth or at least a way to it, is clear enough, even if a student of [Romantic literature] finds . . . this Freudian view to be partial, reductive, and a kind of mirror image of the imagination's truth. The deepest satisfactions of reading [Romantic literature] come from the realizations of new ranges of tensions in the mind."

—Harold Bloom

Contents

Acknowledgments

It took a long time to write this study, and it passed through more than one metamorphosis along the way. Seeking to say something that would "make a difference," reluctant to let go of a kind of radical hopefulness and romantic Freudianism (a 60s-style combination), I can only be grateful that this freighted volume has, in the old-fashioned phrase, seen the light.

In the process I profited from conversations and exchanges with many people. Bill Daleski, Baruch Hochman, Shlomit Rimmon-Kenan, Shuli Barzilai, Peter Jones, Ian Donaldson, Reese Jones, Martin Kayman, Sandra Gilbert, J. Hillis Miller, Shoshana Felman, Harold Bloom, Geoffrey Hartman, Elizabeth Freund, Steven Reisner, Henry Sussman, Hana Wirth-Nesher, Zephyra Porat, Karen Alkalay-Gut, Peter Rudnytsky, Jeffrey M. Green, Debbie Lifschitz, Murray Schwartz, Doris K. Silverman, Earl Ingersoll, Keith Cushman, and Jack Stewart were among the colleagues who helped clarify problems in literature, in psychoanalysis, or in the relationship between the two.

Some of the preparatory work for my book was done at The Institute for Advanced Studies in the Humanities at Edinburgh University on a Sabbatical from Tel Aviv University. I am grateful to both institutions for that opportunity. The staff at Fairleigh Dickinson University Press / Associated University Presses, particularly Harry Keyishian, Martin Green, Julien Yoseloff, and Christine Retz have been encouraging and cooperative throughout.

Going back to an earlier period, after completing my doctorate I undertook a course of Theoretical Studies at the Israel Institute for Psychoanalysis in Jerusalem. At the institute, one particularly gifted candidate stood out. (She was a woman with a beautiful mind, but it wasn't the beauty of her mind that I first noticed.) Ruth Stein became a colleague and friend during those studies, more than twenty years ago, and recently became my wife. Ruth's involvement in my book showed characteristic energy and focus and demanded, implicitly, a corresponding rigor on the part of the writer. A writer who was grateful, at the same time, to benefit from a partner whose dedication to creative activity included a practical insistence on getting the job done.

Acknowledgments are due to Laurence Pollinger Limited and the Estate of Frieda Lawrence Ravagli, and also to Cambridge University Press and the Viking Press for permission to quote from the published works of D. H. Lawrence.

Parts of chs. 2 and 7 appeared as "The Disappearing Drive: Rereading Literature and Psychoanalaysis / Lawrence and Freud" in *Rereading Texts / Rethinking Critical Presuppositions, Essays in Honour of H. M. Daleski,* edited by Shlomith Rimmon-Kenan, Leona Toker, and Shuli Barzilai (Frankfurt: Peter Lang, 1997): 101–18. Thanks are due to the editors and publisher for permission to use this material.

Ch. 3 was first published as "On Freud's 'Negation' and Keats's 'Negative Capability': The Secret Affinities of Metapsychology and Romance" in *Literature and Psychology* 33, 4 (fall 1997): 16–44. Thanks are due to the editors of that journal for permission to reprint the essay.

Permission for the use of the cover illustration, *Blind Spot*, comes from the artist Larry Abramson, and Linda Zisquit, curator of the *Artspace* gallery, Jerusalem.

The Death-Ego and the Vital Self

1

Introduction: The Romance of Desire, or the Unattainable in Twenty-Nine Takes

I

A SIMPLIFIED NOTION OF DESIRE UNDERLIES MODERN CRITIQUES OF romance. Northrop Frye describes romance as a genre marked by its "perennially childlike quality . . . its extraordinarily persistent nostalgia, its search for some kind of imaginative golden age."[1] His definition of romance as a "wish-fulfillment dream" relies on the language and thought of early psychoanalytic texts like *The Interpretation of Dreams* (1901) and "Creative Writers and Daydreaming (1908)."[2] Frye's "golden" romance derives from Freud's affirmations of pleasure as the motive for narrative and narrative as the anticipation of reality. Based on early psychoanalytic theory, Frye's attractive fantasy of a pleasure-romance is a creation of his own romance with romance. His "nostalgic" genre cites Freud's unitary concept of psychic motivation. In the earlier phase of psychoanalysis, our unconscious drives (expressed in our motives) and our unconscious fantasies (expressed in our dreams) take *pleasure* as their ultimate goal.

II

Frye advances criticism by uniting a *genre*, the romance, and a *psychic state*, the search for the satisfaction of a want (in both

---

Theoretical Forenote: This is about our need to study the connections between romance and desire more closely. We can achieve this by examining Freud's presentation of desire in Beyond the Pleasure Principle. *Freud's essay, both a reading and a rendering of desire, contains five fragments of Romantic narrative which, taken together, compose a psychoanalytic romance. Lacan helps us bridge drive and desire.*

senses of the word).[3] The acceptance of pleasure as the motive for narrative makes Frye's critique unsatisfying. After the epochal formulations of *Beyond the Pleasure Principle* Freud abandons his belief in an encompassing pleasure-law. He becomes obsessed with the dualistic theory of the drives, its clash of opposing needs. Enigmatically, Freud hardly applies his ideas about inner forces to outer creations. He rarely integrates the death drive into readings of fantasy or interpretations of art.[4] That which finds scant articulation in practical criticism emerges as a gap, not to say an *abyss*, in psychoanalytic theory: Freud never modifies the simple early conception of the pleasure-dream by the complex later idea of conflicted desire. Orthodox post-Freudianism widens the gap by resisting the death-drive altogether and dismissing or at least condescending to one of Freud's most evocative ideas. (Heretical branches of psychoanalysis, Lacanian and Kleinian, take the death-drive seriously, but these are other psychoanalytic schools, other clusters of psychoanalytic narrative.) Literary critics repeat a major oversight of psychoanalytic thought by avoiding the dissonances of the later forces. Critics of romance—Frye, Jameson, Parker—repeat Freud's original lapse. Their work advances our understanding of a genre, but accepts a reductive view of its motive.

III

Freud's radical essay of 1920 enriches our understanding of human motivation. The new conception doubles the older, presenting destruction and creation as objects of fantasy, death and life as goals of desire. The dark demands of *Beyond the Pleasure Principle* and the bright quests of earlier theory lend themselves to a critical reading of the way psychic motive translates into literary expression.

IV

The new approach allows the tracing of not only expressive form but compressive energy, not only the opposing elements of the divided drives but the force of division itself. Splitting the drives, Freud breaks down, reconsiders, and recreates the elements of psychic motivation. The dividing and reforming of the dualistic drives, the entrance into a theory of uncontrolled energies, justifies the application of the non-Freudian term, *desire*, to describe the revised motive-theory.

V

Desire is a Lacanian word condensing Freudian "wish" and "drive" while adding an elusive supplement, a reference to the seeking of that which cannot be found.[5] In the relationship of drive and desire Lacan makes explicit that which is already implied in Freud. Freud introduces that which cannot be found, or that which is impossible to fulfill, in the very naming of the drives. The drive, *Trieb* in German, is a metaphor referring to pulsation or push of energy. The psychoanalytical definition divides the drive into a series of elements contributing to the experience of the body-in-the-mind, the representation of the physical in the psychical.[6] Yet the metaphorical term *Trieb,* correctly translated by the metaphor "drive," deconstructs the elaborate Freudian drive-structure (*instinct*, the more "scientific" term is less useful because more restricted). By the use of a figurative term, Freud implies that the power impelling human action *resembles* a drive. The term "drive" already enfolds an absence, because it always refers partially to that which the describing word is not. In metaphor something is said indirectly because it could not be said directly. We say $a' = b'$ because we cannot say a' definitively. The metaphorical signifier is another word in a series created by the lack of a successful reality-apprehending word, the word of original signification that does not, that perhaps can not, exist. Metaphor inevitably enfolds an elision

VI

The literary technique of metaphor reveals the absence within the drive, yet metaphor is a technique of language aspiring to pure lyricism, transcending time in its search for universal significance. Probing the drives more deeply requires working with action as well as meaning. Another literary technique, imaginative narrative—that is, stories partially created, aesthetic improvements on actual experience—shows the drives working in temporal and social contexts. If we cannot know what a drive is, perhaps we can know what a drive does. We can know the drive *by* the one who is driven. This allows us to suggest that *the driven figure reveals the figured drive*.

VII

We have said that the drive contains within itself an absence; it becomes a readable presence when seen not in its theoretical meaning but in its actual expression. We read the drive not as a separate idea but as action or feeling connected to the driven figure. In *Beyond the Pleasure Principle*, Freud opens a Pandora's box of contradictory energies working against themselves, and working against their bearer, the figure, or character, in narrative. The drives create opposed forces like love and death, ego and reproduction, isolation and connection, the going forward and the going backward. This is not to mention the middle ground between polar forces—for what is between life and death? Perhaps the figure who experiences them.

VIII

The "figure" (an incalculably rich word) in narrative refers to a metaphor or a form or a symbolic character, that is a character who represents or "figures" something else. One of the few elements of fiction that the word figure cannot re/present is "character." A realistic character who brings a fully individuated self to bear on decisions and actions is not a "figure."[7] Such a character does not stand for something else: he is him or herself, a dramatized man or woman no longer a figure in a literary scheme but a person in a fictional world, a center of a realized mimesis. By the classic Freudian structure the realistic character is based on the ego while the romance character is closer to id, superego, or ego-ideal. Romantic fictions trace a struggle between, first, romance figures as representations subject to desire, dramatized persons who move toward the figurative because they signify abstractions, and, second, full characters who, rather than being subjects of desire, can subject desire to a more stable principle of self. The realistic character can possess himself in such a way as to reign over desire. It is not that he is not prone to desire, but that he is not *a figure of desire*. He is not dominated by what he lacks.

IX

What is the desire we find once we traverse both *Beyond the Pleasure Principle* and the Lacanian variations on wanting (themselves immensely influenced by *Beyond the Pleasure Principle*)? Desire remains an elusive abstraction. We may say that we know desire by the one who desires, we know desire by the desirer, and to understand him we turn to romance—a narrative burdened by what it wants. The more we read romance, the more we realize that one of the things wanted is a singularity of purpose. Hence, Patricia Parker deconstructs the romance as an imaginative narrative of *ambivalent desire*, its motives both attained and denied by "a form which simultaneously quests for and postpones a particular end."[8] My study begins with romance as the literary expression of divided desire, projecting conflicts to engage opposing wishes and clashing fantasies.

X

I wish to formulate the relationship between desire and romance so as to focus the encounter between literature and psychoanalysis. The challenge is to find the bridge across 1) our knowledge of the mind as it pertains to motivation, and 2) that literary genre whose descriptions and actions are about the search to satisfy a want—a lack, a craving. One formula might read: If desire is the implied energy of romance, romance is the implied form of desire.

XI

Romance is the genre whose most serious challenges exist not at the beginning, where we are in the position of lack, nor at the end, where we are in the position of gain, but the middle, as we learn to negotiate the transition. We can say that we find romance in those narratives whose events and figures are pervaded with longing, and that such longing has a strong figurative influence. We alter the perceived by the sought. Hence, the romance beginning of "far away and long ago" alerts us to an excursion beyond close empirical examination. A clear example is found in Chaucer, who surely anticipates the realistic novel with his close reading of character in the "General Prologue," but who releases the reader's imagination by evoking early Feudalism and Chivalric valorization in "The Knight's Tale." After Chaucer we encounter the fullness of Spenserian romance, with its magical occurrences, supernatural beings, and carefully layered allegorical meanings. Yet, the plots of such romances proceed as their central wishes are *not* fulfilled, for romance is more about the frustration than the fulfillment of wishes. Later psychoanalytic theory suggests that the blocks to satisfaction are internal, not external, that the obstacles to the fulfillment of desire are inherent in the nature of desire.

XII

The imbrication of desire and romance bridges literary and psychoanalytic texts. The view of desire as energy and romance as form may organize the connection, or attraction, between novelistic romances (like *Wuthering Heights* and *Jane Eyre*) and a work of romantic psychoanalysis (like *Beyond the Pleasure Principle*). *The Uncanny* falls into the romantic category as does Lacan's *Four Fundamental Principles of Psychoanalysis*. The novelistic romance is activated by the play of conflicting desires in a vexed and dynamic form, while the psychoanalytic romance presents in a play of conflicting forms vexed and dynamic energies.

XIII

The connection between novelistic and psychoanalytic romances provides the reason for my working with later (romantic to modern) novelistic romances rather than earlier formal romance. In the novelistic romance desire encounters stronger outer structures (I refer to the social surface of experience) than in medieval or Renaissance romance. The struggle between desire and strong social surfaces in novelistic romance resembles Freud's description of the struggle between the drives and the demands of the surrounding world. Thus the strong social surface that opposes the wishes of desire in novelistic romance finds a precise analogue in psychoanalytic theory.

XIV

Still, we want to know more about the wishes of desire. Lacanian language records the transformation of drive, a motivation which traces the human need for satisfaction, to desire, a motivation which traces the human need for signification.[9] In Lacan, desire exceeds the drives of the body and spills over to our relationship with language. Combining Freud and Lacan, we would say that desire is about language and the body and that desire is the language of the body but also the body of language.

XV

Lacan's desire links a series of representations, a play of signifiers where the objects of the drives fade and disappear, disassemble and change places. This representation series is implied by the Freudian theory of the unconscious with its ideas of displacement and condensation in fantasy and experience. It is within this larger theoretical context, this increase in the meaning and reading of the drives, that we realize that human beings have complex objects of desire, conscious and unconscious, and that the sought object and the found object are (almost) never the same. Lacan amplifies Freud on the question of return, of going back to an original object of desire. Combining psychoanalysis and linguistics Lacan focuses (not that he ever exactly focuses) on the question of the two categories of objects. In Lacan, objects of desire divide between the signified and its signifiers. The reachable signifier is a representation (*only* a representation) of the unreachable signified, the object we really want but cannot have, while the signifier is the object we can "have" but do not really want. We signify our losses.

XVI

This release of desire into language is the Lacanian supplement to Freud. The greater flexibility of "desire" over "drive" enables Lacan to present lack as explicit in the presentations (absentations) of desire. Where Freud takes the drive as energy targeted at a present object, Lacan takes desire as energy directed toward an absent object. Desire always contains its own (Freudian) negation. This is because of the structure of the psychoanalytic quest with its simultaneous conscious and unconscious objects. Lacan is convinced that the unconscious object is undiscoverable, that the imago itself reveals an absence, so that the Mother is that which is not, the *manque a être*.[10] The Lacanian goal is the lack-of-an-object, the signifying representation in the unconscious that points to something that language can never attain and contain. Moreover, the actual return to the maternal image would entail a collapse of autonomy;

the return to that which is beyond language would exact a psychic cost in the collapse of being.

XVII

So the play of objects, the signifiers, exists above a kind of final prohibited object, which is not part of the play, the signified. Now at this point the Lacanian registers of human experience, the Imaginary, Symbolic, and Real orders of being, come into play (the centrality of the word "play" in Freudian-Lacanian thought derives to no small degree from the boy's *fort/da* game in *Beyond the Pleasure Principle*). What Lacan calls the Symbolic is precisely the fall into language and its "play of signifiers." (It is a loss of the Paradise of the All, oneness with the universe and the Mother, the very word F/all suggesting the intrusion of the Father into the wholeness between Mother and child.) At the same time the Imaginary is the continuing search for the signified, for the point before the fall into language and its necessary distinctions. If the Symbolic is about the verbal play of language, the Imaginary projects the visual signifiers returning to the original signified. The signified itself exists only in the omniscient and catastrophic Real, the not-to-be-articulated signified, and yet the Imaginary has a special bond to the Real. The goal of the Imaginary is the original object of desire who exists in the Real as a catastrophic fantasy. He or she can only be reached in terrifying or spellbinding experiences. In the Imaginary the subject feels unborn, yet a terrible beauty is born.

XVIII

When we turn to the Lacanian orders, we recognize that Freud supplements Lacan no less than Lacan supplements Freud. To make some distinctions in a system that can be very obfuscated, I propose that there is an intrinsic link between the Imaginary and the death drive, on the one hand, and the Symbolic and the life drive, on the other. Once we bring Lacan and Freud together in this way we make some crucial distinctions between the energies, actions, and expressions of desire. The crucial point about the Lacanian orders inheres in the suggestion that not all desire is equally desirous. If we turn to the series of signifiers we find that if the Symbolic signifiers involve play (in both senses of the word), the Imaginary signified involves a yield (in both senses of the word). To return to the signified is to regress to a point that predates choice, to backtrack to the point that precedes the possibility of play. When we regress to the Imaginary, we turn from our own desire. Lacan finds desire in the Symbolic, and claims that we find desire in recognition of the desire of the other, "that man's desire is the desire of the Other" (*É*, 264). The corollary is that we lose our empowering relation to desire if we subordinate it to the other. If the Symbolic progresses by the finding and making of desire, the Imaginary is a regress involving the losing and undoing of desire. Imaginary desire is altered to another category of wanting because it is attached to a prohibited object. He or she dominates the forbidden desire that becomes, therefore, vexed and disturbed. In the Imaginary desire is transformed to a category I will call anti-desire,[11] desire against desire, belonging to a subject who becomes a non-subject in his troubled wanting.

XIX

Of course, there is such a thing as Imaginary desire, but the difference between the Imaginary and the Symbolic is the difference between the flow or course of desire and the goal or source of desire. To go to the source is to go against the current. The Imaginary is about resistance to the course of desire, the stilling of a current in midstream. The Imaginary that begins from within desire must, because of internal injunctions, realize itself against desire, must finally take form as the desire to cease desiring. The hypnotic quality of the Imaginary appears in late Victorian and early modern art—in for instance certain Symbolist and Pre-Raphaelite paintings[12]—while the dynamism of the Symbolic finds its fullest expression in literary narrative. Static image and dynamic narrative combine in novels and films to create an exciting intercourse of the Imaginary and the Symbolic.

XX

Yet let us beware: the Imaginary rarely brings us to the source itself for that is to bring us into the Real. To come to the source of desire is to come to an elusive order that cannot be locked into any image. We recognize the Real not because it is, in Percy Shelley's word, "imageless" (when reached it finds its images), but because of the shattering affects it produces.

XXI

As we have seen, the Lacanian orders enable the formulation of some literary-generic distinctions. The movement against the current, the static holding to original objects of desire, refers to mythic goals. I would take the mythic as a version of a basic psychic story remaining close to primary process and intimate with regression.[13] In literature the mythic is rigid, static, terrible: it awaits at the climaxes of Greek tragedy. The mythic achieves the paradox of narrative-dramatic stasis, a stillness of catastrophe; it gives verbal form to our deepest images of fear. But the fluidity of the Symbolic expresses itself in the varied desires of altering forms. The Symbolic empowers the subtle complexity of romance, yielding more fluid narratives not restricted to the mythic action that is bordered by terror. We are within the calmer borders of romance so long as the characters are motivated and the events are dominated by a pervasive wanting. The kingdom of romance is ruled by desire. We step outside the kingdom of desire, and outside the formal considerations of the present study, when the narrative entails that self-conscious critique of desire that characterizes the realistic novel.[14]

XXII

In the mythic romance of the Imaginary we return to original objects in a kind of trance. When the struggle is lost we are relegated to pure myth. On the other hand, the novelistic romance based on the life-drive and the Symbolic moves away from myth. So we encounter two clusters of concepts. The death-drive, the Imaginary, and mythic romance (on the way to myth) on the one hand, and the life-drive, the Symbolic and novelistic romance (on the way to the novel) on the other. My conception of novelistic romance encompasses Lawrentian notions concerning the inherent vitality of the novel, while mythic romance evokes stories of stasis and return recalling figures like Oedipus and Narcissus. *Oedipus the King* neither transcends nor elaborates myth but rather employs dramatic form for a devastating statement about the inescapability of myth. Oedipus puts out his eyes when fate crushes desire. Mythic power moves backward, short-circuiting narrative possibility to assert that the source of desire holds the death of desire.

The present study focuses on neither the rigid fatality of myth nor the lucid, perhaps satirical, self-consciousness of the novel, but instead on various mediated points between. We can perhaps approach novelistic romance with Lawrentian ideas in mind, agreeing with Lawrence that the life within "the living novel" is the life of desire. Yet Lawrence would not have written so eloquently about the vital novel had he not been conversant with deathly myth. Imaginary myth involves the return to original objects, where death awaits on the icy slope, while Symbolic romance demands an effort of climbing, an energy.

XXIII

It should be clear by now that desire takes contradictory forms because it poses a conflict, a struggle of desire against anti-desire. Freud formulates this conflict in the profound but broad terms of life against death, while the Lacanian categories are formulated with a deliberate obscurity that restricts their usefulness. I find that the forms of desire are communicated most compellingly, not in such theoretical expositions as those developed in *Beyond the Pleasure Principle* and elsewhere,[15] but in the narratives of psychoanalysis. The narratives of *Beyond the Pleasure Principle* develop in the course of its exposition, yet, like expository wild cards, they develop an independent life of their own. They are achieved in the literary techniques of metaphor and metonymy, in dreams and the reading of the dream, in dramatized actions which become "fictional" when interpreted as representative of human action and motivation. I believe that the large principles of life and death, and Imaginary and Symbolic, can be filled in, finessed and gradated, through a reading of the fragments of narrative in psychoanalytic texts. In such fragments the theory of desire begins to turn into a narrative reality of desire. I seek the nuclei of romance narrative, the germinal tissue of the romance story in original recitations with an almost organic capacity for growth. I take all my germinating narratives from *Beyond the Pleasure Principle*, although similar or related elements may be found elsewhere in psychoanalysis or in other disciplines. But *Beyond the Pleasure Principle*, as an essay on desire, perforce turns to narrative.

XXIV

There are five such fragments in *Beyond the Pleasure Principle*, but I shall reserve the listing of them for a chapter on that essay, for to name the fragments is to develop the meaning of each. I will say here that they divide overall into two categories: four narratives of return are aligned against a single narrative of advance. The narratives of return are regressive stories. They consist of a (reading of) dream, a game, a drama, and a romance. In each case, the return includes the embracing-again of original pain (I avoid the ungainly term "unpleasure," whose linguistic structure valorizes pleasure). The regressive stories activate the Imaginary in narrative enactments of the death drive. Freud brings the Imaginary forward in various genres to suggest the universality of the death drive. The four fragmented narratives on death and the Imaginary are about the desire to return to an absence. One of my strictures against Freud's reading refers to his understanding of return as the desire to transform absence to presence. I contend that return is a desire for absence itself. I also claim—as already intimated, but it is an important point that bears repeating—that the motivating force of return is not actually desire. Rather, romance develops from a strange motive operating against desire because of unconscious fear and hatred of desire.

XXV

Beyond the Pleasure Principle shows one story of life. That story takes the form of an original biological romance describing the genesis of being, a genesis it reproduces in a record of biological experiments and in philosophical love poetry borrowed from Plato's *Symposium* and the Hindu *Upanishads*. This bold and eclectic exposition is Freud's only true narrative of desire. That he uses so very eccentric a genre is puzzling only at first. For what he does, perhaps in a completing inversion of the Platonic search for a transcendent ideal, is seek the irreducible origin of human wanting. He stresses the significance of "conjugation," of "amphimixis," in the organic origins of life-reproduction. I take the significance of this as relating, in "the figurative language" of biology with its "unlimited possibilities" (6:60), to the necessity of transcending, in the sense of exceeding the borders of, the individual organism in the generation of life. As a philosophical elaboration of the significance of the trans-individual force of regeneration I speculate on this notion (it is philosophical psychoanalysis, true metapsychology disguised as biology) as the originating spark of what has come to be known as the Sartrean-Lacanian "other." The other raises the difficult psycho-philosophical question of recognizing an existence outside the conscious self, the differences between the *en-soi* and *pour-soi* in Sartre, which Lacan subsequently reworks in his psychoanalytic schematics of the "o/Other." The point of Freud's bio-narrative is that life comes first *from* the other but most of all *with* the other, for only through intimate physical union with another can the recrudescence of vitality occur. Of course, this is hardly a new idea in itself, but Freud brings it down to the origins of biological life in a scientific parable about single-celled organisms, which he then applies to universal life by way of Platonic philosophy. Through some metaphorical alchemy biological process becomes psychological knowledge and leads to Love. Our intrinsic bodily wanting of this vivifying union-in-otherness is desire, life-desire, felt as a spark, an equality, a balance. Other forms of desire exist in opposition to this true desire. The clash of desire against anti-desire proliferates in various forms and genres of romance.

XXVI

D. H. Lawrence is the romantic novelist who most resists writing romances, taking romance as a dreamlike and unreal fiction, its world pervaded by the wishes that alter reality. The paradox develops because Lawrence affirms the life-drive so strenuously, investing his deepest conscious energies in the romance motif that crosses from the text to the world. It is for the same reason that the life-romance *Jane Eyre* seems to be a less "pure" romance than *Wuthering Heights*, even as Emily Brontë is more skillful than Charlotte at integrating realistic elements into her text. What do I mean by a "pure" romance? A pure romance is one that finds its resolution in literary expression itself. On the other hand another order of romance, life-romance, finds its resolution in an extratextual reality (or dream of reality). Therefore, between the death-drive and the live-drive, the death-drive constitutes the weaker desire but yields the stronger romance. The death-drive thrives in the text of the novel because it is fulfilled in the text of the psyche. That is, its objects are textual objects, psychic or literary. The forbidden object of desire does not constitute an other but remains a part of the self, part of the self that the ego, in an operation of narcissistic love, takes as its own object. The psyche as a system of images and words, operating according to both the Imaginary and the Symbolic orders, is a self-enclosed system, a closed text because its objects are internal, original, unconscious. The romance hero who goes back to original objects stays within himself. This same notion of a closed system, problematic and even antilife out in the world works forcefully in literature, and can produce extremely significant literature, precisely because of its coherent integrity (this does not mean simplicity). The life-drive, however, does not remain restricted to either the psyche that originates it or the text that expresses it; unfaithful to its original objects it moves beyond enclosures, impelled toward the other who waits outside. Thus, if the death-drive triumphs, as in *Wuthering Heights*, the romance is fulfilled, but if the life-drive triumphs, as in *Jane Eyre*, the romance is over.

XXVII

In literary (as opposed to actual) terms, and in relation to the achievements of romance, neither of the Lacanian orders is preferable to the other. One of the paradoxes of a literary reading of these categories concerns the attractions of the death-direction, the force of the lesser desire—nothing is more haunting that our desire to come to the end of desiring. My chapter on "Negation and Negative Capability" emphasizes the tonalities of death in literary romance.

XXVIII

The distinction between desire in the Symbolic and non-desire (the desire not to desire) in the Imaginary, may be useful in terms of a crucial issue in literary-psychoanalytical studies. I shall employ this distinction to refer to the question of *the-name-of-the-subject*, the problem of how to designate the subject at the center of our discussion. The Lacanian "subject," the Freudian "ego," and the post-Freudian "self," will all be employed in the terminology of the present study, but they shall be employed according to a procedure of my own, a metapsychology I have developed from the interreading of literature and psychoanalysis. I take the subject to be a kind of neutral center of experience, not only as the speaking subject, but as the feeling subject and the remembering subject as well. I suggest that the subject is often subject to the ego, the force of will and energy whose task is the protection of the organism. Yet the subject can find autonomy by reaching selfhood. The subject becomes a self by unifying with desire.

XXIX

The sense of self, the experience of self, seems to me inseparable from what Freud and Lacan together present as desire; the self is the gift of desire (not the other way around). *The self is the desiring self*; the self is a self only when it desires; desire creates the self. To put it in Blakean language, *the desirer* is the heart of the subject, for while the ego's desire not to desire can subsume self, *desire is self*. Finding the self in its desire is the goal of life-romance; mourning the self lost to the ego is the force of death-romance.

2

Desire and Anti-Desire in *Beyond the Pleasure Principle*

Psychoanalytic Romance

Romance has been described as the quest toward a goal that both reveals and conceals its identity.[1] Yet the ambivalence of romance concerns, also, the direction its hero takes. For he is one who seems *directionless*, one who simultaneously quests toward and away from the very same objects. What does he wish to find and what does he wish to lose? In his perplexing *Beyond the Pleasure Principle*,[2] Freud appears to serve two mistresses: one familiarly beautiful, named "pleasure," the other, too elusive to have a proper name, called "the beyond." Like a bewildered knight of romance he takes a path of deviations and retreats, approaching and avoiding each beloved in turn.

In his discursive *work* (Lacan, a younger French knight, introduces discursive *play*), Freud appears to abandon his first love, pleasure, she who had extended her protection to all human actions and fantasies. As the essay progresses, the hero finds his heroine less persuasive but returns to her at journey's end, coming back after having ventured unto destruction, catastrophe, and helpless suffering. Yet he is tempted by her rival, a darker force too exciting to be a lady, the irrepressible "beyond." Having acknowledged that psychoanalysis encounters many phenomena that exceed the pleasure principle, Freud's thought-voyage is at once a speculation that *collapses*, and a narrative that *discovers*, the beyond.

Theoretical Forenote: This is the heart of the present study. It attempts an elucidation of Freud's hidden texts, his five brief romances, fragmented or displaced but germinal, and carrying stronger suggestions about death and love than those attained in the metapsychological speculations composing the larger proportion of his essay. I name each narrative by a metaphor that implies an act of doing or being or creating because their meanings are achieved actively in experiences of life or language.

He undertakes a mystifying excursion in prose, writing an essay that is the bane of many and the passion of a few, a discursive journey of contrasting expositional modes. When he works abstractly, talking about matters such as the Nirvana principle or the principle of constancy, he affirms his own observations and returns to the fundamental law of psychoanalysis: that in our search for stability we choose the pleasure principle. He comes back to pleasure through a certain speculative discourse that can be described as a *metapsychology*, but which in its search for a secure hypothesis about mind is more of a *psychology* (his theorizations while not proven lack the transcendent *meta*-quality).[3] As a theoretical psychology based on carefully considered assumptions, Freud's speculations on the pleasure principle (together with its derivative, the reality principle) are part of normative psycho/analysis. We are therefore not surprised when Freud concludes his wide meditation in a circular manner, saying "the pleasure principle seems actually to serve the death instincts" (*SE,* 7:63). He unifies his earlier ideological commitment and his later discovery to return to the starting point.

If death is pleasure, what is the "beyond" as destination? Where does one find it? By what mode of travel does one reach it? Paul Ricoeur and Jacques Derrida have each noted that in Freud the pleasure principle (pleasure as a biological law) differs from specific instances of pleasure as in, say, sex.[4] I would make a related distinction between the death-principle (death as a biological law) and specific instances of death as in, say, narrative. The psychological discussion, *the discursions on death*, trace the biological movement back to the pleasure principle, while the diverse and figurative expressions of death, the essay's *narratives of death*, lead forward to the beyond.

The conflicting forces in *Beyond the Pleasure Principle* are uncovered (and partly created) by its different writing techniques. Discursive consideration of the "motive forces" in the psyche invariably leads to the single theorem, the all-explaining principle, discovered over again as the knight encounters opponents to the sovereignty of his lady. He confronts enemies like the death-drive (a black knight, a dark abyss, the past), the life-drive (a white knight, a green field, the future) and at a crucial moment that changes the life of his thought, an encounter with the two knights riding together. He then yields the field and is, errant knight, seduced by their radical ideas. Nor can he convince them, finally, to accept the sovereignty of the bountiful lady, Mistress Principle *née* Pleasure. He himself, the knight of intellectual adventuring, had returned to her because he wanted to remain faithful to a kingdom under the reign of law, a harmonious state. His wanting to believe in the pleasure principle was in itself *an illustration* of the principle, his first law providing a kind of intellectual peace or stasis. Yet after this strenuous excursion he returns to her no more.

For the knight is enchanted into strange fantasies, stories of dark and bright magic. The meta-element in *Beyond the Pleasure Principle*, taking "meta" as a prefix for "after," "transcendent," or "beyond" appears in its flights of narrative. These parts of the essay, narratorial, figurative, imaginative, constitute its true metapsychology. In *Beyond the Pleasure Principle*, Freud transcends the psychological in the literary. His writing becomes figurative in discussions of dreams and children's games (*SE*, 2:12–17), in descriptions of the compulsion to repeat and the citing of a Renaissance romance (3:18–23), and in the biological metaphors by which he reads the operations of life-energy (6:46–61).

Writing figurative narratives Freud breaches the beyond to attain a permanent foothold within it: the narratives describe psychic return but are undiluted by intellectual retreat. Increasingly preoccupied by the drives it is as if he himself were a driven figure, an author obsessed by a figurative conception serving as the metapsychology—or metaphysics—of our inner world.[5] The prose-journey of our knight, then, is perplexed by its conflicting desires; he is beset at the same time by an urge for stability and a fascination with the uncontrolled. The literary (narrativistic, metaphorical, dramatic) expression of its clashing desires justify our considering *Beyond the Pleasure Principle* as the exemplary achievement within an original genre: the psychoanalytic essay as a form of romance.[6]

The Fate of the Ego

The knight draws maps of the landscape providing structural, economic, and dynamic paths of entrance. The *structural* plan is Dantean and like Dante he describes a cosmos with higher, middle, and lower ranges of being (exchanging the macrocosm for a microcosm Freud's id, ego, and superego, or ego-ideal replace Dante's *Inferno*, *Purgatorio*, and *Paradiso*). The *economic* method quests for a unified principle of energy, while *the dynamic* view corroborates the existence of opposing drives, self-preservative and sexual, the satisfying of "hunger and love."[7]

Freud tries to find convergence between the economic and dynamic paths, but one leads to unity and the other to duality. He seeks the high way, faith in pleasure as an understanding of nature, but the roads resist unification. Sexuality becomes life while self-preservation expands to death:[8] each drive-path becomes a full road, a principle in itself. Continuing onward he tries to subdue each new principle to pleasure, bending death to *Nirvana* and life to libido, yet the two roads stretch endlessly and reach beyond pleasure. Can the knight follow a map of contradictory paths? More crucially, can he conceive *of the opposition between related forces* as the unstable dualism organizing the kingdom?

He soldiers forward examining all apparent refutations of pleasure, testing her reliability. He uncovers material confuting pleasure in the transference, the repetition of the past that occurs *inside* the emotional relations between patient and analyst. In the transference, we repeat not only unpleasant experiences of tension, confusion and incompetence, but terrible experiences of failure and rejection; we are seduced by analysis into catastrophe.

The knight unmasks the mythic terror behind painful repetition: an uncontrollable inner force called the compulsion to repeat. From his revealing encounter with the monster on his path, Freud looks down into the abyss of death. He makes an interpretive connection between the chimera above and the depths below. He concludes, in oracular fashion, that we return to negative events to prepare for final nonexistence, echoing nonbeing in being. We repeat the inorganic state preceding organic life to follow a primary drive toward universal retrogression: "*an instinct is an urge inherent in organic life to restore an earlier state of things*" (*SE*, 5:36, italics Freud's).

The idea that all things dissolve to original nonbeing—cosmic entropy—underlies the death-drive. Yet the death-meditation appears *after* the discussion of the repetition-compulsion in the essay. The sequence is perplexing for how do we arrive at the quiet of the grave from the vexed tensions of the compulsion to repeat? How can one write about the turmoil of war as if it were equivalent to the quiescence of peace? Freud transforms a signifier (the repetition-compulsion) to a signified (the death-drive) according to a presupposed theory (the pleasure principle). He slights the autonomous significance of the repetition-narrative.

Hence the curious feeling of anticlimax as we pass from the narratives of chapters two and three to the meditations of chapter five. We are left disappointed by the blunt enormity of the claim "*the aim of all life is death*" (*SE*, 5:38). Freud the scientist in search of conclusions eclipses Freud the critic examining verbal evidence. The internal meanings of the pleasure-refuting narratives are slighted. The description of literal death ends the play of signifiers and reverberates in a hollow fashion. Literalizing death, Freud elides its infinite meanings.

The most significant connection between the repetition-compulsion and death is not made directly but does exist within the text. In both the death-meditation and the death-related narratives, the ego plays the central role. We recognize that the profundity of chapter 5 pertains not to death itself but to the role of the ego within it. Freud had always seen the ego as the psychic agent of survival (the early self-preservative instincts are also called the ego-instincts). But the function of the ego takes a tragic turn in *Beyond the Pleasure Principle*.

In his daring assay Freud formulates the idea of the death-ego, the dark *Todesich*, which orchestrates the apportioned ends of our destiny. The meditation becomes most compelling as Freud asserts that "the organism wishes to die only in its own fashion" (*SE*, 5:39). He determines that the ego preserves the organism for death, but a reversal of his terms may prove equally revealing: *that death preserves the organism for the ego*. The being-within-death, the holding to death in various figurative ways, gives the ego its sovereignty. Thus, the ego holds us to the fate of our isolation, to our lonely self-concentration, to the inward focus of a narcissism intensifying, perhaps, with advancing age.

Reading retrospectively from the death-meditation to the compulsion to repeat, we recognize that both describe dramas of the isolated and isolating ego. To transpose the analyst into a figure from the past is to subordinate him to the mythic closure of non-temporality; the analysand holds the analyst to the stopped time of a self closed into itself: the transference is history as total egocentricity. The narratives of the ego that preserve us in and for death occur beyond—or before—the pleasure principle. They replay traumatic memories in a repetition that is also a kind of supernatural punishment. As in a *hex*, the stark myths of the past put a paralytic spell on the full romances of the present. The *Todesich* generates narratives that become metaphors for death by their arousal of catastrophic feelings.[9]

We can understand the catastrophic by recognizing its connection to the demonic. Freud describes the demonic as the attribution of our unconscious self-destructiveness to an outside force, a kind of malevolent magician who causes us to act against the conscious within. If the demonic is a metaphorical term for the *cause* of self-destruction, the catastrophic is a term for the *effects* of self-destruction. (We are considering here a literary-metaphorical term meaning an overturn or revolutionary reversal—cata/strophe—as, in particular, the plot of tragedy.) Its effects occur largely on the level of affects, and refer to the unbearable feelings we impose on ourselves as self-punishments. In catastrophe, the disintegration incipient in experience is actualized. It is as though the weave of life were completely unraveled, and we were devastated not only by the appearance of the unwoven but by the disappearance of the weaving-capacity itself.[10] These elements may emerge in the experience of personal disaster or in the recitation of analysis or in the reading of literature.

We could conclude, thus, that catastrophic experience results from our dark fate, from the way the demonic usurps selfhood; fate, Greek *Moira*, the apportioned, appears identifiable with the force Freud describes as the "demonic," the unconscious return to prohibited pleasure. Yet tracking the paths of the knight we realize something he does not realize himself. That it is not an estranged and hostile force in the unconscious, the *demon*, that drags us before the tribunals of catastrophe. Rather, submitting the organism to the ordeal of the death-narratives is part of the normal functioning, is indeed an essential operation, of the ego. The ego will bend us to its will in the innumerable deaths that trouble our isolated fates. From the vantage-point of the ego, all successes are brief detours from dying; our triumphs are merely life's augmentations of death. The ego drives us through deaths long before we die; it pulls us into narratives that anticipate and accompany death, but that cannot be equated with death in a totalized signifier-signified relationship. How can we define these deaths without dying? We can describe them as literary catastrophes built inescapably into human experience.

We know the rhythm of fate closing in on the subject from Greek tragedy. Its inescapability suggests that fate is woven into the character, that fate is an intrinsic part of our human being (being as an active participle not a noun), part of our consciousness and unconsciousness. If there is a force that arranges our destiny it is what Freud calls the ego, the great compromiser negotiating its way between brute id, oppressive superego, and relentless reality. It is the fate of the ego ("of" as "belonging to" not "occurring to") on its path toward death that rehearses our *undesired* experience. But what is the *undesired*? Not the return to prohibited desire. The repetitions of the transference do entail, of course, a return to prohibited desires, but this does not tell us enough to explain the formation of another drive, a new motive, an independent narrative taking us in a completely different direction from the more familiar forces.

The prohibitive material surrounding the Oedipus complex develops an independent life because it serves the ego so well. If there is a force of desire which supersedes the ego, there is also, an opposition to desire within the ego. This opposition to desire, this anti-desire, constitutes another force, an inescapable but independent corollary of life-affirming desire. (The drives are, somehow, inseparable but independent, each having a relationship of indispensable Otherness to the Other.) The force of anti-desire is not to be subsumed by the pleasure principle or the life-drive; the second power justifies in its autonomy the dualistic theory. The second drive is accurately described as *anti-desire*, because it is another force *not* an *un*/desire, *not* a lack of force, *not* a negation or a subsidiary force serving the reality principle. The ego, the force of self-preservation wants to preserve itself as preserver. The second drive is nothing less than the ego asserting its sovereignty, *and the fate of the ego is not a stage but an end*.

Desire is the keenest threat to the sovereignty of the ego; the ego, both serving and mastering the id, its master and subject, its shadow and double, is the demon-director who terrifies us out of desire. (The knight says do not look to the demons outside but to the demon within; but we may add to the wise Shakespearean admonition that the demonic is a fundamental motive of our being.) The ego operates this way to rehearse a finality, but its rehearsals show their significance long before the last performance.

The function of the ego, then, is to resist love and the act of love, to resist the full immersion of body and psyche in the life-process, for in the energy of life (or love) self-preservation is discounted. Self-generation opposes self-preservation. How does the ego interfere with desire? It terrifies us out of desire by throwing us back to its proscribed origins. Narratives against desire, traced in their forms and formlessness, comprise one of the subjects of the present study. The demon-dramas of the transference are against desire even as the longed-for original objects of desire await at the culmination of the transferential process. We encounter the interdictions of desire at its origins. The backward motion creates a world of action and story; it achieves a structure (often a destroyed structure), and a plot with a mythic beginning and a final end.

When there is a change from myth to romance, romantic elaborations provide the Aristotelian middle and, as Geoffrey Hartman points out, the middle is life. Mythic beginnings and endings create narratives describable by Coleridgean phrases like "life-in-death" and "death-in-life." Freud formulates the idea of the death-ego, but the way he conceives the relationship between its literal and figurative operations is debatable. He describes the return to the *narcissistic scar*, but his metaphor presents an injury located in the past; the recurrent drama of the transference opens, however, a *narcissistic wound*. In the play of transference (drama not game) the past usurps the present.

The tale of Oedipus remains the mythic exemplar of *anti-desire*. In that story, the poetics of anti-desire, like Aristotle's poetics of tragedy, dispose themselves by a rhythm of emotional crisis. Repetition and catastrophe (repetition *of* catastrophe and repetition *as* catastrophe) replace recognition and reversal. When we are consigned (for we do not consign ourselves) to *anti-desire* we drown in its depths, anticipating our endings in a catastrophe that surpasses death.

Who should know this better than our knight, discoverer of hidden meaning in the dreams of Oedipus and Hamlet. In *Beyond the Pleasure Principle*, he comes to cloudy Thebes again, contemplating the narcissistic scar and other oedipal traces. Yet he avoids, not for the first time, an immersion in the Theban darkness. Thebes stages oedipal dramas in a theater of the self, dominated by internal figures. The ego returns to the time before childhood to encompass oedipal and pre-oedipal traumas. The drive toward earliest experience can be expressed only in literary narrative. Our fates, after all, are our stories (every unhappy psyche writes its own unhappy narrative). Within the drive-that-becomes-narrative we approach again the dramatis personae of myth, the love-figures merged in the blind history of the ego. In these dark tales, we love again the-Other-that-is-no-other.

On this strenuous excursion the knight interprets the Theban stories incompletely and abandons the city prematurely: the fatal gap in his knowledge of that country opens because of his fear of Jocasta.[11] The knight passes from Thebes, with its dramatization of death, to the less-treacherous abyss of literal death.

For Oedipus suffers beyond death in a kind of primordial agony, his pain inseparable from the form of dramatic narrative and the formlessness of psychic revelation. With its eponymous title, the narrative *is* the hero; Oedipus is *sutured* between a furious plot of the present and an archaeological plot of the past. The play is not about the redemption of suffering, only about suffering. What drives Oedipus? Why does he go back to Thebes? It requires no great intelligence to foresee the nightmares on the three-pronged road. Coming to a sacrificial altar, Oedipus enshrines anti-desire to demonstrate, as a cultural admonition, the fate of the desiring self.[12]

Desire Beyond the Ego

Dismayed by the grim meditation, the knight (a courtly figure, a devotee of *Trouthe*) discerns a paladin and a lady, ardent in a green field, and recalls the kingdom that renounces gloom. The lonely sojourner enjoys a burst of insight: "It cannot be so" [that death is the all-in-all] (5:39). The ego determines the destiny of life in death, but the living organism supersedes its mortal coil. Organic life self-generates through a sought counterpart; we live forever in the extension of self that is separate from the self. The living element Freud calls the "germ-cell," taken in a larger germinal or germinating sense, achieves an immortality framed by death through a spark of reproduction: "We must regard as in the highest degree significant the fact that this function of the germ-cell is reinforced, or only made possible, if it coalesces with another cell similar to itself and yet differing from it" (5:40).

The last phrase resounds to lead authoritatively to the Other drive. (Each drive is Other because neither drive is *the* drive; the dualism divides life, the final accounting to be given at its end.) There is that in the organism which transcends the power of the ego. When the knight follows the life-road only (when he follows either road without keeping his eye on the Other), he comes full circle. Earlier in the journey, death had returned him to the overarching Principle of Constancy, the conviction that the organism wishes to live with an absolute minimum of stimuli. Constancy allowed a properly chivalric return to Lady Pleasure.

Now, contemplating the undeniability of life, the knight embraces the unitary idea again: he reduces being to the sexual striving of the One Life. Meditating on its great power he collapses life, as he had collapsed death earlier, to a monistic principle. "If the self-preservative instincts too are of a libidinal nature, are there perhaps no other instincts whatever but the libidinal ones? At all events there are none other visible" (6:52). He returns to his "On Narcissism" position, and sees not love in relation to death, but two kinds of love in relation to one another: self-love and other-love. In self-love the active ego takes the passive self (the desirer enclosed) as an object, yet narcissistic love must be a preliminary stage to other-love if it is not to become death. *The self only realizes itself through another self.* "On Narcissism" returns to the pleasure principle; the knight expands life to an all-inclusive *Libido* as earlier he had expanded death to an all-inclusive *Nirvana.*[13] Dame Pleasure reigns supreme in two brief jousts where all-inclusiveness triumphs, but, ultimately, she will lose the prize of the pageant to Madame Beyond, dark lady of the two costumes.

For our knight continues to be driven by dualism. He writes about the biological dualism of a natural process while his writing encompasses the conceptual dualism of a philosophical idea. Both forms of dualism relinquish the certainty inherent in known quantities. Freud actually does what he later fears he may be forced to do and works "upon an equation with two unknown quantities" (*SE*, 6:57). To increase the radius of being, to widen the circle of the known, the life of the mind like the life of the body requires interaction with the other, taking the other as one who is finally beyond the self.

Our knight of Trouthe goes ahead then, with a hypothesis for which there are no proofs at all. He writes of the struggle between life and death, a universal contest where neither power dominates. The fierce clash of antagonistic forces will, hereafter, obsess the knight. But, the force of the obsession will derive from intellectual—or imaginative—conviction rather than empirical evidence. Thus, Freud makes a dramatic admission in the later *Civilization and Its Discontents*: "To begin with it was only tentatively that I put forward the [dualistic] views I have developed here, but in the course of time they have gained such a hold upon me that I can no longer think in any other way" (6:119). Freud's dualism transcends his intellectual will to express his creative desire.

From our present standpoint, we can place his ideas in contexts he did not himself employ. Here, the philosophical notion of otherness foregrounded by Sartre, Lacan, and other theorists, expands the range of the Freudian life-narrative. We can induce that outside and inside the organism there is that which flourishes beyond the ego. The sexual drive finds resolution in the reproductive creation shared with a similar yet different, contrasting yet completing, other. The encounter with the biological other in propagation yields the conceptual other in the theory of the drives. The other as an external unknown quantity separates from the ego as an internal unknown quantity; the other is different from the ego, but intrinsic to our being. The self is that which responds to the other, that which is amplified and increased by the drive toward the other, by desire.

The energies of desire are visible, traceable; yet there is no death process analogous to the reproduction process: there is neither an observable death-drive nor any representation of a death as such in the psyche. Life and death are inseparable yet not congruent, not the same in kind, yet linked in relationship. Both forces take place beyond the conscious will; yet the organism actively participates in the forces of reproduction in ways that do not obtain in relation to the forces of death. It is as though we could affirm the life-forces but were powerless in regard to the death-force. We can enhance our desire because sex involves the physical expression of the directed will. But death proceeds by passive participation in an unwilled movement, as if we were obeying the phantom will of another. This would make the ego an alien other at the same time as it is our essential being. The ego is against desire as it is for survival, but it is for survival as an endgame; we feel the force of the ego as if it were against us, bowing to an alien will. The death-drive of the ego is desire only in the sense of anti-desire; the ego is the location of the desire not to desire.

But we still have not demonstrated the full nature of this perplexing death drive, for how does it come about that the *undiscoverable* death drive remains the *inescapable* death drive? Freud returns again and again to two contrasting points and creates a serious ideological clash, perhaps the chief *aporia* of his thought: 1) there is no proof of the desire for death and 2) the drive toward annihilation remains the power which upholds the dualistic theory of the drives.

This gap is felt dramatically in the long footnote on the drives that completes chapter six of *Beyond the Pleasure Principle*. A comprehensive statement, it traces the drives and their vicissitudes to conclude:

> [the final instinctual] opposition appeared between the libidinal (ego- and object-) instincts and others, *which must be presumed* to be present in the ego and which may perhaps actually be observed in the destructive instincts. Our speculations have transformed this opposition into one between the life instincts (Eros) and the death instincts. (6:61, italics mine)

Freud forcefully asserts the dualistic idea despite the absence of evidence for the death drive, itself the essential second term for the theory of double desire. He bases his final theory on a presumption whose existence "must" (what is the role of the imperative in evidential reasoning?) be observed; yet the death-drive can be discovered only by a transformative inversion from inner to outer, from the silent inward "death instincts" to the clamorous outward "destructive instincts."

My claim is that the *only* place where Freud does encounter expressions of invisible death is in the experiences recorded in *Beyond the Pleasure Principle* and elsewhere. The discovery occurs through subtle and elaborate literary representations beyond the abstraction known as the death drive. The representation of death occurs in modes of writing other than the discursive, for death exists within drives that find both mythic and romantic expression.[14] We can conclude our introductory discussion by noting that desire transcends the ego in a new synthesis. The synthesizing forces of desire occur not in the ego but within the self, the self itself being the creation of desire. It is the fate of the ego to fulfill itself in death and the fate of the self to fulfill itself in another self. This occurs when desire overflows the dominion of the ego. If myth is the narrative of the ego, romance is the narrative of the self.

Narrative and Drive

Freud often writes of Eros, the mythic name for sexuality, yet never refers to Thanatos, the mythic name for death.[15] He resists accepting that death, like love, finds its significances in rhetorical expression, in fragments or totalizations of myth or romance.[16] *Beyond the Pleasure Principle* shows five narratives of desire, four stories about the desire to endanger the self and one story about the desire to perpetuate the self—four tales of death and one tale of life. The stories leading toward death also lead beyond the security or quiescence identified with pleasure. They fill in the gap left by the avoidance of the word "Thanatos," the mythic romance of death. Indeed, Thanatos remains unnamed in the essay it dominates. The strongest energies in *Beyond the Pleasure Principle* are destructive energies. The death narratives may be described as the-dream-of-the-wound (from the traumas of war veterans), the-play-of-substitution (from the patterns of transference), the-game-of-disappearance (from the *fort/da* game) and the-romance-of- death (from the story of Tancred and Clorinda); the counter-narrative of creative desire (from Freud's recountings of life-sparking biochemical experiments) is the-romance-of-life. The five narratives constitute different categories of being-in-the-world: dreaming, action, encounter, creation-and-destruction, relationship.

First Narrative: The-Dream-of-the-Wound

Freud begins his study of exceptions to the pleasure principle with the "traumatic neurosis" suffered by World War I veterans. A psychological condition caused by physical injury, its symptoms are diagnosed as "subjective ailment (in which it resembles hypochondria or melancholia) as well as . . . general enfeeblement and disturbance of the mental capacities" (*BPP*, 2:12). The syndrome amazes Freud because the neurotically tormented soldiers return in dreams to the scene of their wounding. The repetition of injury in dreams poses a refutation to his dream-theory, yet Freud responds by making an appeal to his own authority and refusing "to be shaken in [his] belief in the wish-fulfilling tenor of dreams" (*BPP*, 2:13).

The-dream-of-the-wound arouses Freud's indignation because it resists the law of the dream: "Anyone who accepts . . . that their dreams should put them back at night into the situation that caused them to fall ill has misunderstood the nature of dreams" (2:13). He closes a brief discussion with some fragmentary and preliminary remarks: "we may argue that the function of dreaming . . . is upset in this condition, or we may be driven to reflect on the mysterious masochistic trends of the ego" (2:13–14). Either this dream-process is not a true dream-process (yet what else could it be?) or it introduces those strange twists of the self that Freud will only begin to encounter five years later in "The Economic Problem of Masochism," an essay that reveals little that is new about self-destructive energy and death.[17]

This discussion of oneiric repetition might seem minor, yet it introduces the subversion of pleasure which is the subject of the essay. Moreover, Freud not only slights the ideological significance of traumatic neurosis, but omits any direct transcription of traumatic dreams, eliding the dreams behind the discussion. The dream-of-the-wound is a narrative of absence, the real story is omitted and the beyond fills a space—a vortex—of nonpresentation. The first literary narrative in *Beyond the Pleasure Principle* is an unexpressed expression of Thanatos and Freud's reading is a noninterpretation of dreams. Perhaps because of its subversive powers, Freud resists the dream as an open, fictional narrative. In his resistance, he resembles Nelly Dean during Catherine's confession in *Wuthering Heights*. In both cases a dream of origins is recited, while the essential auditor withholds the response of full listening. Freud, like Nelly Dean, affirms the significance of a dream by his distance from it. Anticipating subsequent turns of story and symbol in *Beyond the Pleasure Principle*, traumatic neurosis makes us reconsider the darkness in wishes and the destruction in dreams.

Second Narrative: The-Game-of-Disappearance

Observing that the "repetition of . . . distressing experience" (2:15) organizes the games of a young child, Freud examines another refutation of the pleasure principle. While most commentary focuses on the *fort/da* game-of-the-reel,[18] the boy actually plays several games. The *fort/da* should be read within the four-part series of toy-game, reel-game, mirror-game, and rifle-game. The series begins with the boy's

> disturbing habit of taking any small objects . . . and throwing them away from him into a corner, under the bed, and so on, so that hunting for his toys and picking them up was often quite a business. As he did this he gave vent to a loud, long-drawn-out "o-o-o-o", accompanied by an expression of interest and satisfaction. His mother and the writer of the present account were agreed in thinking that this was not a mere interjection but represented the German word "*fort*" ["gone"]. I eventually realized that it was a game and that the only use he made of any of his toys was to play "gone" with them. (2:14–15)

The only game the boy plays entails the losing of his toys, a loss he compensates with the sound "o-o-o," and which Freud translates into language as "fort" or "gone." The initial game sets the rules of the game as loss and symbolic compensation. There is no hint in the general game, the overall game which configures the generic series, of any returning of the object. For the boy, *play itself is loss*, as in later games motion equals disappearance and encounter leads to separation.

Freud *alters* the game when he reads it as a preliminary losing and a subsequent finding, a game where the child causes others to return his lost objects. For in actuality the boy plays only "throw-away," while the adults complete the circle by playing "bring-back." The boy, Freud's one-and-a-half-year-old grandson, Ernst, signals no desire for the action the adults perform, so the observers close a circle the player would leave open. The toy-game raises questions related to autonomy and open-form; it demonstrates some significant differences between action and interpretation, between the game-text of the player and the critical reading of the observer.

The *fort/da* or reel-game is more distinct than the toy-game for it describes a specific object and a particular goal:

> The child had a wooden reel with a piece of string tied round it. It never occurred to him to pull it along the floor behind him, for instance, and

> play at its being a carriage. What he did was to hold the reel by the string and very skillfully throw it over the edge of his curtained cot, so that it disappeared into it, at the same time uttering his expressive "o-o-o-o." He then pulled the reel out of the cot again and hailed its reappearance with a joyful *da*["there"]. This then was the complete game—disappearance and return. As a rule one only witnessed its first act, which was repeated untiringly as a game in itself, though there is no doubt that the greater pleasure was attached to the second act. (*BPP*, 2:15)

In a cogent interpretation, Freud argues that the reel represents the mother and the game symbolizes "the child's great cultural achievement—the instinctual renunciation . . . made in allowing his mother to go away without protesting" (2:15). The game reverses the pain of loss. Acknowledging the boy's frequent playing of disappearance without return, Freud discovers an emotional return despite the lack of a physical return. The boy always brings back the feeling of pleasure, which Freud takes as the yield of the game. Returning the mother to control the experience of loss, the boy reverses their relationship by throwing her away from him and reaches pleasure through revenge. Going from active to passive, the boy transforms himself from victim of abandonment to master of return.

Yet Freud's reading maintains the centrality of pleasure against the evidence of the game. His motivation may reside in the similarity between observer and observed, for he faces an intellectual loss if the symbolic action of the boy subverts the hypothetical dominance of pleasure. (Freud's "work" is intimately bound with his grandson's "play.")[19] Freud returns to the pleasure principle when he reads the game as a reparative reversal of abandonment, describing the "joyful return" of the transitional object as "the true purpose of the game" (2:15). Ernst may be read as Freud's own transitional object, determining that the pleasure principle is *da* (here) and not *fort* (gone). The child brings back *pleasure*, while Freud as the real master of the return brings back the *pleasure principle*.

Thus Freud insists that "the complete game" consists of "disappearance and return" (2:15) even if the boy plays "disappearance" far more often than "return." He finds the game completed whenever pleasure is attained, and describes mastery and revenge as its indirect paths. This raises serious problems about whether *mastery and revenge are persuasive paths to pleasure*. For what can the boy "master" here? How does one master disappearance? By returning? But the whole inescapable point (as much as Freud tries to escape it) is that *most of the time the boy does not return*. What does that leave as a path to mastery? A total disappearance? What kind of mastery would that be? Would not disappearance entail, rather, the moving into a scene not only outside previous recognition but outside the power of mastery?

Similarly, revenge finds its place in the theory of the drives as a category of aggression, the death drive in reversed externalized form. By invoking revenge, that return to pain through an inversion of pain, Freud already shatters the dominance of the pleasure principle and anticipates the significance of the compulsion to repeat. (Despite the discovery of the repetition compulsion, Freud never retrospectively revises the reading of the game.) Mastery and revenge adduce such radically altered forms of pleasure that they constitute something *other* than pleasure.

Looking closely at the action of the scene, we find a movement into a suspended state that leaves the boy lost-and-not-found. Placing its player in a symbolic structure enclosing invisible space, the game intuitively organizes a state of irresolution and incompleteness. The going out into the unknown is represented again by the open vowel-sound, the round fullness of a long "o-o-o," interpreted by Freud as *fort* (gone), while Lacan, in a major revision, takes this as the child's discovery of language and the birth of the Symbolic Order.[20] Despite the brilliance of Lacan's insight, one wonders why the boy, if he has discovered the Symbolic Order, retreats from it into the oceanic oneness of his infant's crib, preferring the regressive to the progressive syllable. One answer would be that sound and language are not the same, and that the formlessness of his utterance suggests the vocalization of endlessness rather than the discovery of language.

Questioning the reading of its purpose and structure, we may query, also, the reading of *representation* in the game. Agreeing that it replays the relationship between the boy and his mother, its testing of reality would focus, nevertheless, on the maternal figure within the context of the boy's developing self (with her significant presence experienced from birth and earlier she was never a figure to *toy* with). The lack of differentiation between child and mother would lead to experimentation with transitional objects as symbolic separation, the disappearance and return felt within the being of the child.[21] The crucial signification here would be less concerned with the achieved control over the mother than with the experienced reality of the self. As the symbolized subject of and in the game, *the reel (real)-thing is the boy*.

We may, then, *reverse* the Freudian reading by seeing the boy as not throwing the mother away from himself, but himself away from the scene of abandonment. The realness of his play takes him away from the reality of his pain, but rather than reproducing the scene to control it, he reproduces a scene too elusive to be controlled; he repeats the pain of abandonment (he throws himself into emptiness) while opposing it with union (he throws himself into the mother). He goes from complete separation to union-in-separation, from a bare reality to a rich scene-of-the-imagination composed of symbolized-object, ritualized-action, and signifying-sound. Thus, pace Lacan, the word is not the entire or even the most significant substitutive element; what the boy does is present active, visual, and verbal expressions of the innate creative imagination—*if the unconscious is a language, the language is not composed of words only*. In the end the *reel* (the undetermined imagination) takes him away from the *real* (determined experience).

Seeing the boy as the active agent symbolizing himself, the mother appears not as the *projectile from* but as the *receptacle for* the desiring self; the boy's "curtained cot" provides a striking feminine-maternal figure. The curtained cot holds the boy in an indeterminable and unmasterable state (*not* exclusively or even primarily a return to the womb), a state of disappearance into an unknown reality apprehended by his active imagination. The boy moves from a real mother who abandons him to an imagined mother who receives him. This return to the imagined figure brings no pleasure but only a wordless state signified by a sound. The young boy, discovering not only the reality of the imagination but the being in nonbeing, acts out the disappearance of the self in a staged self-annihilation. These are experiments in death projected from the unconscious imagination. They condense the experiences of death in art and art in death.

To complete the reading of the game-series: in the mirror-game the boy makes *himself* disappear from the looking-glass while saying, "baby—o-o-o-" (baby is *fort* "gone"); Freud interprets this third game superficially by never pursuing the implications of a complete game based on a vanishing self-image. Since there is no indication that the boy ever returns to the mirror in reality, the mirror-game *finalizes* disappearance. In the rifle game, the boy throws away his father, in the form of a rifle, saying, amusingly, "go to the fwont." Following the other games, Ernst hopes, certainly, that his rival-father will never return at all and throws him into the many-faceted game of no-return.

Moving into dramatic criticism, Freud discusses tragedy as an adult form of play, making "painful experiences . . . enjoyable" by allowing them to be "recollected and worked over" in the mind (2:17). He hypothesizes the tragic as a completing and compensating structure, yet surely our experience of the tragic is of an incomplete, indeed a *shattered, form*. Do our repeated experiences of *Oedipus Rex* and *King Lear* render such searing works "enjoyable?" One could argue, rather, that our confrontation with tragic form reveals the unattainability of closure after great pain, and that the tragic re-opens wounds that never heal.

Third Narrative: The-Play-of-Substitution

The-play-of-substitution refers to transference as a narrative and repetition as a trope. (The term takes play as drama not game, for it describes a process that is necessary rather than free.) The displacements and condensations of the compulsion to repeat produce the essay's *literary* elements: the fragments of story, image, and character-creation that provide its fractured dramas. There are two literary modes in *Beyond the Pleasure Principle*, the one contained within the other. The frame for the literary dimension of the entire work would refer to the literary elements in the analyst's exposition; contained within that frame are the literary elements in the patient's experience. Since the relation between the two frames is itself dynamic and uncertain the overall structure is a kind of interrupted inset.

The crucial literary element in both frames is *narrative*, and by literary narrative I refer to a told fiction, a story fashioned of linked events. My use of the term fiction remains Aristotelian, for it indicates a telling that lifts its story out of a historical and specific context to a level of universal generalization. (Herein is one of the significant meeting points between the *literary* and the *scientific*.) Within the larger category of narrative the literary elements that emerge most forcefully include the trope—the essay develops a repertoire of literary-psychoanalytic images—and the character, the literarily-created presences or selves that emerge in *Beyond the Pleasure Principle*. The main narratives of the-play-of-substitution are the transference, its counterpart in the compulsion to repeat (if the transference is about narrative form, the compulsion to repeat is about narrative energy), the narcissistic scar, which recounts the drama of "neurotic" repetition, and the demonic, which recounts the drama of "normal" repetition.

The word transference invokes the concept of metaphor; the two terms are nearly synonymous, for the Greek root of metaphor, *metapherein*, means transfer or change. The psychoanalytic transference refers to the carrying-over (*Übertragung*) of feelings from their origin in the early experience of the patient to the person (body, voice, presence) of the analyst. Feelings appropriate to an earlier figure, and remaining attached to a psychic image from the past, are displaced to the therapist, an actual figure in the present. Such a passage from id to ego involves the metaphysical (through its introversion as the *metapsychical*) transfer of unconscious desire from the timeless past to conscious desire in the time-bound present. This achieves a carryover from inner to outer modes of being, an ontological exchange.

The exchange is achieved through metaphor, in the final analysis *is* a metaphor, about the relationship between the manifest signifier in the present and the latent signified of the past. To use Jacobson's terms, the metaphorical relationship of past and present is one of correspondence, yet the actual content of the relationship is built on the axis of contiguity, on the series of events in the manifest plot of the present that reveals the hidden structure of the buried plot of the past. In the transference the latent metaphorical relationship is contained in the manifest metonymical structure.

The carryover from past to present involves the transformation of invisible to visible. The transference occurs across the same division between the conscious and the unconscious that organizes dreams, errors, and symptoms. The difference between the invisible past and the visible present is reminiscent of a romantic abyss; the past-signified is imperfectly captured by a present-signifier, while the temporal chasm refers to irrecoverable memories of being.

The content of the transference is invoked by the narrative trope of the narcissistic scar. Like all the literary elements in the essay, Freud's conception is at once image and story, for it begins in the traces of memory and ends in the gestures of action. The narcissistic scar describes the child's feelings of inadequacy within the Oedipus complex. This drama reveals its tragic elements when the child's original passion leads to primary rejection—his first affair ends as a failed affair.

> The early efflorescence of infantile sexual life is doomed to extinction because its wishes are incompatible with reality. . . . [It] comes to an end in the most distressing circumstances and to the accompaniment of the most painful feelings. Loss of love and failure leave behind them a permanent injury to self-regard in the form of a Narcissistic Scar

which . . . contributes more than anything to the "sense of inferiority" which is so common in neurotics. (3:20–21).

The narrator-analyst tells a composite tale garnered from the innumerable tales of protagonist-patients. We note the literary mode of the discourse; the psychoanalytic generalization takes form as romantic tales of childhood. Concerned with the disappearance of love, they tell Wordsworthian stories of original loss. Yet the analyst's single story is fashioned not from the *recitation* but rather from the *repression* of stories. The analyst reconstitutes the lost signified of the past from the found signifiers of the present and tells a tale never told.

We recall that the patient repeats *because* he cannot remember; rather, he acts his story, drama replaces narrative because actions can be performed in a mindless fashion while narration requires thought. (Judging from *Oedipus Rex*, the difference between act and utterance is memory; it is only with the combined memories of the community and the protagonist that something like full speech is possible at the end of the play.) Freud does a retrospective reading of the unconscious signified of patients whose actions repeat unconscious memories that may never become available.

Freud traces past memory through present action as it is acted out in response to the analyst. The patient repeats his narcissistic scar in actions that express his unconscious desire for rejection. The patients "seek to bring about the interruption of the treatment while it is still incomplete; they contrive once more to feel themselves scorned, to oblige the physician to speak severely to them and treat them coldly" (3:21). The enacted signifier, the patient's objectionable actions, may be traced to the hidden signified, the memories of rejection and failure within the unconscious.

The depths of the unconscious hold images from the past—in their elusiveness and power they may be described as phantoms—about which we can only speculate. These ghostly figures belong to the genre of romance, for we simultaneously do and do not comprehend their nature, do and do not desire to return to their proximity. This is the intriguing area that Freud introduces, but does not explore. He acknowledges that the compulsion to repeat transgresses the pleasure principle and restricts himself to the economic question, thus slighting the dynamic examination of the area of displaced rejection. Abandoning the exploration of this "unknown quantity" Freud misses (or deliberately avoids) *the poetics of the transference*.

To enter into the world of primordial failure and rejection is to go into the Hades of the mind, Mephistopheles' Hell, the one we cannot get out of. This grim area is not cordoned off by chance, nor can we be sure that the analyst, wise as Virgil, will be kind and capable enough to take us through. My own intuitive reading of what goes on in the forgotten world of pleasure-denying memory begins with the readable present. It recognizes that the past will defeat us if we use it to deny the present, but that we will defeat ourselves equally if we use the present to deny the past.

Manipulating events for the sake of imposing a catastrophe on himself, the patient—that is, the suffering subject, the self in its vulnerability—arouses the coldness of the analyst. The patient gets himself rejected by an authority with power over fate itself. This may be interpreted as the repetition of a pattern of pain, the desired return to the experience of failure. Despite the evocativeness of his metaphor, the narcissistic scar, Freud has misnamed his trope; the scar finds its drama when reopened as a *narcissistic wound*. The patient wishes to submit himself again to the refusal of the parent; returning to rejection is a refinding of the famil/iar in the deeper sense. The parent triumphs again over the abject self.

Returning to the scorn or rage of parents, the subject returns to the catastrophic moment when parental support was denied. This achieves a complex and tragic purpose: to return to rejection is to return to the closeness of the family constellation, albeit in the destructive phase of the failed Oedipal complex; thus, the return achieves the all-important *intimacy of failure*. He returns to the point when the life-line of identification was refused and the closure of the Oedipal complex denied. To return to this point is to return to a lack of differentiation, and, thus, to lack of vitality, to the absence of a separate force of being. The psychic return of the transference leads to the death of the independent self.

It bears repeating that while Freud brings in the transference as an example of the transcendence of the pleasure principle, he does so in relation to the affects of pleasure and pain. But he only begins the exploration of the literary content of his narrative metaphors. My contention is that it is precisely in the exploration of these literary elements that we find the form of that second force necessary to the completion of the Freudian dualism. For the destructive transference is a kind of compelled quest for death. Death can be acted out in symbolized form; the transference has in common with other symbolized forms the aesthetic situation that allows us to *feel* but not *bear* the consequences of experience, the transference produces affects without actuality, and transferential narratives produce a death-without-dying. In the brilliant third chapter of his essay, Freud brings forward additional stories, images, and characters connected to variations on the transference.

He continues to show the relationship between rejecting analyst and rejected patient. We remember the instance Freud provides where the boy who could not produce a child becomes the man who will "produce a plan or a promise of some grand present" that he is unable to fulfill. Here the analyst is in the maternal role, with analysis as the grand *projét* that cannot be realized, and the relationship reopening the narcissistic wound. The analyst is the mother who makes the boy feel impotent.

Freud's rhetoric takes further turns, and we move compellingly from patient to analyst, from child to parent, from slave to master. For the sake of a composite reading, I shall refer to these two main characters in Freud's narrative as "the Stronger" and "the Weaker." We find ourselves reading a series of narratives, for if at first Freud presents the destructive transference as experienced by "neurotics," he now describes the destructive transference as incited by "normal people." For the Weaker member of the pair, "the neurotic," the energy of destructive repetition takes the name of the narcissistic scar, for the Stronger member, the "normal" person, such energy is described as "the Demonic." The Weaker returns to a pain inflicted *by* the other, while the Stronger inflicts pain *on* the other.

The second order of catastrophic narrative, the story of the Stronger one in the transference, contains elements of Freud's self-characterization:

> . . . . we have come across people all of whose human relationships have the same outcome . . . the benefactor who is abandoned in anger . . . by each of his *protégés*, however much they may otherwise differ from one another, and who thus seems doomed to taste all the bitterness of ingratitude, the man whose friendships all end in betrayal by his friend, or the man who time after time . . . raises someone else into a position of great private or public authority . . . and then himself upsets that authority . . . the lover each of whose love affairs with a woman passes through the same phases and reaches the same conclusion. (3:23)

We know that Freud had severe disappointments of his own, both with colleague-protégés, the most famous being Jung, and with patients, the most famous being Dora. The Weaker suffers the rejection he himself precipitates, and endures the experience of *being annihilated by the other*; the Stronger rejects without intent, himself abandoned as he is forced, by a relational pattern beyond the conscious will, to abandon the Weaker. The Stronger suffers from the experience of *annihilating the other*. The transference produces, in the Stronger, an illusion of mastery; but the compelled annihilation of the Weaker continually opens an infernal, empty space before the Stronger. All illusions of mastery are subverted as the failure of the Weaker leaves the Stronger before a vacuum of eternal futility.

Describing the patterns of transference Freud's language sounds subjective and incensed; his analytic text is as driven as the people it analyzes. It is as though the writing were taken out of his hands and placed in the hands of one of the reverberating figures of *Beyond the Pleasure Principle*—the self-opposing demon:

> What psycho-analysis reveals in the transference phenomena of neurotics can also be observed in the lives of some normal people. The impression they give is of being pursued by a malignant fate or possessed by some "daemonic" power; but psychoanalysis has always taken the view that their fate is for the most part arranged by themselves and determined by early infantile influences. (3:23)

The child/parent relation and its transferential repetitions has annihilating consequences for both partners; child and parent return with repetitive need to bitter disappointment. The infernal machine of pain indicates the human proclivity toward death-in-life. The one in the parental role achieves an intimacy with the one in the childish position; by intimate displacement he remembers his own experiences of annihilation. Thus, he knows indirect agony despite his relief that he is no longer the one destroyed.

Fourth Narrative: The-Romance-of-Death

The-play-of-substitution achieves direct repetition, but the displacement of memory to form may occur in an indirect manner. Borrowing a phrase from Nietzsche, Freud points out:

> This "perpetual recurrence of the same thing" causes us no astonishment when it relates to *active* behaviour on the part of the person concerned. . . . We are much more impressed by cases where the subject appears to have a *passive* experience . . . in which he meets with a repetition of the same fatality. There is the case . . . of the woman who married three successive husbands each of whom fell ill soon afterwards and had to be nursed by her on their death-beds. (3:22)

He describes the woman as passive because she appears to lack control over her husbands' illnesses. Power has been transferred from the acts of the individual to the forces of destiny. This transforms the reporting genre from a drama of fate that explores a metaphor to a story of suspense that accepts a mystery. Instead of reading Sophocles, we are viewing Hitchcock. The degree of our influence over the surrounding world determines the difference. Oedipus sets great powers into motion, but dreadful consequences develop from blind actions. The oft-widowed woman, on the other hand, appears the victim—or beneficiary—of outside forces. Hitchcock might show her secretly poisoning her unfortunate husbands, but that would simplify matters. At issue, rather, is the phenomenon of an environment that serves and represents the unconscious will. The paradox is that the subject may feel helpless in relation to surroundings that fulfill her needs and reflect her desires.

Freud's evocative rendering of Tasso's *Gerusalemme Liberata* explores this question. The knight-hero of the poem, Tancred, engages in actions amid surroundings that depict the experience of return. Yet he hardly sets out in pursuit of repetition; it is rather as if repetition were in pursuit of him:

> The most moving poetic picture of a fate such as this is given by Tasso in his romantic epic *Gerusalemme Liberata*. Its hero, Tancred, unwittingly kills his beloved Clorinda in a duel while she is disguised in the armour of an enemy knight. After her burial he makes his way into a strange magic forest which strikes the Crusader's army with terror. He slashes with his sword at a tall tree; but blood streams from the cut and the voice of Clorinda, whose soul is imprisoned in the tree, is heard complaining that he has wounded his beloved once again. (3:22)

This excerpt is different in kind from the literary elements I have described thus far. Tasso—or Freud speaking in Tasso's voice—establishes a separate style of narrative because the destructive powers of repetition are now expressed in a series of metaphors that call attention to themselves *as* metaphors. The extraordinary beauty of the passage derives from literary self-reflection, for the series of transformations indicate purposively the magical scope of figurative language. This is literature conscious of itself, and as Freud notes elsewhere, the literary contains all the symbolism of everyday life "and something more besides."[22]

What is the "something more besides" of the literary? To answer the question fully we need to distinguish the literary from the romantic. The literary as it has been presented in this study refers to a universal narrative, to stories and tropes whose signification refers back to a hidden signified. We may say, while aware that this relation may be reversed, that the narratives and tropes we have explored consist of a literary signifier and a psychoanalytic signified.

The function of analytic interpretation is to diminish the autonomy of the signifying structure, whether dream, game, or encounter—thus psychoanalysis conceals a desire to *reduce* the Signifier to the Signified (Freud admits his interest in the literary theme is always far greater than his interest in literary technique).

If the other narratives are literary (with romantic elements), the passage from Tasso brings in *the pure literary-ness of romance*. Tasso presents the signifier as a force of generation that can change itself again and again. Here we may point to a way of understanding the difference between *the literary* and *the romantic*. If in *the literary* the signifiers are displaced from a traceable signified, in *the romantic* the signifiers are transformed from a signified that becomes more and more elusive. (Among categories of the literary, the romantic is distinguished by its creation of autonomous worlds-within-worlds.)

Related to the idea of the romantic is the experience of the demonic. The demonic/daemonic is both the threat to and the culmination of romance. As the power that keeps driving us back to our original fate-of-rejection, the mythic demon undermines the free-play of signification. Yet there is considerable complexity here when *the mythic demon* sounds so similar to—and is deeply related to—*the romantic daemon*. We ourselves swim or sink in deep waters here but perhaps the point is that we have to return to the demon again and again to find the daemon, that myth is the father of romance. Freud himself releases his writing into something greater as he keeps returning to the stases of the pleasure principle and death.

Not surprisingly, *Beyond the Pleasure Principle* culminates in references to Plato's *Symposium*, for Freud's invocation encompasses both the malicious *demon* of religious legend and the inspirational *Daemon* of Platonic thought.[23] As Freud writes about the psychoanalytic "demon," he appears inspired by the literary daemon, for his prose resolves itself in the poetic paraphrase of Tasso. The complex object of desire behind Freud's expository/imaginative essay alternates between the pleasure principle (of stasis, of nirvana, of death) to which all psychic experience returns and the unnamable beyond which extends past earlier conceptions of desire. The demon is static, the daemon dynamic.

In *Gerusalemme Liberata*, we have an example of demonic romance because the driving force is an environment with its own will-to-power. The uncanny magic forest, *den unheimlichen Zauberwald*, is the place of eternal transformation. Here power is in outside forces because the hero, an errant knight not wandering but driven, has no access to the content of the forms he encounters. This play of unreadable signifiers is the terror of literature without end. It is about a wondrous yet terrifying creativity released when the signified is occluded. The ignorant knight is also the unknowing subject or blind I, suffering because of the uncrossable gap between symbol and symbolized. (It is worth considering the amazing English letter *I*, a glyph that can indicate *ego*, *one*, *eye*, and *phallus*.) The infernal trick in the-romance-of-death is that while the signifiers keep changing, the signified is always the same. The demon-mythic-Mother-in-the-beloved is enclosed in the wondrous transformations of the daemon-romantic-beloved-in-the-changing-world.

To fully explain why I call this narrative the romance-of-death it will be necessary to exchange the enchanting obscurities of literature for the clearer explanations of psychoanalysis. It is not by chance that Freud uses the charged adjective of the uncanny to describe the magic forest. We know that at the end of the line of uncanny significations awaits the seductive but fearful body of the mother. She is there but not-there—we only find her by returning to the narcissistic wound. Yet placing Clorinda in relation to the mother, we may comprehend her unhappy fate. The relationship of the beloved and the mother is both inside and outside an elusive equation.

At the same time, Tancred may be taken as representing *the reversal of pain*; if we link him to the foreshadowing figure of the abandoned child, we realize that his efforts entail an unconscious distancing from the narcissistic scar. He inflicts injury to avoid receiving it, and changes the narcissistic wound to a narcissistic wounding. Tancred illustrates the relationship between the death instincts and the destructive instincts: through a process of reversal the desire to die is transformed to the desire to kill. Enacting the process Freud attributes to that other child, the boy in the game-of-disappearance, Tancred takes revenge on the abandoning mother in his repeated attempts to injure the beloved.

Yet there remains a final issue here, perhaps the deepest conclusion reached from the romance-of-death. The point is this: so long as the self, boy or man, child or knight, remains attached to the mother he will need to injure the beloved. The narcissistic wound should be understood finally as a breach in the integrity of the ego. So long as the ego cannot separate into independence it will return obsessively to the source of the breach. It is as though Tancred represents the boy who dismantles the Symbolic to return to the Imaginary toward which he feels, nevertheless, passionate destructiveness. The knight injures the beloved as a last episode in a series of stories beginning with a rejected child. In that context the injuring of the beloved may be—a gesture toward the mother—a refusal of the separateness of sexual love. But in the transformative magic of romance the beloved may *be* the mother; she may represent the male's repressed hostility toward the mother who demands the loyalty of his manhood. Or the changing tropes of the poem may condense beloved and mother in a dream image that requires no differentiation.

What we do know is that the knight is fated to injure the beloved, and that she is disguised and disguised again until we do not know whether he wants to kill his love or the hidden obstacle to his love. What is clear is that the knight is in the forest of his own psyche that transforms objects by desire and fear, and that Freud gives us, inadvertently, a reading of romance as the love affair the self has with its own inner objects, and that death is the name of the romance.

Fifth Narrative: The-Romance-of-Life

Freud creates the last narrative using the figurative language he describes near the end of the essay. That description comes, in deferred fashion, after its application. While acknowledging the inconclusiveness of his speculations on the instincts Freud wishes for a more scientific analysis:

> The deficiencies in our description would probably vanish if we were already in a position to replace the psychological terms by physiological or chemical ones. It is true that they too are only part of a figurative language. . . . Biology is truly a land of unlimited possibilities. (6:60).

Previous to this Freud had already written a powerful narrative of vital process, affirming and transcending the pleasure principle, and *created from the figurative language of biology*. *Beyond the Pleasure Principle* offers fragments of a narrative which *in toto* presents a vital story, a romance-of-life.

Freud writes, thus, of the equality of forces necessary for procreation. He refers at length to the propagative "germ-cells" in living things; but, since he writes of evolved as well as rudimentary organisms, the discussion expands to general biological regeneration. The distinction is made between the *reproductive body* and the *functional ego*. The ego is the abstract power producing the momentum of separate organic existence. We can distinguish the *vital body* that wishes to *recreate* bodily existence from the *deathly ego* that wishes, ultimately, after the separate life, for the *cessation* of bodily existence. (The four earlier narratives enact the thanatotic desires of the isolate ego.)

On lower as higher levels, the reproductive body fulfills itself in conjunction with another body, similar yet different, and produces a new creation. There is no *re/production* (though there is *production*) without the creative alignment of a second body, the coming together of equal balanced forces:

> We must regard as in the highest degree significant the fact that this function of the germ-cell is reinforced, or only made possible, if it coalesces with another cell similar to itself and yet differing from it. (5:40)

Life is generated in relation to the other. In literature we encounter this idea in metaphysical love poetry (which may parallel metascientific theory), and recall the alchemical and erotic polarity eloquently counseled by John Donne, for "whatever dies was not mixed equally." This dependence on the other for a balanced force of being evokes the novels of the Brontë sisters and D. H. Lawrence. Freud allows us to interpret the passionate struggles of *Jane Eyre* and *Sons and Lovers* in a context of a universal psycho-biological reduction. The balance of separate, attracted forces, dependent and independent, underlies the creative tension of human love.

Having presented a narrative on the balanced equality of otherness, Freud begins another narrative, similarly composed from microbiological metaphors, on the theme of immortality. He reviews the biochemical experiments of Weismann, who divided the living organism into the "soma," the dying individual body, and the "germ-plasm," the species-preserving body. What rivets Freud's attention is the discussion of the potential immortality of the living plasm. Indeed his discursive foregrounding of the eternal life-force suggests a kind of metabiological poetry. Bringing forward the work of an American biologist, Woodruff, Freud elucidates the poetry implicit in science. Woodruff is fascinated by the potential longevity of unicellular organisms, like the

> ciliate infusorian, the "slipper-animalcule," which reproduces by fission into two individuals. [Woodruff] persisted until the 3029th generation (at which point he broke off the experiment), isolating one of the part-products on each occasion and placing it in fresh water. . . . Thus in so far as *figures* of this kind prove anything, the immortality of the protista seemed to be experimentally demonstrable. (6:47—emphasis mine).

By the word "figure" Freud might refer to the 3029—an oddly random number—generations, or, he may refer to the figurative language of biology. The signal word "figure" refers to our human capacity to reproduce experience as an abstraction composed by number, metaphor, image, character, or thought. ("The figure" or "to figure" achieves the philosophical unification of our various representational endeavors and refers to nothing less than the human attempt to *render reality*.) Freud's conclusions reveal a theoretical fascination with a metaphysical life-idea rooted in biology. It indicates his superseding interest in the erotic as a universal power.

Hence, he notices two salient points. The first principle concerns *revitalization-through-union*: the unicellular organisms can find immortality through coalescence only—the secret of eternal life is "conjugation." Interpenetration reverses "senesence" if it occurs before the point of devitalization. Rejuvenescence occurs with the unification of two organisms, for life is restored by the joining of one creature to the other (a process Weismann calls "amphimixis" in single-celled creatures). Nor is this exclusively relevant to primitive organisms: "Conjugation is no doubt the fore-runner of the sexual reproduction of higher creatures." (6:48)

The second principle is *deterioration-through-isolation*. Cells die when restricted, suffocated by their own self-deterioration; isolation intensifies the death-process. Death results from the accumulation of metabolic wastes in the separate creature. However, exposure to another unicellular creature resuscitates the animalcule; it flourishes again within the nutrient fluid (including the waste products) of another organism. The intimate proximity of organisms changes the death process to a life process. The life-process is the death-defeating coalescence of living things. Here in the experimental laboratory, we reduce to its fundamental source a classic theme of Western love-poetry, as in Catullus who speaks of "true love inviolate/against time itself, a symbol of eternity."[24]

Theorists of romance discuss its liminality, employing the feminine trope of dilation to capture a timeless space of waiting. The fertile romantic landscape suggests ongoing contribution and reception. Outside time, the motif informing the romance of the germ-cell is creative generation; its theme is not repetition but reproduction, because creative inter-generation is the universal design for the bringing of newness, a new life outside or a new life between in the eternal life-spark. This is the vital romance of biology.

Considering that biological rhythms reveal invisible processes in advanced creatures, Freud applies the relevance of the experiments to human beings. His narrative becomes a cosmological speculation on individual destiny and species destiny, on coalescence and dissolution, on the *life-force of intimate union* and *the death-force of separate isolation*. If we apply these notions to the sexual and emotional lives of human beings, we recognize immortality as the feeling of permanent commitment to a shared life, immortality as the product of equality. These two concepts lead inevitably to a third idea. Thus, if the "germ-plasm" sequence concerns *equality* (the balanced union of separate entities), and the experimental descriptions bring forward the idea of *immortality* (the vitality of an eternal bond), the final conception brought forward in the romance-of-life concerns *unity* (love re/pairs original disunion).

The unity-theme is pursued when Freud turns to Greek philosophy to cite Aristophanes' meditation on love in Plato's *Symposium*. He theorizes that originally there were three sexes: male, female, and male-female. Zeus decides to cut the man-woman in two, "like a sorb-apple." After the division, "the two parts of man, each desiring his other half, came together, and threw their arms around one another eager to grow into one" (6:57–58). Freud suggests a cosmic theory: "Shall we follow the hint given us by the poet-philosopher, and venture upon the hypothesis that living substance at the time of its coming to life was torn apart into small particles which have ever since endeavored to unite through the sexual instincts?" He posits a primal disintegration, with creation followed by division, something incomplete and splintered in immemorial organic origins.

Biology presents cosmic life and death dramas in a language of invisible substrata. To understand this language is to understand a notion, both an experience and a conception, that we might call *sub-scendence*, the inversion of transcendence. This subscendence or intrascendence would have us moving into and recognizing the invisible living particles that underlie reality as an inversion of the higher spiritual forces that overlie reality.

Metaphysics becomes microbiology when we base ourselves on what is underneath reality instead of what is above it. But, both figurative languages search for universal truth. That truth traces two paths. One is the path of the single life, dramatizing its loneliness in the psychodramas of the isolate hence incomplete self. The other is the way of union, joining with the completing other, recognized as other, similar but different. Two become one, while one becomes nothing.

Penultimate: On Lacan and Freud, or, the Real Beyond

The present chapter has explored life and death as dynamic patterns expressed in literary terms. What is of special relevance to Lacan is the literary infrastructure I have described as the play-of-substitution. My term refers to play as in drama not play as in pleasure, for the Freudian transference rarely shows the free-play of a game. Such a substitution-play may remain within a stark and rudimentary area of experience, carrying the inwardness of the past into the outwardness of the present, thereby regressing to a stage *before* the pleasure principle, or it may make a positive advance on old experience, achieving a difficult psychic configuration that progresses *toward* the pleasure principle.

To journey still further and go *beyond* the pleasure principle we need to explore the relationship between certain Freudian and Lacanian concepts. The duality of a transference leading backward to archaic or forward to reconfigured objects may be elaborated further by reference to Lacan's Imaginary and Symbolic orders of experience.[25] Thus, the repetition-compulsion may 1) regress to visual psychic images that, in Lacan's terms, present objects of fantasy apprehended in the *Imaginary* mode, or 2) progress to verbal *Symbolic* encounters, modified and adjusted by language, which are characterized by the perception of others as subjects rather than objects. (In Lacan, objects become subjects when recognized in their own separate desire.) Lacan identifies the Imaginary with a fixity of images and the Symbolic with a flexibility of words: the dynamism of language fragments (in a positive shattering) the stasis of visuality. Thus we may claim that the Imaginary is about the repetition-compulsion in locked position, while the Symbolic describes the repetition-compulsion in open position, playing out of itself.

Yet there is a third position that seems most relevant to our discussion, for it is just here that we definitively leave the pleasure principle behind. I refer to the order Lacan designates as the *Real*. To understand the Real we need to comprehend the philosophical idea, shared by Freud and Lacan, that our way of apprehending reality is through a semiotic process or creation that structures itself *before* something that is not in itself subject to apprehension. This apprehensible surface is the perceived *Vorstellung* or fore-placing of representations. The *Vorstellung* in its entirety creates a network, conceivable as a screen or curtain, of ideas placed before reality by Imaginary (visual) or Symbolic (verbal) process. Indeed, the *Vorstellung* affirms the inextricable connection between the Imaginary and the Symbolic as the idea is represented by—or in—the image.

The Real may be comprehended, thus, as a tear in the curtain, an opening caused by the disruption of the semiotic process that first projects the Imaginary and then transforms it to the Symbolic. If unable to translate the fixity of primary imagery to the fluidity of secondary language, we are thrown back to a prior point before representational process. This leads to the terrifying or uncanny feeling of an unencompassable perhaps violent break in the necessary process of signification. The Reality of the Real is unavailable to the semiotic process that refines the rawness of pre-represented material to representative intelligibility (using the language of metaphor—or any language—one both approaches and distorts the Real).

The Lacanian Real refers, moreover, to that which Lacan, translating from the Freudian "*Verwerfung*" (German), calls "forclusion" (French), or *foreclosure* (English).[26] The foreclosed idea cannot be integrated into either the conscious or the unconscious dimension of the psyche, and can only be discovered as a shock or trauma from the outside. Hence the Real defeats the semiotic processes of the psyche. Most critics agree that the Real is closer to the Imaginary than to the Symbolic, and that the Real underlies the Imaginary as the Imaginary underlies the Symbolic. The Real is that which the Imaginary transforms, and would consist, therefore, of those dimensions of psychic connection, the parental imagoes behind the oedipal dynamic, which the semiotic processing of the orders accesses. Notably, both orders begin with *the maternal image*, with the Imaginary going toward her in fusion and the Symbolic going away from her in translation. This is a significant echo of the directional opposition within romance.

This is not to deny the threatening father, who parallels the desired mother in the Real, and who is integrated as an approving rather than annihilating presence through the Symbolic. As the longing for mother-love is refracted into the Imaginary, a sign exchange of gain-and-loss, so the fear of father-death is translated into the Symbolic, a word exchange of acceptance and identification. In psychic chronology, the maternal image precedes and predominates the paternal, so that the Imaginary is closer than the Symbolic to the mysterious Real.

The Real appears in a disruption of Imaginary fusion. That is, the Real, placed authentically in a stark and original oedipal context, reveals itself when the original object of desire appears in some essential isolation to resist or *defeat* the Imaginary. Lacan identifies the Real with Trauma (from the Traumatic Dreams of *Beyond the Pleasure Principle*)[27] and Trauma is that which cannot be legibly inscribed in the psyche.

Coleridge and Freud, Ending on a Literary-Psychoanalytical Note

Freud achieves tragic profundity in the connection between the compulsion to repeat and the death drive. Yet, his powerful reading moves to a final signified without sufficient critical attention to preceding signification. His reading omits, in particular, the acceptance of *pain (not unpleasure*—the destructive transference being more than a subsidiary inversion of pleasure) as a goal while the destructive-creative pattern (emotionally destructive, dramatically creative) becomes *a vehicle of desire in itself.* Hence Freud resists examining the death pattern as it is played in life, as it diverts part of our life-time into what Coleridge on his epitaph calls *death in life*. For, in a reversal that is more than an afterthought, *Life-in-Death*, the spectral plague from *The Rime of the Ancient Mariner*, finds a final name in the elegiac chiasmus of Coleridge's gravestone inscription:

> O, lift one thought in prayer for S. T. C.;
> That he who many a year with toil of breath
> Found death in life, may here find life in death![28]

As his epitaph identifies "life in death" with Christian salvation, Coleridge inverts his prior formulation, rendering *death in life* as his last designation for the dark passages of existence—the same dark passages formerly constellated by the feminine death-figure from the *Rime*:

Her lips were red, *her* looks were free,
Her locks were yellow as gold:
Her skin was as white as leprosy,
The Night-mare *LIFE-IN-DEATH* was she,
Who thicks man's blood with cold
(ll. 190–195, p. 88, italics Coleridge's).

The lines have more relevance to the Freudian text than might at first be imagined, for Coleridge's ghostly messenger embodies a significant elision from the Freudian text. Freud's extended scientific meditation and Coleridge's allegorical romantic journey find hidden parallels, telling twinned stories of death without dying, doubled tales occurring under the corrosive portrait of woman and dis/ease. Thus the third chapter of Freud's speculation returns to the second chapter because it repeats a significant absence—namely of the mother, found and lost at the center of the child's empty reel or, most accurately, *Spule*, the turning spool around a hollow core.

Similarly, the transfers of the transference, described in narrative figures and figurative narratives, revolve around an *unnamed* figure, known in absentia, for example by the traces of pain within disappearing presences, as in the injurious synecdoche of the narcissistic scar raising the mother like a wounding ghost. The romantic poem finds its intertextual relation *to Beyond the Pleasure Principle* by supplying a formal presence for Freud's absented content, for Coleridge's picture, his blinding portrait of the deleterious Mother, haunts metapsychological space like an unspoken *revanant*.

3

The Secret Affinities of Metapsychology and Romance: Freud's "Negation" and Keats's "Negative Capability"

> What was your dream? Tell it me and I will tell you the interpretation thereof.
>
> —John Keats

IN AN EVOCATIVE PERCEPTION, WALTER BENJAMIN FINDS THAT WRITING transforms both remembered and forgotten aspects of experience:

> . . . the important thing for the remembering author is not what he experienced, but the weaving of his memory, the Penelope work of recollection. Or should one call it, rather, a Penelope work of forgetting?[1]

Referring to the suppression of experience by writing, Benjamin also recognizes suppression as intrinsic to writing. Describing "remembrance" as "the woof" and "forgetting" as "the warp" of the "work of spontaneous recollection," Benjamin finds that the weave of the text encompasses, or is encompassed by, an absent text, its unwoven yet inescapable dimension. The absent text refers less to the forgotten than the unremembered: the necessary omissions of creative transformation make, or unmake, a shadowy counterpart to memory.

Thus denied, writing inhabits the affirmed writing from which it is formally excluded. A phantom connection[2] develops when the

---

Theoretical Forenote: The Death-Ego and the Vital Self *is about the subtexts and intertexts of* Beyond the Pleasure Principle. *The present chapter is a kind of miniature of the larger study. A comparison between a brief metapsychological essay, Freud's "Negation," and a Romantic idea, Keats's "Negative Capability," reveals the ways in which Freud closes the meanings that Keats opens. While already implied in Freud's closures, the open meanings only emerge in our reading of Keats.*

written and the unwritten include precisely what the other omits, and illumined and shadowed texts haunt one another in a reciprocal expression of the unsaid. Such a *fantasmatic* connection may exist within the single text (as in Benjamin's reading of Proust) or may develop between writings with shared reciprocal powers of completion and disruption.

Ghostly encounters between texts raise the question of negation—of how to comprehend the different ways of negating. In works that cross generic lines (yet draw a line between metapsychology and romance), Freud's essay on "Negation" and Keats's letters on "Negative Capability" establish a revealing intertextuality. Implicating one another in a continuing dialectic, each original text brings the negative (the avoided or annulled) into its discourse, the inclusion-by-omission leaving conceptual gaps filled by the other. The ensuing connection leads to intricacies of double and triple negatives, but its significance extends beyond mind-teasing conundrums. For the juxtaposition of Negation and Negative Capability allows the continuation and reparation of Benjamin's work of creative forgetting.

Metapsychology

Freud creates metapsychology when he places fantasy before reality in the formation of the self. In his revised psychology, unconscious fictions divorced from "the indication of reality" replace sexual violation as the source of psychic disturbance.[3] Anticipating the Oedipus complex, Freud discovers the origin of childhood trauma in "sexual fantasy" on "the theme of the parents." The new conception collapses the *neurotica*, or belief that repression of physical abuse underlies neurosis, leaving only dream-interpretation and the metapsychological "beginnings" theoretically "secure" (*OP*, 218).

Thereafter, metapsychology, the component of psychoanalysis "far-removed from empirical reality," privileges fantasy and dream while providing theoretical frames for psychic dynamics. Meta/psychology, Freud's invented term, comes "after" psychology, the science of mind; it displaces yet echoes meta/physics, the traditional study coming "after" physics, the science of energy and matter.[4] Representing the *imaginative* (bordering on the visionary) dimension of psychoanalysis, metapsychology grows into Freud's "ideal and problem child"; employing figurative discourse and intuitive logic, metapsychology introduces into psychoanalysis the speculation regarded ambivalently by psychoanalysis.[5]

Such paradox characterizes psychoanalysis from its origin. Freud's enraptured response to Goethe's "On Nature" essay, its central presence "an eroticized Nature . . . an embracing, almost smothering . . . mother" determines his embrace of natural science. Desiring to "eavesdrop" on Nature, Freud searches for esoteric knowledge of an omnipotent force, beginning his career in a Faustian (and Frankensteinian) mode.[6] His frequent references to Goethe and other romantics betray a lifelong susceptibility to the nostalgia of Germanic *Sehnsucht*.[7]

Sometimes restricting metapsychology to technical diagrams for the psyche, Freud will invoke the term—nevertheless—when he transcends restrictive schemes.[8] A recent theorist notes the figurality of the "metapsychological constructions" Freud describes, alternatively, as " 'metaphors' . . . 'fictions[s]' . . . 'scientific phantasies' . . . and 'our mythology' "[9] More than the self-reflexive theory of itself in psychoanalysis, Freud's theoretical revisions both delineate and transgress psychoanalytic borders, operating as the *negation* of psychoanalysis in its strict scientific sense.

First conceived as an excursion "behind consciousness"[10] metapsychology prepares later anthropological, biblical, and folkloristic explorations: inner journeys behind time and space parallel outer journeys beyond time and space. Freud's revised psychology focuses on the theory of the instincts (the mythology of psychoanalysis) and the structure of the unconscious (the archaeology of psychoanalysis); emerging when interpretive desire exceeds empirical constraints, metapsychology escapes demonstrative necessity. (Women and female sexuality, texts and subtexts of uncertain explorations, inhabit the "dark continent" of psychoanalytic geography.)

Referring to an undesignated area beyond psychology, metapsychology shares the threshold or liminal quality of romance, the literary form structured by an elusive achievement, its plot an uncompleted quest for an unnamable object; romance conceals an endless and beautiful "subterfuge," its deceptive narrative serving art but escaping desire in indirect articulations of the unknown. The unconsummated quest that typifies a literary genre characterizes its parallel psychoanalytic genre. Expanding Freud's range of speculation through endlessly elaborated but never-foreclosed concepts, metapsychology can define itself by an incapacity to define itself as *the romance of psychoanalysis*.

Psychoanalysis, the prior Freudian invention, contradicts and parallels metapsychology when its opposed ideological content resides in a similar linguistic form. Deliberately fashioned on chemical analysis, the name of Freud's new science emphasizes "analysis" as breaking-down, the separating into component parts (*LP*, 368). Scientific "analysis" combines with the mythological "psyche" in an oxymoron revealing its ideological purpose, for the nominal structure of psycho/analysis de-mythicizes *Psyche* into *the psyche*. A word meaning spirit, capitalized and personified in reference to a mythological character (Psyche the female goddess represents the soul in Pagan mythology) is abstracted, transformed, and subjected to analytical dismantling.[11]

Meta/psychology, the counterpoint of psycho/analysis, reasserts the rejected element and mythifies the psyche again. A mode of analysis affording no verification, metapsychology resists Freud's much-desired scientific *Weltanschauung*, the empirical method based on "carefully scrutinized observations" that reject "revelation, intuition or divination."[12] In diametrically opposed fashion, metapsychology introduces far-flung conjecture and, indeed, obscure symbolism into psychoanalytic thought.

The pessimistic *Analysis Terminable and Interminable* provides a trenchant example; when Freud acknowledges the fearful difficulty of "taming" the id to submit to the ego, he expresses ironic despair in a striking rhetorical figure:

> We can only say: *"So muss denn doch die Hexe dran"* ["We must call the Witch to our help after all"]—the Witch Metapsychology. Without metapsychological speculation and theorizing—I had almost said "phantasying"—we shall not get another step forward. (*SE*, 23:225)

Nearly admitting that far-reaching consideration of mental conflict itself partakes of fantasy—on the verge of a confession—Freud cites Goethe's *Faust* to invoke the hex of a dangerous muse. Intuitive speculation (with an element of the witch, the feminine demon who suggests not only general irrationality, but the compelled assertion of the female) emerges at the limits of scientific psychoanalysis.

Freud's term, moreover, interweaves metapsychology and romantic literature when the elusive "Witch Metapsychology" recalls Shelley's remote "witch Poesy" ("Mt. Blanc," 44) and finds a sister *Hexe* in the epistemological Power residing in a blank mountain. Interconnections between metapsychology and romance, or, more precisely, metapsychology and the internalized romances of romantic poets, appear as Freud and Shelley provide an identical name for the uncaptured force within a beloved discipline.

Sometimes obscured by metaphor, metapsychology can be shrouded in silence. During the isolated years of World War I, Freud planned a definitive volume on a favored subject in twelve *Preparatory Essays for Metapsychology*. He published only five of the articles, however, *destroying the other seven*; nullifying the majority of the explicatory studies on metapsychology, Freud left an extraordinary blank in his prolific career. "The rest is silence," he writes to Ferenczi, nor is it coincidental that one of his last metapsychological papers is "Mourning and Melancholia." Including the never-presented phantom theory of sublimation, metapsychology is haunted by the ghosts of lost texts.[13]

The scriptive gap may be explained by the revelation in resistance, the hidden affirmation in negation. In his slightly earlier (1913) "Theme of the Three Caskets," Freud finds a connection between the problem of silence and the mystery of the Eternal Feminine (Goethe's *Ewig-Weibliche*). A lyrical essay comparing myth, folktale, and Shakespearean tragedy, in "The Theme of the Three Caskets" "dumbness" appears as a "representation of death." Affirming the psychoanalytic trope that finds underlying unity in apparent opposition, Freud can interpret Cordelia's inscrutability as a sign of Lear's imminent death—when "contraries are . . . represented by . . . the same element in the . . . unconscious," the "Goddess of Death" may replace the "Goddess of Love" (*SE,* 12:298–99). He proceeds beyond duality to refer to "the tri-form Artemis-Hecate," a goddess of many dimensions representing more than "a wishful opposite" that "harks back to a primaeval identity" (*SE,* 12:299). The aged king encounters the implacable silence of the triple-goddess, the figure of woman who gives birth, love, and, finally, death to man; more than being her own double-opposite, woman takes an endless series of roles, ending as "the Mother Earth who receives [man] once more" (*SE,* 12:301).[14]

If we place the aging Freud, facing the mass casualties of the Great War, in the position of Lear, the silence in psychoanalytic self-analysis appears more than eloquent. Psychoanalytic silence involves the annihilating love of an old man for a beloved daughter: incest, death, and a life-long sense of inadequacy before the feminine are among the concerns evoked in metapsychological explorations and non-explorations. Experiencing Cordelia's silence at the limit of his endurance, Lear cautions that "Nothing will come of nothing," but in an ideology placing repression at the center of its dynamic, nothing is more significant than nothing.

Silence raises terror and beauty in an essay that resists classification, but arouses the aesthetic categories associated with the sublime—a sublimity that challenges the therapeutic and theoretical dimensions of psychoanalysis, revealing gaps within the metapsychological text. But as critics like Felman, Brooks, and Irwin have demonstrated, such gaps may be filled by literary texts speaking in spaces opened by metapsychological silence. The juxtaposition of literary and psychological works allows reciprocal illumination between the two disciplines. Felman finds that in the relationship between literature and psychoanalysis each form represents for the other the "unthought . . . the possibility of its own self-subversion";[15] each discipline realizes itself through the inclusion of its shadow-like other. Indeed "Negation" and "Negative Capability," metapsychological and romantic texts on a similar subject, reflect one another like facing mirrors that create depth rather than duplication and bring one another closer to an unreached completion.

Negation

Freud's discussion of negation examines both "denial," an undeliberate mechanism of defense, and "negation," a deliberate rhetorical device. Echoing Shakespeare's "the lady doth protest too much," psychoanalysis takes forceful denial as invariable confession.

> [The analysand says] "You ask who this person in the dream can be. It's *not* my mother." We emend this to: "So it *is* his mother." In our interpretation, we take the liberty of disregarding the negation and of picking out the subject-matter alone of the association. (*SE,* 19:235)

Freud finds the negative word in the patient's utterance to be not a negation but the condition of an affirmation; such negating words as "no," "not," "ridiculous," "impossible" can partially dispel repression and permit prohibited thoughts to enter consciousness. We interpret the protest, "I do *not* hate my father," by ignoring the disclaimer while focusing on the statement otherwise expressed. The negating word represents a conscious denial of an unconscious revelation. But where the analysand imposes the conscious on the unconscious, the analyst seeks to release the full strength of the unconscious. Making a positive out of a double-negative, the strategy of the essay is to reverse the negative, liberating the expression of negated desire. Freud, as analyst and writer, subsumes negation into affirmation, his object to *negate the negation* of the analysand.

The function of negation is to loosen "the restrictions of repression," facilitating the entrance of prohibited thoughts into the mind: "A negative judgement is the intellectual substitute for repression" (*SE,* 19:236). The analyst affirms the analysand's underlying counter-thought, discovering the term (a kind of magic word) that releases the repressed. Connecting the effects of repression to their causes, negation reveals a hidden reality, finding its significance in the relationship between denial in language and the prohibition of desire. Necessary for both the integration of the analysand and the interpretation of the analyst, negation allows the gaining of knowledge in analysis.

The power of Freud's brief metapsychological essay resides in its invocation of a subversive unconscious. "Negation" reads the language of the unconscious as the Lacanian discourse of the other, locus of hidden desire and denied will. Within the repressed unconscious, readable as the reversal of the expressed conscious, analysis finds the force of a counter-self: the negated is the psychic other.

But this psychic other is revealed to be dispelled. Where negation clarifies both repressed meaning and the motive for repression, Freud reveals his own deeper goal by diminishing the negated as a continuing force in psychic life. Thus his reading of the negative consists of a *reversal* of the negative. Slighting his own concept of ambivalence, Freud's determined assertion of affirmation takes on the quality of intellectual desire, its goal a reassuring certainty in interpretation: "What [the analysand] is repudiating . . . is, of course, the *correct* meaning of the obsessive idea" (*SE,* 19:235—emphasis mine). His method takes that which is most assertively distanced from consciousness as a revelation of the unconscious: "[W]e ask . . . what was furthest from your mind at that time?" (*SE,* 19:235). Leading the analysand to affirm the denied wish may negate the power of the wish—ultimately and with the necessary *working-through*—because bringing the repressed into consciousness can defuse the repressed: in the ideal case to reverse negation is to master negation.

But mastering the *process* of negation remains complex, even if Freud presents the *meaning* of negation as reachable through a simple reversal. The process of negation brings forward all the difficulty of the repression it simultaneously lifts and perpetuates:

> Negation is a way of taking cognizance of what is repressed; indeed it is already a lifting of the repression, though not, of course, an acceptance of what is repressed. . . . The outcome of this is a kind of intellectual acceptance of the repressed, while at the same time what is essential to the repression persists. (*SE,* 19:235–36)

Lacanian critics find a connection between ambivalence around negation and Hegelian dialectics: going beyond negation entails incorporating negation. The earlier stage in the development of a dialectic must be both surpassed and integrated. Thus Jean Hippolyte emphasizes that the German *aufheben* ("lifting" in Strachey's English translation) can also mean annul or cancel. Elaborating on this, Richard Boothby argues that through negation "the effects of repression are at once breached and maintained."[16] Thus, sympathetic critics encounter Freud at the point in the dialectic of "Negation" where the negative is nearest to acceptance (the point at which "Negation" is closest to "Negative Capability"); stopping the dialectic at that juncture, some of Freud's critics see him preserving negation in order to enrich thought. Yet the continuing dialectic of Freud's article moves away from ambivalence toward resolution.

Thus the interpretive device of inversion—itself a mechanism of exegesis—uncovers not only the restricted "correct meaning" of the analysand's idea but a longing for correctness in psychoanalytic interpretation. The analyst's restrictive interpretation confines in practice the free association that has been compared to negative capability in theory.[17] The desire of psychoanalysis for certainty in the interpretive process rests on its desire for certainty about the interpretive object. Indeed, while psychoanalytic signifiers proliferate to include day-dreams and night-dreams, errors, symptoms, and the revelations of analytic discourse, the signified always returns to prohibited desire. Freud's interpretive desire is to "discover" emotional desire; it is as if the intellectual desire of the analyst were the double of the affective desire of the analysand, and the double of desire desired the negation of desire.

The psychoanalytic goal is to solve a causal mystery by uncovering the precipitations of maternal figure and incestuous drive: "We emend this to: 'So it *is* his mother.'" Negation, brought forth by the analysand as a *disruption* of simple interpretation, is reversed by the intervention of the interpreter to a *validation* of simple interpretation; reversal allows the establishment of a direct link between signified and signifier, focusing negation so as to strengthen but narrow its figurative significance. After it is affirmed, the linguistic structure of negation is negated in turn as a prelude to the negation of its psychic content, the "bringing about a full intellectual acceptance of the repressed."[18] Thus, Freud aspires not only to negate the analysand's negation, but "to succeed in conquering the negation" *altogether* (*SE,* 19:236).

The simple reversal of negation is not limited to the analyst's reading of the patient's "obsessive" thoughts, for the same process occurs when negation is freely chosen:

> With the help of the symbol of negation, thinking frees itself from the restrictions of repression and enriches itself with material that is indispensable for its proper functioning. (*SE,* 19:236)

The phrase "the symbol of negation" denotes its intellectual function, its exploiting of negation to take possession of the negative in thought or feeling; Freud moves from his therapeutic to his theoretical mode, designating negation as a cognitive device, necessary to efficient thought, and a rhetorical device, necessary to comprehensive writing. Negation is essential to the inclusive thinking that empowers "judgement" (*SE,* 19:236), while judgment consists of the capacity to determine the attributes and reality of things.

The recognition of the attributes of things refers back to the archaic and oral division made by the "pleasure-ego" between that which must be devoured and that which must be repelled; the desire of the primitive ego, driven by the unmediated desire for pleasure, is to introject the good and make it part of the self, while projecting the bad to maintain it as separate from the self. Building on the most fundamental level, the recognition of the negative is preliminary to its rejection.

At a more advanced level, the "pleasure-ego" alters to the "reality-ego," its concern not the nature but the *reality* of things. The necessary location of the real is found by distinguishing between a "presentation" within the ego and a "perception" outside the ego. An inner presentation may be a creation of memory or an external perception is interpreted as a material "reality," recognizable when it can be grasped not only psychologically but physically; the real is necessary to the essential provision of the act of possession, making the desired object available "so that [the subject] can get hold of it whenever he needs it" (*SE,* 19:237).

The goal of Freud's article is gradually disclosed: the discovery of the *real* in the empirical sense. We test reality to protect ourselves from the illusions of fantasy, our deceptive capacity to "bring before the mind once more something that has once been perceived . . .

without the external object having still to be there" (*SE,* 19:237). In this formulation (and his speculations on fantasy constitute one of Freud's contradictory and creative arguments with himself), the imaginative powers of fantasy appear to have no originating power (as if there were no Primary Fantasy to act as a metapsychological counterpart to Coleridge's Primary Imagination).[19] In the evolving logic of "Negation" the power of inner presentation is secondary, its function not "to *find* an object . . . but to *refind* [it]" (*SE,* 19:237). The desired object was possessed in reality then lost to the mind's capacity to fabricate nonreality. Our object in the encounter with the outside world is to find the beloved object again; hence, the acute reading of that world is the ego's essential function. It is important to remember that as the reality-testing part of the psyche, the ego is nothing less than the internalization of reality—that is, the ego is our *inner reality*.

Fantasy, which plays a central role in the genesis of the Oedipus complex and the theory of infantile sexuality, is relegated to secondary status. "What is unreal, merely a presentation and subjective, is only internal; what is real is also there *outside*" (*SE,* 19:237). Demoting the inner world—generally the privileged domain of metapsychology—"Negation" privileges the actual over the imagined. Emphasizing the role of the ego in assessing the external world, the essay finds in the separating of the "bad" from the "good" a stage toward separating the real from the unreal, itself essential to the organism's final goals of surviving and thriving.

Thus Freud climaxes the article with his most dramatic repudiation of negation. The primitive dualism of the pleasure-ego moves to its most inclusive and powerful level of abstraction when connected to the dualistic theory of the instincts: herein the urge to introject becomes the desire to unite, part of the life-instinct, while the desire to expel becomes the impulse to attack, a product of aggression:

> Affirmation—as a substitute for uniting—belongs to Eros; negation—the successor to expulsion—belongs to the instinct of destruction. (*SE,* 19:239)

The drive toward negation has now been intensified to the drive toward destruction (prejudicing the case further, Freud refers to "the negativism . . . displayed by some psychotics"—*SE,* 19:239). Thereby, we exploit the "symbol of negation" not merely to encounter but to reject the negative elements, the repressed, the destructive, the aggressive, it reveals. The logic of the process poses the negative against itself; the symbol of negation allows us to locate and dispel the negation that interferes with the positive, and positivistic, apprehension of the world.

Altogether Freud sets the powers of a consciousness enriched by the release of the negative (taken as a necessary entrance into thoughts and emotions one would rather deny) against the reality of fantasy and the desire for destruction. The consciousness strengthened by unconscious material recognizes the deceptions of the creating mind and the destructions of the aggressive drive—negation becomes a defense against fantasy and dark desire. Thus "Negation," an essay written six years after *Beyond the Pleasure Principle*, appears to retract the drives toward destructive fantasy traced in that work, as in the rejection and punishment fantasies reinstated by the compulsion to repeat (although even in *Beyond the Pleasure Principle* Freud not only returns to but retreats from such drives).

Reaching the point where dispelling the negative appears not only desirable but possible, Freud demonstrates his enormous rhetorical skills; yet using negation against itself weaves an inescapable double-bind, for negating negation generates, unavoidably, an affirmation of negation. The negative elements of deceiving fantasy and destructive drive are invoked to be negated, yet Freud has demonstrated, superbly, that negation achieves not a dispelling but an *evocation* of that which it denies. A trace of the negative remains non-negatable within Freud's essay, its shadowy continuation fully embodied and deeply explored in Keats's letters on Negative Capability.

Negative Capability

"Negation" and "Negative Capability" negate one another in an intricate dialectic. Where both seek dark knowledge in unrecognized areas of being, Keats validates forms of negativity Freud rejects; the poet's speculations serve as the "unthought-out shadow in psychoanalytic *theory* . . . the self-subversive blind spot of psychoanalytic *thought*."[20]

Freud views the interaction between inner and outer perceptions as active, the ego "deciding" between the internal and the external, while Keats conceives a passive connection in a play of contraries refusing final decisions. The theoretical lexicons of Freud and Keats indicate the similarity-in-opposition of their ideas. Central terms, like Freud's *drive* and Keats's *sensation,*[21] examine mental experience beyond abstract cerebration; both writers combine psychic and somatic perception in a union of body and mind.

Desiring "a Life of Sensations rather than of Thoughts," Keats takes a metaphor from the pain or pleasure of the body to describe an excitement of the mind.[22] Similarly, Freud defines "drive" as "the psychical representative of somatic forces" ("Instincts and Their Vicissitudes," *SE,* 14:112), physical needs received by the psyche. Drive and sensation alike are located and structured within the *body-in-the-mind*. An essential difference emerges when drive denotes the body's insistent *demand* on the mind, while sensation alludes to the mind's disinterested *experience* of the body. The drive registers the experience of a self aware of and defined by its desire (Freud's ego always a "body-ego"—see *The Ego and the Id, SE,* 19:27), the self as *subject*; while Keats's sensation is received not by the desiring but by the experiencing self, the self perceiving as if at a distance from itself, in a space of waiting, as *object*. Keats has the ability to observe the most intense desires with uncanny objectivity.

He develops his informal and spontaneous views in letters interweaving the themes of negativity, imagination, and creative identity.[23] The three themes become one when the creative imagination integrates the negative in a suspension of identity. Negative capability (a paradox of negative being) establishes a creative emptiness, a receptive space in the self and the poem where the identity dissolves, allowing the imagination to realize itself in objective form.

Keats's letter to Benjamin Bailey examines the connection between sensation and the imagination, the nature of the relationship between deeply-felt physical perceptions ("axioms in philosophy are not axioms until they are proved upon our pulses" [*LJK,* 1: 279]) and literary creation. Asserting that "What the imagination seizes as Beauty must be truth" and "The Imagination may be compared to Adam's dream—he awoke and found it truth," Keats writes apodeictically, privileging imaginative acts as not translatable into the language of analysis; but he develops his ideas to reveal that acts of the imagination find their power in *re-creation*, the intensity of physical perception intensified further in imaginative recollection:

> have you never been surprised with an old Melody—in a delicious place—by a delicious voice, fe[l]t over again your very speculations and surmises . . . do you not remember forming to you[r]self the singer's face more beautiful tha[n] it was possible. (*LJK* 1:185; *L1*—corrections the editor's and mine)[24]

The mind finds truth and beauty in the luminous depth of recreated impression, its significance beginning in Keats as in Wordsworth with *the return of the impressed.* In a parallel-and-contrast with Freud, meaning and loveliness are not refound but remade, the salient difference in the independent power Keats attributes to the act of creation:

> the simple imaginative Mind may have its rewards in the repeti[ti]on of its own silent Working coming continually on the spirit with a fine suddenness. (*LJK,* 1:185; *L1*)

Not entirely dependent on the material world or another dimension of mind (the dual sources of Freudian fantasy), the creative act takes place within an "empyreal reflection;" this otherworldly outwardness reflects—in a parallel to Coleridge's primary and secondary imaginations—the "silent Working" of inward creation.[25] Keats's creative imagination, both in its nascent energy and its express achievement, represents a middle term in a merging of subjective and objective states. Separate from both the reality of nature and the identity of the self, the creative imagination establishes an independent dimension of being.

The reader or viewer of works of art that demonstrate negative capability enters the same undetermined and creative state of being. Keats introduces negative capability, a state of mind experienced in both the presentation and the reception of literature, out of unlimited admiration for Shakespeare. Admiring artistry that arouses a "momentous depth of speculation" (*LJK,* 1:192, *L2*), Keats refers to the capturing of dizzying uncertainty in subject/object relations, an indeterminacy in the experience of the artist and audience; the theory expresses itself in his own poetic practice, as when he writes of "dim-conceived glories of the brain / [that] Bring round the heart an indescribable feud" ("Elgin Marbles," ll. 11–12).

The doubling in the experience of the artist and his audience is significant when Keats comes to literature, as Freud comes to dreams, in the dual role of dreamer and reader; the relationship between reading and dreaming implies a poetics of imaginative—or fantasy—creation. Reading Shakespeare, Keats discovers that yielding of individual identity which allows the apprehension and substantiation of infinite *identities*. In opposition to Coleridge's rigorous intellectualizations, Shakespeare demonstrates the elision of the reasoning judgmental self and the corresponding release of the imagining accepting self:

> several things dovetailed in my mind, & at once it struck me, what quality went to form a Man of Achievement especially in Literature & which Shakespeare possessed so enormously—I mean *Negative Capability*, that is when man is capable of being in uncertainties, Mysteries, doubts, without any irritable reaching after fact & reason—Coleridge, for instance, would let go by a fine isolated verisimilitude caught from the Penetralium of mystery, from being incapable of remaining content with half knowledge. (*LJK*, 1:193–94; *L*2)

The negative refers to a fullness of experience allowing the copresence in worldly or aesthetic experience of "uncertainties, Mysteries, doubts"; negative capability maintains a perception together with its own incipient unraveling, sustaining rather than resolving contraries, functioning not to integrate but to include. Incorporating uncertainty into a larger unity, negative capability brings affirmation and negation together in a perception-conception that completes and subverts itself. Concerned neither with distinguishing between the positive and the negative, nor with separating the inner from the outer, Keats's negative capability dispenses with the dichotomies of "Negation." Granting contraries and suspending distinctions, negative capability allows a freedom from moral judgment and philosophical determination that releases (in the sense of canceling to create) self-identity.

Distinguishing (not making distinctions necessitates making distinctions, the negative and positive intrinsic to one another) between the Wordsworthian "egotistical sublime," the poet who always puts his stamp on reality, and the Shakespearean poet-without-an-ego, the vehicle for universal truth, Keats claims the highest poetry for writers who have "no self." The "poetical Character" dispenses with character:

> it is not itself—it has no self—it is everything and nothing—It has no character—it enjoys light and shade; it lives in gusto, be it foul or fair, high or low, rich or poor, mean or elevated—It has as much delight in conceiving an Iago as an Imogen. What shocks the virtuous philosop[h]er, delights the camelion Poet. It does no harm from its relish of the dark side of things any more than from its taste for the bright one; because they both end in speculation. (*LJK*, 1:387; *L*3)

In the letter to Woodhouse, Keats describes the ability of the creative imagination to assume a variety of identities as the true source of negative capability. The imagination demands the release of the containing controlling self; the dissolution of the fixed ego liberates the artist:

> A Poet is the most unpoetical of any thing in existence; because he has no Identity—he is continually in for—and filling some other Body—The Sun, the Moon, the Sea and Men and Women who are creatures of impulse are poetical and have about them an unchangeable attribute—the poet has none; no identity. . . . When I am in a room with People if I ever am free from speculating on creations of my own brain, then not myself goes home to myself: but the identity of every one in the room begins to [so] press upon me that, I am in a very little time annihilated. (*LJK,* 1:387; *L3*)

The romantic paradox of Keats's creative identity consists of its being simultaneously nothing and everything, "annihilated" into "The Sun, the Moon, the Sea and Men and Women;" the negative circles around the positive in the fecundity of obliteration, the imagination born from the death of the self. With the yielding of the ego comes the power of creative imagining, the space of annihilation opening to the space of creation. This space, the vast abyss or feminine "gap" of the unknown demands recognition *as the unknown in its otherness*. Beauty is beyond the "bourne" of knowledge and cannot be preserved, but only devoured, by those who "hunger . . . after truth" (*LJK,* 1:185, *L1*).

Where Freud's idea of mental creation, fantasy or the imaginative fulfillment of desire, *substitutes* for a reality that remains empirically fixed, Keats's idea of mental creation, imagination or the creative perception of nature, *supplements* an alterable reality changed in and by the creative mind. Creation merges with perception in Keats, enhancing the surrounding world ("more beautiful than it ever was") without replacing it altogether; in Freud, fantasy distorts desire to disguise it in a manner more reductive than enhancing. Keats's imagination finds experience and knowledge beyond empirical reality, while Freudian fantasy precedes the encounter with an inescapable reality.

Yet Keats inevitably affirms his identity by his negation of identity. When the beneficial consequences of an explorative play of identity provide the context for negative capability, the capacity to integrate the negative becomes positive. The Poet develops, after all, from that which is "the most unpoetical of any thing in existence." Thus Keats ends his letter to Woodhouse by saying "I am ambitious of doing the world some good. . . . in the interval I will assay to reach to as high a summit in Poetry as the nerve bestowed upon me will suffer." Though he is quick to gainsay this: "even now I am perhaps not speaking from myself: but from some character in whose soul I now live." Yet the letters and poems of Keats attest to the attainment of a poetic identity—a resounding something out of all his theorizing about nothing; the positive emerges from the Keatsian negative, as the negative, the continuing affirmation of powers of fantasy and destruction, remains undispelled in all of Freud's positive and positivistic reality testing (or *texting*).

Romance

Examining the conflict between inner and outer being, Keats and Freud share the double vision of the romantic. "The opposition between the hidden and the visible," that "common characteristic of . . . [psychoanalysis] and Romanticism,"[26] troubles two writers who observe realities and dreams. But where Freud masters the dream in the labor of interpretation, his own *dream-work*, Keats resists the mastery of dream in a *dream-play* of real and imagined worlds. Freud seeks power and meaning *through* vision, where Keats looks for pleasure and meaning *in* vision, the difference conferring the similarity-in-opposition of mirror-images on "Negation" and "negative capability."

Hence the romance figure of the questing-knight becomes self-reflexive in the work of Keats and Freud: both writers pursue an elusive object hidden in the meaning of dreams. Their shared persona divides, nevertheless, into opposed self-portraits, for Freud appears as the *conquering* and Keats as the *conquered* knight. The heroic image illustrates the use of romance tropes by metapsychology, but strikes a significant contrast when Freud's knights penetrate and destroy dream-disguises, while Keats's knights are dismayed and disoriented before dream-realities.

Freud seeks the path from the known to the unknown dream, his instrumental purpose to follow "*the royal road to . . . the unconscious*" (his emphasis). Taking the dream as a means not an end, he discovers the clinical technique that "never fails" to supply a correct interpretation:

> If the first account given me by a patient of a dream is too hard to follow I ask him to repeat it. In doing so he rarely uses the same words. But the parts of the dream which he describes in *different* terms are by that fact revealed to me as the weak spot in the dream's disguise. (*The Interpretation of Dreams,* in *SE,* 5:515—emphasis mine)

The dreamer's narrative invariably reveals itself at the point of difference, the altered place in the retelling, yet it is never the altered but always the original word that signifies:

> [the analysand] hastily covers the weak spots in the dream's disguise by replacing any expressions that threaten to reveal its meaning with less revealing ones. In this way he draws my attention to the expression which he has dropped out. (*SE,* 5:553–54)

As the omitted phrase is of greatest importance, alteration reveals itself as a form of negation. Indeed, unmasking the false discourse of the conscious to expose the true discourse of the unconscious, difference in the dream-narrative functions precisely like negation in the general narrative. Since the narration of the dream repeats the manifest dream-disguise not the latent dream-thoughts, repetition is the reinforcing of psychic defense by language. *The failure to repeat* leaves an absence that betrays significance, the altered detail a break in the protective armor of the psyche.

Accordingly, the interpreter parallels his role with that of a triumphant knight discovering his opponent's place of vulnerability. Describing his own task during the dream-narrative's moment of revelation, Freud employs a Wagnerian reference, further expounded upon in an editorial note:

> The ["weak spots"] serve my purpose just as Hagen's was served by the embroidered mark on Siegfried's cloak. . . . [Note] There was only one spot on Siegfried's body where he could be wounded. By a trick, Hagen persuaded Kriemhild, who alone knew where the spot was, to embroider a small cross on Siegfried's cloak at the vital point. It was there that Hagen later stabbed him. (*SE,* 5:515 Wagnerian reference to *Nibelungenlied*, XV and XVI)

The moment of vulnerability is the moment where the analyst can deliver the coup de grace, striking a fatal blow to the disguising tale of the dream-story, thus removing the narrative form that obscures its all-important content. The aesthetic form of the manifest dream needs to be dismantled for Freud to liberate its hidden significance. Thus, finding the "solution" involves the succumbing of form to content in the defeat of the signifier and the release of the signified. Freud's self-presentation brings forward the knight-interpreter—with a hint of melodrama—as *the slayer of the story*. (The same self-reflection applies to the Tancred-Clorinda sequence in *Beyond the Pleasure Principle*; like the knight, Freud destroys the disguised signifier to release the actual signified.)

Conversely, the doubts of Keats's negative capability concern interpretive uncertainty before the art-dream with its threat of mysterious mastery. Where Freud describes the manifest dream as "brief, meagre and laconic" (*SE,* 4:279), in Keats dreamer and reader may feel "meagre" before a rich and destructive vision. The dream in Keats often includes a transfixed dreamer-observer. Porphyro, the determined knight of *The Eve of St. Agnes*, sinks to his knees, "pale as smooth-sculptured stone" (297), before the virginal Madeleine, his sleeping beauty envisioning the spiritual form of her future beloved.[27] His sexual penetration of Madeleine's dream-world yields a heady mixture of sensuous and spiritual delights, an imaginative cornucopia. Nevertheless, Porphyro and Madeleine finally "glide" from the brutal castle "like phantoms," having disappeared from both the imaginative and the historical worlds: "And they are gone: ay, ages long ago / These lovers fled away into the storm" (370–71). Surrounded by the deathly realities of coarse indulgence or plaintive frustration, the dream remains an irrecoverable vision.

Porphyro initially disturbs Madeleine's dream by playing "an ancient ditty, long since mute, / In Provence call'd, "La belle dame sans mercy" (291–92), usually cited as referring to Alain Chartier's Medieval poem, yet surely anticipating Keats's own version of the ballad. Returning to the evocative encounter between dreamer and observer, "La Belle Dame Sans Merci" presents the disorientation of its protagonist through the perplexity of its narrator.

> O what can ail thee, knight-at-arms,
> Alone and palely loitering?
> The sedge has wither'd from the lake,
> And no birds sing
>
> . . . .
>
> I met a lady in the meads,
> Full beautiful—a faery's child,
> Her hair was long, her foot was light,
> And her eyes were wild.
>
> I set her on my pacing steed,
> And nothing else saw all day long,
> For sidelong would she bend and sing
> A faery's song.
>
> She found me roots of relish sweet,
> And honey wild, and manna dew,
> And sure in language strange she said
> "I love thee true."
>
> She took me to her elfin grot,
> And there she wept and sigh'd full sore,
> And there I shut her wild wild eyes
> With kisses four.

And there she lulled me asleep,
  And there I dream'd—Ah! woe betide!
The latest dream I ever dream'd
  On the cold hill side.

Neither transcending nor participating in the material world, neither in nature nor out of her, the knight is in a spiritual limbo and an imaginative purgatory. He is twice-disoriented, first by the vision of beauty, later by a dream of death: the perplexed speaker encounters the disheveled victim of a double dream. (Like amazed listeners to romantic stories from Coleridge's Wedding Guest through Mary Shelley's Walton and Emily Brontë's Lockwood, Keats's narrator represents the hapless reader in the court of incomprehensible events.)

Taking us from struggle to usurpation, the poem concerns an encounter between a knight and the unearthly figure in his answered quest who is personified by the feminine beauty of the visionary "fairy's-child." The knight attempts to capture the vision, leading her on *his* steed, the ballad rendering a parable of the relations between poet and poem, dreamer and dream. The garlands and bracelets are nature's circles, a closing of transcendent vision in verdant chains. But while he can only encircle her from without, her enchantments are internal, transforming him with magic nourishment until he comprehends her "language strange" and enters "her elfin grot." Inside the mysterious place of her possession, the conflict continues between vision and dream, in a play on seeing and sleeping where each closes the eyes of the other, quieting the visual control of the beloved. In her superior power, the Belle Dame brings an inner sequence like a revelation from the fairy-world, canceling its framing vision and awakening the knight to a threadbare trace of romance, an anticlimax following a nightmare or dream at the end of dreaming. (The reversal in the poem's theme contrasts with the repetition of its technique, its balladic cadences explaining everything but resolving nothing.)

I saw pale kings and princes too,
  Pale warriors, death-pale were they all;
They cried, "La Belle Dame Sans Merci
    Hath thee in thrall!"

And this is why I sojourn here,
  Alone and palely loitering,
Though the sedge is wither'd from the lake,
    And no birds sing.

The technique of poetic self-cancellation finds exile from the dream at the terminus of the dream, and alienation from nature at the heart of nature; its presentation of the dream undreamed and nature denatured renders "La Belle Dame Sans Merci" into the specimen poem of negative capability. The poem shows the knight gaining imagination at the cost of his being, following a seductive witch to her very source; the Keatsian imagination is perilous not because the knight is incapable of following the vision to its essence, but because death *is* its essence. At the extreme point of fantasy, pure imagination desires the fall outside nature into a beautiful and sterile absolute. Opposed to Freud's notion of fantasy as a weak substitute for a disrupted nature, Keats's nature-intensifying imagination achieves its supreme beauty in the stress of abandoning the nature that never allows itself to be abandoned. But the unearthly beauty of the fairy's song leads to an imaginative borderland where a defeating spirit demands full submission, the forsaking of identity achieving not a transformation but a loss of self. No longer a knight of the imagination when loitering is the antithesis of questing, neither can the protagonist remain a natural creature.

If Hagen-Freud imposes an interpretation through the gap in the dream-disguise, the "horrid warning" of Keats's "Pale warriors" imposes obedience, with gallant dreamers blanched like ghosts before uninterpretable death. The poem's readers are baffled by a lyrical yet monitory text with an encircling power superior to the knight's garlands:[28] the repetition of the first stanza by the last encloses the poem's readers in its imaginative purgatory, just as La Belle Dame never returns the power of voice to its dumbstruck first speaker. The dream isolates the dreamer and scorns the natural world through a "death-pale" reality, the realm of the dying known *only* by the imagination, encouraging us to fall "half in love with easeful death." The "horrid warning" comes from a bloodless aristocracy of art counseling against a fantasia of nonidentity (or infinite identity) that transcends mortality to lose humanity.

For Keats negative capability opens "magic casements," yet disorientation awaits the dreamer who loses himself in the fancy's "perilous-seas forlorn." In the later *Fall of Hyperion: A Dream*, negative capability takes a turn toward self-flagellation, as Keats rejects the poetic stance encouraging social irrelevance and self-obsession. *Hyperion*'s protagonist presents himself with masochistic shame before Moneta, the captious goddess who describes pure vision as sickness, attacking the visionary poet as "a dreaming thing / A fever of thyself" (168–69). The true poet takes on himself "the miseries of the world" (148), and actively opposes the self-pitying fantasist who "venoms all his days,/Bearing more woe than all his sins deserve" (175–76). The goddess calls on the passive dreamer to negate negative capability.

As the dreamer arrives at the end of his dreaming, the master comes to the end of his mastering, silenced before language that eludes transformation:

> There is often a passage in even the most thoroughly interpreted dream which has to be left obscure. . . . This is the dream's navel, the spot where it reaches down into the unknown. The dream-thoughts to which we are led by interpretation cannot . . . have any definite endings. (*SE,* 5: 525)

Not quite fading into one another, negation and negative capability are interdependent: negative capability maintains an imaginative freeplay that would be meaningless without a distinction-making structure; the open-minded and rigorous search for the positive is the negative of negative capability, while the continuing inclusion of the negative marks the negation of "Negation." Neither concept survives a submission to the other.

Nor can the two conceptions be equated when negation is at the heart of metapsychology: Freud's revision of the Faust-Prometheus myth returns to the scientific ambition of mastering nature, though in the internalized pragmatic form of self-mastery: "where id was there shall ego be" (*SE,* 80). Freud diminishes the obscuring influence of unconscious fantasy to increase the clarity of vision essential to survival. Less interested in clarity than fullness of vision, Keats finds meaning in the obscure shadowing of a vision-without-closure; negative vision is expressed by a generosity of style, a sweep of profuse outpouring unimpeded by fear of contradiction and yielding fixed identity to a continuing quest. Not centrally concerned with survival, Keats denudes the ego of an essential function. If Freud finds meaning and power in the determination of the *real*, Keats finds meaning and beauty in the undetermined nature of the *true*. In the paradox of their relationship metapsychology illuminates the shadows of romance by the language of romance. Encountering romance at the borders of death, metapsychology waits at that romantic threshold, in fear of its identity.

In a reminiscence of dream-symbolism, negation and negative capability are themselves and not themselves, establishing an intercourse between something and nothing to recall Benjamin's "opaque repetition." At the end of the negation of the negative its reassertion awaits, the reduction of fantasy and death opening the way for demonic return in later writings of Freud. But as the poet of no identity becomes an identity so Keats too can negate negation. At the end of the negative awaits the positive and at the end of the positive awaits the negative; their dialectic depends on the play of contraries. Each concept finds continuation in the absent other.

Conclusion

"Negation and Negative Capability" portrays a way of thinking and reading; it suggests that we may go *beyond* psychoanalysis by going *through* psychoanalysis. The questions of advance and return, desire and anti-desire, request different applications in experience and literature. In relation to "life" we seek naturally the enhancement of life, and may turn to psychoanalysis for such enhancement. But death and life build no hierarchies in the realm of the imagination.

The writing of Keats protects us against the prejudices that diminish aesthetic response. No values are privileged in Keats except for one characteristically double idea: that we be sufficiently open to truth to see beauty and sufficiently open to beauty to see truth. I find the Platonic wisdom of such concepts unsurpassable. Keats is always open to the way death affects the imagination, and here an imaginative openness that Freud lacks becomes evident. Freud is curiously reluctant to see death in imaginative terms though fully capable of seeing love imaginatively. Hence, the absent Thanatos in the Freudian body of work. To give Thanatos its due we need to turn to writers like Keats, Emily Brontë, and D. H. Lawrence.

4

Revenge, Desire, and the Exclusion of Romance: *Frankenstein*

Her Imagination, Her Monster

Mary Shelley introduces the 1831 *Frankenstein* by describing her childhood self. Her early being is divided, for she experiences herself as both a writer, inhibited by an observing presence, and a dreamer, excited to escape that presence:

> My dreams were at once more fantastic and agreeable than my writings. . . . What I wrote was intended at least for *one other eye* . . . but my dreams were all my own; I accounted for them to nobody; they were my refuge when annoyed—my dearest pleasure when free.[1]

Shelley prefers the imagined to the written because she submits rendered ideas to an observing gaze. Its presence, experienced as a sort of imagined authority, shadows her own imagination, even as the pleasures of creativity require freedom from observation. The possessor of the *other eye*, the inhibiting observor, surely refers to Mary's father, the philosopher William Godwin, a figure she idolized throughout her life.[2]

In an adulatory dedication Shelley establishes Godwin as the austere presence overseeing her novel:

Theoretical Forenote: A "waking dream" compels Mary Shelley to enter into the-play-of-substitution. She recreates her unempowered self in Victor Frankenstein and an empowered self in the Creature. Echoing Shelley, Victor Frankenstein attempts to spark a romance-of-life with cosmic lightning bolts. The creation turns catastrophic before a vivid and Oedipal dream-of-the-wound. The Creature, the rejected emanation of Victor's re-denied virility, has no choice but to enact the-romance-of-death with Justine and Elizabeth, duplications of the Mother-in-the-psyche (and body) which divide Victor the Father from his creaturely son.

To
William Godwin
Author of Political Justice, Caleb Williams, &c.
These Volumes
Are respectfully inscribed
BY
THE AUTHOR

Her complex inscription designates William Godwin, the object of the dedication, by name, while she herself, its subject, remains an anonymous and generic author. Whereas the receiver of her homage has written more volumes than may be gracefully recounted, hers is a comparatively brief first creation. The inscriber registers her ambition to emulate the inscribed, naming herself after the profession barely attained by the daughter but securely possessed by the father. Her dedication brings *Frankenstein* before an "other eye" to compromise the independence of her novel: she inscribes the paternal gaze.

Placing her father at the head but not in the body of the text, she indicates his simultaneous presence and absence. Positioned outside the novel, the paternal name, also the Lacanian Name-of-the-Father, the force of law that evolves from the integration of and resulting independence from parental figures, *remains unintegrated in the writing itself*. Rather, Mary returns to the childhood eye of disabling authority while her own writing lacks strong authority. Indeed the novel develops according to the imperative in the name of this particular Father, the admonition found in a complete sentence that warns: *God/Win(s)*.

Later in the introduction Shelley describes an additional inhibition from an unexpected source. She is enjoined to write by Percy Shelley and Lord Byron, achieved writers and literary authorities. Urging her to write a ghost story, they consign a secondary genre to an unexperienced young writer. The revered male poets arouse in her less an anxiety of influence than an anxiety of the imagination. Percy increases his wife's sense of inadequacy by subordinating her literary efforts to his imaginative mastery. Her novel is inspired by the desire of others.

Having been blocked by the paternal presence supervising experience, the father who shadows reality, she is now blocked by the beloved presence supervising the imagination, the lover who shadows fantasy. She faces a second version of the restrictive gaze. Closed off from both the reality-ego, the actual world identified with her father, and the ego-ideal, the dream world identified with her husband, she finds inspiration in the hidden *id* (the *Es* or *it*) of unindividuated drives and unknown desires. In a striking anticipation (one of innumerable parallels between things Freudian and things Frankensteinian), Mary Shelley's *it* embodies Sigmund Freud's *it*. Emerging from an area beneath the conscious mind and civilized process, the id may be associated with the inhuman in a cultural sense. Whether presented abstractly as the Freudian id or imagistically as Shelley's Monster, the *it* is an inward force turned to usurping power, the alien demand within organic process.

Shelley appears overpowered by an imagination with a will of its own, its independent force taking her in a dark dream of ownership:

> My imagination, unbidden, possessed and guided me, gifting the successive images that arose in my mind with a vividness far beyond the usual bounds of reverie. I saw . . . the pale student of unhallowed arts kneeling beside the thing he had put together. I saw the hideous phantasm of a man. . . . behold the horrid thing . . . looking on him with yellow, watery, but speculative eyes. I opened mine in terror. The idea so possessed my mind, that . . . I wished to exchange the ghastly image of my fancy for the realities around. ("Introduction," 9)

In her waking dream Shelley feels overwhelmed, held against her will, by three different forces: first (dis)possessed by her gothic imagination, she is then terrified by the "phantasm" it conjures, and possessed again by the "idea" produced by the *combination* of a demonic force and a deformed figure. The "hideous phantasm" represents the presenting imagination, an act of inspiration is dramatized by the fantasy it inspires. The conjuring foreshadows the novel's infolding techniques, its stories-within-stories and visions-within-visions. The artist overwhelmed by his work dramatically represents Shelley herself, while the Creature reveals himself as the concretization of a creative phenomenon. As a "hideous" visionary power (more a subject than an object of vision), the Creature's "yellow, watery, but speculative eyes" eyes *see more than they reveal.* Their vague regard suggests a neutral gaze, not assertive but curious, as of one watching the one who watches him.

As she allows her creativity to be interfered with, her greatest creation—the figure of the Creature—is belated and defaced. Apparently incapable of conscious resentment, she enacts hostility in compelled behavior of symbolic import. Her usurping dream shatters the constraints of her conscious will. As an unwilled response to authoritative demands ("have you thought of a story"), the Creature enacts unconscious defiance. More than expressing guilt for the subversion of authority, his ugliness exiles him from the arena of authority. He is now outside the higher realms of aesthetic experience; a version of the gothic grotesque, he can hardly compete with poets of the romantic sublime. By the presumed aesthetic inferiority of her chosen genre Mary Shelley protects herself from competitive aggression toward male poets.[3]

Yet more is involved than this. Her dream-sequence, in addition to providing the genesis of the narrative, provides a frame for its dreams. The Creature Shelley creates is identical with the Creature Victor creates, save that the one is an actual and the other a fictional nightmare. (The same dream dreamt by different dreamers, the second is a fiction or "waking dream" of the first.) The dream sequences consist of an experienced daydream and its fictional representation, a dream-within-a-dream. The waking dreams of both Shelley and Victor follow the patterns described in *Beyond the Pleasure Principle.* Each dream replays an injury.

Regarding Mary Shelley, the dream-of-the-wound concerns the trauma of birth.[4] For Mary, producing a novel may recall, as some critics claim, the nightmares of being born and giving birth, particularly as expressed by the helplessness of parturition and the intimacies of death and birth. Birth and creativity are parallel experiences because each emerges from organic and psychic sources too deep to be consciously controlled. Moreover, the act of birth presents an area of otherness, rich and strange as well as bloody and repellent, separate from male experience. The separateness of birth suggests its fecundity as a source of specifically female creativity, the beginning of a Symbolic order of the feminine.

The Creature returns her, moreover, to the imaginative autonomy of childhood; she defaces creativity in order to recover it. Her submission to authority causes her to deform the idealized visions of the child into the uncanny apparitions of the young woman. She attains creative identity through horror when the Creature is the form of an unconscious power. With the overdetermination of dreams and art, the Creature can be connected to the hidden sources of production, his hideous mask projecting dangerous rebellion and monstrous originality.

Shelley, enacting biographically what she depicts fictionally, resists her brilliant Creature. Never fully accepting responsibility for her "hideous progeny," she prefers to view the powerful Symbolic elaborations of her novel as imposed upon her. One of the most brilliant and influential images in the literature of Romanticism languishes in a partial authorial vacuum, half-claimed by its creator.

The Four Narratives of the Text

In their separate critiques of *Frankenstein,* Anne K. Mellor and Barbara Johnson share feminist concerns but arrive at opposed editorial determinations. Comparing the 1818 and 1831 versions, Mellor asserts the superiority of the earlier text; she climaxes her argument by citing Percy Shelley's emendations to the second edition:

> He typically changed [Mary's] simple, Anglo-Saxon diction . . . into . . . more refined, complex, and Latinate equivalents. He is thus in large part responsible for [its] stilted, ornate . . . prose style.[5]

The contrast between Mary's attractively direct "Introduction" and Percy's distantly formal "Preface" supports criticism of his overelaborate prose. Nevertheless, its superimposing of one linguistic register on the other makes the *Frankenstein* of 1831 the more interesting text. Percy's editing anticipates the subversion of creativity by authority that echoes *within* the several tales of the novel.

In a reading that affirms the 1831 edition, Barbara Johnson emphasizes Mary's self-referentiality:

> the desire for resemblance, the desire to create a being like oneself . . . is the autobiographical desire par excellence—is also the *central* transgression in Mary Shelley's novel. . . . Frankenstein's Monster can thus be seen as a figure for autobiography as such. (italics Johnson's)[6]

The autobiographical approach integrates Mary's introduction into the comprehensive structure of *Frankenstein.* Conceived thus the frame-narrative—generally viewed as comprising three stories[7]—expands to an enclosure of four tales-within-tales; in the series of tales desire is divided between the ambitions of the autonomous self and the longings for the authoritative Other. The division leads to repressive conflicts between inward energy and outward demand.

The struggle for independence reflects itself in the narratives of the artist (Mary Shelley), the explorer (Walton), the scientist (Victor Frankenstein) and the anomalous child-turned-Monster (the Creature). Negative authority commences with Mary's father, William Godwin, continues with Walton's sister and Victor's parents, and culminates in Victor's accession into fatherhood. In all four narratives outward interference is destructively *internalized.*

The internalization of authority is paralleled by the repetitive return to its outward representation. In a self-destructive pattern, Mary's characters submissively negate their independent selves, yielding autonomy in fear of losing love. Her protagonists can rebel fiercely against restriction of endeavor, yet will reverse themselves again in apparent denial (Walton) or attempted destruction (Victor) of independent creativity. It is only the Creature who can achieve an affirmed aloneness and hold, eventually, to a separateness of self. Shelley's own stance toward independent creativity is locked in the intricacies of the novel as a whole.

Placing the "Introduction" inside the novel we expand its narrative structure to encompass an autobiographical dimension. The structure resembles a hall of mirrors reflecting a play-of-substitution, a diffusion of parental roles through the different layers of the narrative. Victor Frankenstein and the Creature duplicate one another while imitating an authorial self divided between submission and assertion. Victor's compulsive experiments repeat Shelley's own compelled creativity, while her suppressed imagination takes form in a maligned Creature. The Creature reflects the divided sensibility of both creators: disfigured by conscious inhibition, he is made of unconscious energy.

Thus, if Mary's narrative criticizes Shelleyan romanticism, it is by way of an *unconscious* rebellion. The refusal of authority in *Frankenstein,* taking form in the involuntary eruption of the fantasy-monster, requires a reconsideration of Mary's ideological position. Feminist critiques oppose an earlier underrating of Mary's intellectual achievements by an overrating of her counter-revolutionary intentions. Thus, readings that find Mary deliberately subversive of Percy's romantic ideals overstate the intensity of her ideological concerns. Crediting her with a comprehensive dismantling of male romantic presumptions confers a retroactive radicalization that fails to accord with the anxiety pervading a much-disrupted tale.[8]

Itself a dream-vision variant of a frame-tale, Mary's introduction organizes the novel's inner tales. More than a series of framed insets or "concentric circles,"[9] the novel's stories telescope into one another, disappearing like *matrushka* dolls into Mary Shelley, the outermost figure. She becomes the narrative mother at the outset of the text who also, to some degree, devours the text. As evidence of the vexed irresolution of a divided novel, she both identifies with the revolutionary creature *and* affirms the repressive power of authoritative Fathers and fusionary Mothers. Robert Walton and Victor Frankenstein repeat Shelley's own ambivalence toward imaginative quest, for their cautionary tales are subsumed into the concerns of the introduction. The series of questing heroes proceeds from her, the *author,* yet she is herself beholden to the *authoritarian* gaze inscribed in the dedication.

Accordingly, each tale incorporates its successor because told by the protagonist of the preceding narrative. Beginning the novel after the introduction, Walton is clearly a device for Shelley, the medium for her "waking dream" (the novel as a whole). Walton proceeds to write Frankenstein's story as part of his own epistolary text. Frankenstein's confessional declaration also contains a succeeding story, the Creature's declaration-within-a-declaration, with its pleas for understanding and its threats of revenge. Each tale gives scriptive or declarative voice to the tale within, thus establishing itself as the narrative predecessor—*the parent-narrative*—designed to control the voice of its successor. Reading the four stories synoptically, we see how the encounter between inhibition and creativity is expressed in conflicted relationships. The characters in *Frankenstein* substitute for one another in mirroring repetitions of both the self and the authorities that restrict the self.

Fields of Ice and Light

The arctic traveler Robert Walton writes in the intimacy of epistolary style. All his letters are addressed to his sister, Mrs. Saville, and are shadowed by the presence of their implied reader. Opening his communications in the second person, Walton demonstrates his devotion to their designated receiver:

> *You* will rejoice to hear that no disaster has accompanied the commencement of an enterprise which *you* have *regarded* with such evil forebodings. . . . (Letter I, p. 14, emphasis mine)

The introductory second-person pronoun invokes a pervasive consciousness of the Other that parallels Shelley's dedicatory inscription to William Godwin. Walton brings his writing before the admonitory *regard* of the Other; he seeks confirmation, a sympathetic response or approving gaze in writing, from an elder sister who surrounded his youth with "gentle and feminine fosterage"

(15). Acting as a representative of familial authority, she disapproves of the journey he documents.

Walton responds to her negative observations ambivalently, distancing himself in action from one he approaches in writing. Indeed, his entire enterprise appears torn between different *fields of desire,* areas of the natural landscape characterized by metaphorical elements that in themselves represent dimensions of wanting. The fields are places where the hero sojourns or stops or arrives, signifying harbors along the path of the romance journey. Part of Walton wishes to escape the demands of relationship, hence he wants to disappear on the fields of the sea or lose himself in the fields of ice, but part of him seeks the higher order of human connection represented by distant fields of light.

He begins with a narrative that answers to the inhibiting reader who wishes to hold him in *Sa-ville, her town, her territory*. Leaving her physically, he is beholden to her psychically, held to the field of the sea (Freud's "oceanic" experience). In the sea, escape is condensed with regression: the oceanic path leads toward original objects. Because of its dangers, its death-draw, the sea *goes toward* an original object of desire even as it sustains an *escape from* that object. Walton both escapes from and goes toward the walled town (Walton) of primary entrapment The play of leaving and approaching provides the emotional underpinning of *the-game-of-disappearance*.

He responds to the threat of primordial drowning—to the domination of will and mind by a maternal figure—by approaching the fields of ice, the deeper escape into solitary being. In a parallel with both *The Rime of the Ancient Mariner* and *Jane Eyre*, Walton finds protective solitude in a frozen landscape; he experiences the enthrallment of *isolation* as an exalted *ice/elation*. The entrance to the fields of ice establishes a figurative transformation of the-game-of-disappearance, the vanishing strategy in the *fort/da* game. Walton remains bound, however, to Mrs. Saville: he leaves her physical but not her psychic presence. Moving into the ice, he leaves the scene of merger for the solitude of journey. The ecstasy of ice represents the attempt at independence.

The icy environment represents, furthermore, the world of the fated *Todesich*, the death-ego. The sea of frigid formations, expressed beautifully in Coleridge's glaciers "green as emerald," and captured in Walton's "vast and irregular plains of ice, which seemed to have no end" (Letter IV, 23), would refer to poetic projections—like exfoliations of crystal—from the self-isolated world: nature as a mirror, an ecstasy, of the frozen soul. Vistas of desolate landscapes, scenes lacking cultural imprint or the physical reality of an/Other, define the *sailing into ice as the romantic representation of the Lacanian Imaginary*. Its romantic representation strengthens the connections between the Imaginary and the Freudian death drive.

But in another intertextual connection the ice leads to disgust and horror. When the Ancient Mariner drops below the sea, the hill, and the lighthouse, he falls into the chaos of an uncharted ocean. Within that turmoil his own sexuality elicits unbearable self-detestation, refracted by "slimy things that crawled with legs upon the slimy sea" (II. 125–26). Walton similarly perceives in the distance—before he encounters Victor, thus without the mediation of his narrative—a rough and gigantic figure reflecting the plains of ice; this is the same Monster who will reveal his visage at the end of the novel: "Never did I behold a vision so horrible as his face, of such loathsome and appalling hideousness" (XXIV, 218). Both Walton and the Mariner face unbearable encounters in their escape from overseeing presences; seeking isolation they abandon psychic defenses and immerse themselves in chaos.

A connection arises between *the maternal and the monstrous*, the closeness of the two figured by the rhetorical swerve from mirror to ice. The Monster is the ironic de/facement of the Mother, the mocking catastrophe at the end of a desperate quest; Coleridge's leprosy woman is the laughing reversal of the desired, the feminine as hell. The relevant intertexts are not only *The Rime of the Ancient Mariner* and *Jane Eyre* but the Anglo-Saxon *Beowulf*, an epic saga that reads like an extended myth. Hrothgar, King of the Danes, warns his people against Grendel and Grendel's Mother, unspeakable "walkers," "alien spirits" who "know of no father." The monstrous is located as the unfathered.

If the ice-scape is about forms of death, Walton's quest continues to the illumined area beyond the ice: "What may not be expected in a country of eternal light." The further advance is toward the symbol of the sun "for ever visible," the empowering presence of paternal light. Walton, with characteristic self-depreciation admits his

> want (as the painters call it) of *keeping*; and I greatly need a friend who would have sense enough not to despise me as romantic, and affection enough for me to endeavor to regulate my mind. (Letter II, 19)

The editors of the Oxford *Frankenstein* define "keeping" as "the maintenance of the proper relations between the representations of nearer and more distant objects in a picture" (234). We discover the difference between intimate and removed objects as we learn lessons from the confusions of the transference. The young man's need is to find one who can reveal the Law of the Father and lead him to independent power; a benevolent male presence can secure inner stability:

> I desire the company of a man who could sympathise with me; whose eyes would reply to mine. You may deem me romantic, my dear sister, but I bitterly feel the want of a friend. I have no one near me . . . to approve or amend my plans. (Letter II, 19)

This paternal strength inhabits "the country of eternal light" and yields "the wondrous power which attracts the needle." These forces may be conferred by the non-threatening friend conducting Walton toward fields of light.

The search for light refers to Walton's earlier struggle with authority. We recall the search for the Father's sanction that emerges in the young man's memory of competing fathers. He compares "good uncle Thomas," whose library was full of travel literature, "the history of all the voyages of discovery," and his actual father, the restricting figure whose "dying injunction" prohibited a "seafaring life." In *Frankenstein* as in *Jane Eyre* ice and ocean are unfathered fields. Walton experiences ambivalent fathering, and continues to replay within himself the conflict between prohibition and encouragement. His inability to write poetry derives from his unhappy fathering, and his failure to find strong self-expression is further indicated by his compliance toward Mrs. Saville. Ambivalence in relation to paternal images appears again in the encounter with Victor Frankenstein. Victor's disheartening discourse contradicts his courageous actions: his striking appearance and dramatic performance condense contradictory and inconclusive stances. The young explorer discovers a divided father for a divided quest.

The Indebted Self

We perceive Victor initially as a figure of idealization. His language of "unparalleled eloquence" and his "lustrous eyes" of "melancholy sweetness" are seductive examples of the male gaze and voice. Walton turns to Victor for a tale of encouragement, but finds only a story of anxiety: a seeming master of authority reveals himself as a mere victim of desire, while his narrative is pervaded by ambivalence toward achievement. In banalities recalling the moralistic ending of *The Ancient Mariner* Victor attacks his own sustained enterprise; Walton's search for the perpetual light beyond the pole, the magnetic field of power and insight, arouses his passenger to a furious outburst: "Unhappy man! Do you share my madness. . . . Hear me,—let me reveal my tale, and you will dash the cup from your lips!" (IV, 29). The shattering of the intoxicating "cup" destroys the Holy Grail, itself both a feminine trope and the ultimate goal of romance. Indeed, the negation of quest pervades Victor's narrative. While negating visionary ambition, he neglects, also, the reality of the body. For Victor soon reveals himself as an idealized shadow of a man, a ruin of desire. His career depicts the search for the ideal as the plot of a catastrophe.[10]

Self-destruction appears to be the unconscious goal of his quest. Miraculously saved by Walton's vessel, he refuses to be rescued unless he is assured of continued pursuit. A final confrontation with his Creature precedes the maintenance of life. The amazed Walton recounts Victor's condition at the time of his paradoxical demand: "His limbs were nearly frozen, and his body dreadfully emaciated by fatigue and suffering. I never saw a man in so wretched a condition" (IV, 25). The bodiless man in pursuit of a massive Creature suggests the hidden relationship between the two figures. The Creature serves as Victor's completing double or intimate antithesis. If Victor in his bodilessness expresses the anxiety of an overextended psyche, the Creature bears the weight of an excessive body. Victor's dis/embodiment is compensated by the physicality displaced to the over/embodied Creature. His continuing hostility to the Creature expresses a fearful hatred of not only the male body but his own body.

Victor's condition is the result of a historical process: a lifetime of emotional coldness brings him to exhausted frigidity. (In a paradox, *Imaginary intimacy is emotionally cold.*) The process begins with the story of his parents, Alphonse and Caroline Frankenstein. The elder Frankenstein first comes to his bride, Caroline Beaufort, as a "protecting spirit;" he appears as a substitute father saving an "orphan" whom he proceeds to take as his wife. The story of the Frankensteins originates in the disturbing fusion of parental and erotic relationships. Alphonse, condensing the prototypes of William Godwin and Percy Shelley, assumes the overbearing position of Father/lover.

The outward benevolence of the elder Frankenstein conceals an underlying authoritarianism: "my father's upright mind . . . rendered it necessary that he should approve highly to love strongly"

(1:33). Dominating toward Victor, the father describes familial responsibility as the index of general productivity: "I regard any interruption in your correspondence as a proof that your other duties are equally neglected" (4:55). Alphonse undermines the independence of others by the application of a domineering will; relinquishing "all . . . public functions" after his marriage, he projects crippling authority into the intimate arena of domesticity.

The domestic scene of the Frankensteins is characterized by familial over-involvement, crossings of the boundaries of identity. Symbiotic relationships undermine the clarity of Victor's self-identity, and, as a result, a vague monotony characterizes his idealization of the past: "Much as [my parents] were attached to each other, they seemed to draw inexhaustible stores of affection from a very mine of love to bestow them upon me. My mother's tender caresses, and my father's smile of benevolent pleasure while regarding me, are my first recollections" (1:33). The conventionally sentimental aura about the Frankensteins, their "patience . . . charity, and . . . self-control," glorifies parental figures to suggest the avoidance of suppressed emotions. Indeed, writing in praise of repressive parents, Victor submits his writing style to the censorship of the past. Filial indebtedness fills his tale with childish admiration, yet drains it of convincing affects.[11] Thus, Victor's language subverts itself, canceling its express meanings by sentimentality and evasion:

> No human being could have passed a happier childhood than myself. My parents were possessed by the very spirit of kindness and indulgence. We felt that they were not the tyrants to rule our lot according to their caprice, but the agents and creators of all the many delights we enjoyed. (2:37)

As his parents subject him to genteel domination, his words require decoding by reversal. Most revealing is the disclaimer that strikes a rare precision by evoking "tyrants [who] rule our lot according to their caprice." Removing the monosyllable "not" (the negating term is often the least significant component of a linguistic utterance), we liberate the meaning of a positive assertion that far outweighs its nominal reversal. Victor loses himself in vacuous assertions, affirming the tyranny they were intended to deny.

Therefore, his language is as if inverted in a psychic mirror, his words uniting him with precisely the images he needs to escape. To valorize parental figures is to be dominated by them. It is as though Victor were writing falsely to pay a certain kind of *psychic debt*. His *indebted self* is motivated by moral guilt directed toward inner figures whose demand for final loyalty denies the separate self. Having been subjected to an erasure of his autonomy in childhood, he erases his autonomy again in his writing. The return of self-erasure in writing is carried out by denial, an avoidance of anger that vitiates strength-of-being and strength-of-writing. Denial leads to sexual and verbal inhibition. Victor's language is vitiated by psychic accountability to internal presences: consciousness of the other interferes with his integrity of style as it interrupts his integrity of self.

Editorial evidence suggests that the strong expressions of idealization-of-abstraction and denial-of-physicality in the novel were formulated by Percy Shelley. Such ideological elements are asserted more emphatically in the 1831 than the 1818 edition of *Frankenstein*. In an irony that imprints the thematic substance of *Frankenstein* onto its formal style, Mary Shelley allows her own discursive fullness to be overridden by a certain romantic emptiness. Idealization and denial, tendencies of which he was self-consciously aware, are the hallmarks of Percy Shelley's contemporary writing, burgeoning in the extreme stylistic richness of *Alastor*.[12] The usurpation of creativity proceeds within Mary Shelley's art as well as her life.

Reflecting Mary Shelley, *his* creator, Victor valorizes authority figures in an affirmation of dependency that weakens the conscious will: "I was their plaything and their idol . . . the innocent and helpless Creature bestowed on them by Heaven . . . whose future lot was in their hands" (1:33–34). In a vague, glorifying style interfering with narrative self-presentation, he merges with parents who raise him as a possession. He identifies with figures who absorb him into themselves, while his prose exemplifies the narcissistic sentimentality it describes: a haze of language blurs the distinction between subject and object. The application of Victor's separate will, like the operation of Mary Shelley's independent imagination, requires violent and unconscious expression.

Describing his adopted sister and lover Elizabeth, Victor connects salvation to possession; like Justine the servant girl, his adopted sister is rescued by a maternal figure who appropriates her in turn. When the aristocratic (if once impoverished) Caroline adopts Elizabeth from a peasant family, she enacts the social magic of the family romance.[13] Elizabeth dramatizes a fantasy of adoption by a valorized family, passing from impoverishment to aristocracy in a transformation of origins. She becomes an adopted sister, a figure who may be taken as an incestuous love object, just as, in the Frankenstein family, the Mother is a kind of wedded daughter of the Father. The family romance paradigm applies to all the women in the novel; the condensation of their origins in the past and their situation in the present renders the feminine figures in *Frankenstein* as simultaneously available and forbidden. The adored male-child, Victor, is entangled in a network of family romances, while his stories of abandoned young women create reflecting images of the Mother in narrative. The series of mirroring women diffuse maternal envelopment into a general environment for childlike merger.

Thus, the blank monotony of Victor's early narrative reproduces the situation it depicts. Its deepest source is the possessing bond of the Mother, Caroline. Her pervasive influence turns the narrative repetitious and unitary as its tales-within-tales return to the maternal source. Elizabeth and Justine are inferior stand-ins for Caroline, deliberately chosen imitations who enhance the mother without supplanting her, while Caroline, or Caroline-within-Victor, like an omnipotent force of reduction, dissolves the distinctions between characters. She adopts Elizabeth as "a pretty present for my Victor" (1:35), and he receives the orphaned child as a "gift" and "possession," a duplication by reversal of the mother's controlling hold.

Repeating that primary connection, Elizabeth becomes his "more than sister," embodying an intimacy beyond "expression." Arranging the marriage of her son and adopted daughter, Caroline shapes her children's future into a form of a merger both sibling and Oedipal, for Elizabeth imitates the mother who fashions others into versions of herself. Victor's narrative of early memory employs fairy-tale motifs to banish adult sexuality, turning incestuous desire to an idyllic dream. The tale achieves a familial narcissism where self and Other fuse in nonrecognition. Hence, Victor describes the death-merger of non-individuation, a narcissistic fusion pervaded by non-distinguishing love, a play of beautified, beloved, deathly substitutions.

Yet his outward docility masks inward rebellion. Many connections emerge between Mary Shelley, the creator, and Victor Frankenstein, her creation. Shelley is neglected, while Victor is over-indulged, yet over-indulgence is a form of parental neglect. Victor is a completing antithesis of Shelley as the Creature is a completing antithesis of Victor. Sharing a repressed desire to violate the natural, Shelley and her protagonist show that traversing nature is part of both literary and scientific endeavor. Yet poetic and experimental explorations each enter—particularly in the romantic era—the body of nature to search for her sources, her causal spirit. Transgression of the natural marks the efforts of Shelley as well as her self-protagonist, Victor Frankenstein. Their efforts come to the same ironic climax: the stunning revelation of a force deformed—an achievement or productive advance is defaced. Defacement both denies and expresses rebellion. Its intensity reveals rather than hides the rebellion it cannot face.

Freudenstein

Victor explains his scientific ambitions in metaphysical terms: "It was the secrets of heaven and earth that I desired to learn. . . . my enquiries were directed to the metaphysical, or, in its highest sense, the physical secrets of the world" (2:39). His goal is to break through the "ideal bounds" of "life and death" (4:54). His ideas, indeed the very rhythm of their expression, bear an astonishing similarity to sentiments of the sixteen-year old Freud: "I have decided to be a Natural Scientist. . . . I shall gain insight into the age-old dossiers of Nature, perhaps even eavesdrop on her eternal processes, and share my findings with anyone who wants to learn."[14]

The careers of the two scientists begin with remarkable similarity; each is inspired by romantic literature to go beyond the *appreciation* to the *divination* of nature. A poetic hymn ascribed to Johann Goethe, the prototype of the scientific man of letters,[15] inspired Freud to become a Natural Scientist. Freud's conception of the scientific vocation entailed a belief in the prototypes of *Naturphilosophie*,[16] but he was himself part of the European movement that altered Natural Philosophy to Natural Science. The shift based itself on the replacement of the analytical mind for the creative imagination in the study of visible and invisible nature. The ideology of natural science replaced the metaphysical by the physical; it took pride in eliding the "meta" dimension. The process was vastly accelerated by the time of Freud's medical studies, undertaken some seventy years after the writing of *Frankenstein*.

Yet Freud's Natural Science bears more similarities to than differences from Frankenstein's Natural Philosophy. Both are related to the romantic doctrines concerning themselves with the invisible essences—variously conceived as elements, processes, or structures—behind nature. By Freud's time, positivistic science had divested *Naturphilosophie* of its lingering mysticism. The religious tinge in Frankenstein's earlier rhetoric is also a superficial phenomenon, stylistic not substantive, a function of grand romantic language. Victor carefully distinguishes science from poetry, and displaces the literary to the "softer" figures of the beloved, Elizabeth, and the sensitive friend, Henri Clerval. The tender regard for a *Weltanschauung* not adopted, the respect and admiration for the literary (Freud in awe of Goethe and Shakespeare) nevertheless conceals a hint of the condescension that empirical science bears toward heuristic intuition. Freud and Frankenstein, intoxicated by the *power of knowledge,* sometimes turn to literature as a displaced value lost to the ambitions of godlike science.

Moreover, the autobiographical writings of Victor Frankenstein and Sigmund Freud refer to strikingly similar authority figures, each text shows how older scientists faithful to the doctrines of logical positivism influence their protégés against a mystical reading of nature. In both cases the development occurs within a structure of relationships, a pattern of succeeding authority figures. For Freud and Frankenstein the passion for research requires a paternal authority who clears the path toward independence. In both cases, the path-clearer is preceded by a false beginning with a less attractive instructor. Victor commences his studies with M. Krempe, a "squat . . . gruff . . . repulsive" pedagogue who makes science seem pettily insignificant in comparison with the grand promises of alchemical illusion: "I was required to exchange chimeras of boundless grandeur for realities of little worth" (4:47). It is only with the appearance of the benevolent M. Waldman, whose voice is "the sweetest [he] had ever heard," that Victor commits himself to scientific study wholeheartedly.

This parallels Freud's early experiences with authority figures and vocational choice. He begins in the laboratory of the Darwinian researcher, Carl Claus, but because of an "obscure antipathy," he later disregards the work performed under Claus's direction. His subsequent mentor, Ernst Brücke, was far more significant for Freud's development. He takes Brücke as an idealized professional model, and remembers vividly the astonishing power of the older man's gaze. Having faced Brücke's anger at his repeated tardiness, Freud recalls—and dreams about—Brücke's regard with uncommon vividness: "The overwhelming thing was the terrible blue eyes with which he looked at me and before which I melted away." The authority figure of supreme talent and integrity is the pathway to the greatness of experimental science;[17] the male voice and gaze open the way for scientific penetration. Victor separates himself from a suffocating family through the singularity afforded by the scientific vocation. An aspect of this applies to Freud, who replaced a weak father with a strong father figure, and arrogated for himself a profession committed to exploration.

Yet Freud's assumption of the role of radical scientist, his masterly identification with himself, is antithetically opposed to Victor's self-masking: the fictional character hides his oppositional energies from himself. A compliant and devitalized son, he sublimates his sexuality in research (his relationship with Elizabeth is asexual throughout). He describes his natural curiosity in the masculinist terms of modern science: "I have described myself as always having been imbued with a fervent longing to penetrate the secrets of nature," (2:39). The texts and teachers empowering his ambitions display the same force of entrance: "But here were books, and here were men who had penetrated deeper and knew more" (2:40). Victor displaces sexuality and physicality to scientific experimentation, an intellectual sublimation that parallels the poetic sublimation of *Alastor*'s questing poet. The poet prefers sexual dreams, as the scientist prefers physical experiments, to the reality of the body.

Victor employs metaphors of entrance after Waldman, a professor of chemistry, counsels his student to replace the mystical alchemy of Cornelius Aggripa, Paracelsus, and Albertus Magnus, with a humanistic interpretation of Natural Philosophy. An empiricist who preserves a poetic element of Romantic *Naturphilosophie* Waldman—his name, which means "woodsman," indicating his natural proclivity—certifies a version of modern science with an aggressive philosophical program: "[Modern chemists] penetrate into the recesses of nature, and show how she works in her hiding places. . . . They have acquired new and almost unlimited powers; they can command the thunders of heaven, mimic the earthquake, and even mock the invisible world with its own shadows" (3:47–48).

Waldman's vision combines godlike or satanic knowledge with a sexual possession that bears incestuous overtones (the violated body belongs to *Mater Natura*). His promise satisfies Victor's dualistic—hence romantic— desire for powers transcending the material realm: "my enquiries were directed to the metaphysical, or, in its highest sense, the physical secrets of the world" (2:37). M. Waldman attracts Victor because his fine appearance combines physical energy and seductive speech. The potent combination of vigorous masculinity and persuasive language evokes the Lacanian Name-of-the-Father in the *voice* of the Father. The-Name-of-the-Father is an abstract power affording escape from undifferentiated familial intimacy by the elaboration of an objective system (language being the central, but not exclusive, system). Skill in physiochemical science provides Victor with an elemental signifying vocabulary, a system of continuing displacements, which offers

Symbolic emergence from the mergers of the Imaginary mode. Introducing semiotic self-reconstitution in the recreative laboratories of chemistry, Waldman promises recovery of the play of signifiers, the free representational interchange Lacan associates with the Symbolic "Phallus." The signifier of signifiers or master-trope that subtends the Symbolic, the Phallus in *Frankenstein* is identifiable with knowledge accumulated by scientific experimentation.[18]

Waldman replaces the elder Frankenstein, who is still a commanding Father, over-connected to the Mother and, thus, unable to play an individuating role. Members of the Frankenstein family mirror one another in fantasies of idealization, their possessive visuality creating a dynamic in the Imaginary mode. Alphonse Frankenstein is a dominating yet Imaginary Father who facilitates fusion with the Mother. That the Father "knew no science" suggests his lack of a mediating language, his inability to foster differentiation.

Absent at the Creation

If intellectual experimentation unlocks the Symbolic, transgression arouses the guilt that returns Victor to the Imaginary. He defeats himself by the gross physical literalness of his creation. Regressing from the brilliance of an "astonishing" discovery, the Symbolic achievement in a lightning-like idea, Victor moves backward to a deformed birth. *The deformation of the Symbolic returns him to the Imaginary.* He initiates a brilliant romance of life, his search for the "spark of reproduction" recalling Freud's discussion of experiments with single-celled organisms. At the same time, the scientific search for an outer principle of life masks the personal longing for an inner force of being. All the more ironic, then, that in *Frankenstein* the-romance-of-life transforms to a protracted romance-of-death, its series of murders an expression of death, its death-romance providing the novel with all the energy of its plot.

Victor's way of seeking life already contains the kernel of death. He rebels against an oppressive environment as one compelled, as one too obsessed by his psychic needs to apprehend his physical surroundings. His compulsive activity, a "passing trance" taking "an irresistible hold on [his] imagination," proceeds regardless of conscious intentions. He disguises the meaning of his project from himself. A mysterious anxiety characterizes the quest of a student of science turned suddenly to a worker in graveyards, a guilty and isolated betrayer of nature, like Coleridge's Mariner or the young Wordsworth of *The Prelude*. His self-interpretation explains little, for he blames his sufferings on a "pursuit" troubling "the tranquillity of his domestic affections" Here, we affirm his admission that he "moral[izes] the most interesting part of [his] tale" (4:56), and find in Victor's explanations, like Mary Shelley's apologies, conventional screens over deeper motivations.

We may fill the interpretive gap by reconsidering his acknowledged goal. He quests for the universal principle of revitalization, a drive apparently realized when he becomes "capable of bestowing animation upon lifeless matter" (4:53). Beneath his general intellectualizations he reveals the need for *personal animation.* Unbeknownst to himself, Victor struggles darkly—unconsciously, shamefully—to revive the feelings, thoughts, and drives that wither in an incest-haunted consciousness. Immersing himself in cemetery and charnel-house, he externalizes the burial that suppresses life and strives against the mergers of repression.

Laboring in "a solitary chamber . . . at the top of the house . . . separated from the other apartments" (4:55), he replaces total union with total separation in a desperate attempt at self-making. In the "slavery" of his divided enterprise Victor cannot transform himself but can only project the de/faced self he both wishes and fears to be. The conditions of his brilliant experiment trap him; in order to resurrect the body he needs—wants—to distort the body. If we read the great meta/physical endeavor meta/psychologically we discern the perplexities of his position. The love-objects surrounding him are part of the self, so that insofar as he loves them he loves himself. The ego takes the self as its object: thus, a self, a part of being subscribed to love, does exist in Victor but it submits to the ego, the *Todmeister;* in his narcissism, Victor withholds recognition of a separate physical being, for the Creature is a true other. Victor's narcissistic love submits to the death it confirms.

In some desperate assault on his deathly self-love, he attempts the resurrection, or creation, of *a love-embodying body.* Victor's emaciated body sacrifices itself to the Imaginary, with its encroaching figures of prohibition, while the Creature's massive body achieves autonomy in a Symbolic expression of sexuality; Promethean independence takes the form of the sexual-Symbolic. (The sexual is Symbolic and the Symbolic is sexual; perhaps this is the meaning of Lacan's gnomic statement "there is no sexual relationship.") But we are left with the question: why is the form of the Creature so very horrible? We know the romantic idea that possibility is always severely reduced with the transformation of radiant potential to disillusioning actuality. Hence the romantic disappointment in all artistic realization. Similarly, the gothic genre derives much of its power from direct expressions—sometimes comparatively obvious—of romantic psychopoetics. The gothic is far more *literal* than the romantic.

Moreover, the ugliness of the Creature expresses Victor Frankenstein's *divided desires*, his wish to both create and destroy a body made as it is unmade. He accomplishes a catastrophic subversion of love. His master's agonized ambivalence explains the misery of the Creature.

Thus, our experience of him goes beyond the graveyard horror of exhumed body parts, and his giantism is less a vindication than a negation of the body. In a self-censuring use of the grotesque, the desirability of the physical is collapsed by its distortion. The grotesquerie of the body spells out its significance, yet the Creature's face is infinitely more vivid than his body. Rather than an animated corpse we encounter an unbearable disfiigurement, a negation of the visual, a de/faced eye/I:

> It was on a dreary night of November, that I beheld the accomplishment of my toils. . . . I saw the dull yellow eye of the Creature open. . . . How can I describe my emotions at this catastrophe. . . . His yellow skin scarcely covered the work of muscles and arteries beneath; his hair was of a lustrous black, and flowing; his teeth of a pearly whiteness; but these luxuriances only formed a more horrid contrast with his watery eyes, that seemed almost of the same colour as the dun white sockets in which they were set, his shrivelled complexion and straight black lips. (5:57)

The Creature is a curious mixture of superhuman vitality and eerie sickliness (his yellow color projects an unwholesome luminosity). It is as though there were no skin between outer and inner being. The facial elements connected to immediate surfaces and their perception, particularly the eyes and the skin, are erased or incomplete. They disappear to reveal invisible energies, psychic, kinesthetic, sanguineous, and the black lips are sensual negation. The Creature assaults the supremacy of visual perception. As the antithesis of the beauty others wish to possess, he deconstructs the beautiful.

To deconstruct visual beauty is to reject the fusion with the maternal implicit in the Imaginary. The loving gaze of the mother achieves the visual possession of the son. Hostility to the visual is a separation from the maternal regard. The search for an antivisual form of being provides an approach to Victor's dream. His dream (a dream-within-Mary's-dream) envisions further horrors. After the creation he flees from the Creature, promptly and comically succumbing to sleep after "lassitude succeeds to tumult." He feels persecuted, yet in this version of the dream-of-the-wound he is perpetrator not victim: he dreams of wounds inflicted rather than of wounds received.

> I slept, indeed, but I was disturbed by the wildest dreams. I thought I saw Elizabeth, in the bloom of health. . . . I embraced her; but as I imprinted the first kiss on her lips they became livid with the hue of death; her features appeared to change, and I thought that I held the corpse of my dead mother in my arms; a shroud enveloped her form, and I saw the graveworms crawling in the folds of the flannel. (5:58)

We view a melodramatic, cinema-style retake of the sequence from Tasso's *Gerusalemme liberata* (the sensationalistic scene reminds us that the gothic novel is the predecessor of the horror film). Parallel to the haunting passage in *Beyond the Pleasure Principle,* Victor's dream is a foreplay of the-romance-of-death. Affirming the oneiric themes and techniques of the earlier sequence, Victor recalls Tancred in the *Zauberwald*; but in Victor's dream there is less metaphorical transformation, the sequence is direct, gothic, almost literal. The lover turns into the mother in murderous confusion. The dream focuses on facial reconfiguration: features cinematically fade, dissolve, reform, fade again. The series is not of two faces but three, beloved, mother, Creature (described as a resurrected "mummy"). From Victor's point of view, face negates face, young lover effaced by dead mother, both erased by the faceless yellow mass, eyeless in Ingolstadt:

> I started from my sleep in horror. . . . I beheld the wretch—the miserable Monster whom I had created. He held up the curtain of the bed; and his eyes, if eyes they may be called, were fixed on me. His jaws opened, and he muttered some inarticulate sounds, while a grin wrinkled his cheeks. . . . one hand was stretched out, seemingly to detain me, but I escaped and rushed down stairs. (5:58)

The Creature has no face, but bears, rather, an antiface, a chaos of disordered features; yet, he does have 1) voice (the pained beginning of speech), 2) expression (his unbearable features are communicative), and 3) gesture (his ungainly body is meaningful.) Able to communicate, he seeks relationship—a soul is part of his endowment. He reaches toward connection intuitively, but is left in the empty space of non-response. Yet if we pause for a moment we will find Victor's rejection of the Creature at this juncture paradoxical. Having killed the Mother through the Creature in the dream, why does he then take flight from the one who performs the necessary task? Precisely for that reason. We recall that the dream he remembers is manifest not latent. The signifying dream is not the signified dream. And, we know from Victor's ensuing actions that the Mother remains dominant in his mind. If the Mother dies in the dream it is a warning to protect her life deep within the psyche. All of Victor's struggles to resuscitate desire return to the source of desire, while the whole point of the Oedipal myth is that the return to the source is the death of desire.

Victor rejects the Creature in order to isolate him, but the Creature cannot be neutralized. He is creative or destructive but never ineffective, distant but never absent. Rather than being absent himself, the Creature *creates absences*, his hostile energies arranging from afar injurious actions like the murder of William and the framing of Justine. Victor abandons his creation only to receive its malevolent messages in vengeful acts. Completing the communication Victor denies, the Creature responds to silence with murder.

Mt. Blanc provides a blinding backdrop to the delayed meeting between Victor and his Creature. (The blinding caused by an excess of Imaginary vision.) The connotations of the *Blanc* mountain, developed in Percy Shelley's meditative address, surpass whiteness to reach nothingness, the mountain adumbrating an empty nature awaiting imaginative completion, a blank field for the creative mind.[19] In *Frankenstein* the white mountain tropes Victor's frigid soul. But as he admires its blank face, desiring to lose himself in a recovery of his own lost beauty, *turning the mountain to a narcissistic landscape*,[20] the Creature bursts from the snowy landscape. The Creature, a flash of fire on the plane of ice, fractures Imaginary coldness because he embodies the feelings, instincts, and ideas it represses.

In the dramatic encounter with his creator, the Creature replaces visuality, the betraying sense, with audition, the redeeming sense. The frequent replacement of the visual by the auditory in romantic tradition (we recall the sounding cataracts of Wordsworthian poetry) foreshadows the replacement of the Imaginary by the Symbolic in psychoanalytic thought. On the glacial surface of the mountain, confronted by the rage and abhorrence of his maker, the Creature dramatically shifts the focus of interaction from face to voice:

> "Thus I relieve thee, my creator," he said, and placed his hated hands before my eyes, which I flung from me with violence; "thus I take from

thee a sight which you abhor. Still thou canst listen to me, and grant me thy compassion." (10:101)

The Creature asks—his speech to Victor a paradoxical combination of plea and threat—for the conferral of true listening. He both demands and begs for the right to tell his story; his rich narrative combines the recitation of a history, the pleading of a legal case, the psychoanalysis of criminal action, and the record of an autodidactic education. His is full speech in the Lacanian sense, designed to bind a listener, to redeem the Son before the Father.[21] His narrative is stronger and more comprehensive than that of Victor because the power of speech is released within it. His exclusion from the false reassurances of the Imaginary accesses first the controlled efficiency of the Symbolic, then the uncontrolled energies of the Real.

The transition from the visual image to the spoken word moderates the dangerous encounter with a denying father; the Creature organizes such passage to release their relationship from the fiendish self-reflections of visuality. The pathos of the encounter is enormous: the Creature says in effect, "you need not look at me, I acknowledge my ugliness and do not even blame you for creating it." For the Creature is irremediably unfathered, an abomination forever denied the-Name-of-the-Father. The bowing before the denying Father is the greater part of the pathos. Victor can never forgive the Creature of his driven force, the son of his desire.

Annihilating Narcissus

The Creature's talents emerge in relation to language and literature; he is a speaker and listener, reader and writer. His hypnotic speech, both accusation and confession, fills the strategic center of the novel. *Frankenstein* lacks a deliberate beginning because it is inaugurated as a kind of compelled dictation; it lacks closure because its Creature remains energetic "in darkness and distance" (24:223). The novel is most fully articulated in its middle tale; its pregnant center gives birth to lyric discourse. The Creature tells stories of love and death in the mid-range of the narrative, while his clarity and depth of style slows the pace of its temporality. His closed-off tale is the excluded romance of *Frankenstein*. Its slow recital describes a romance of self, nature, and otherness; it is as lovely as Mozart at its inception, and tempestuous as Wagner in the later phase. An orchestrated sequence, the Creature's narrative fills the narrative's protected heart.

On the other hand, Victor's story is all beginnings and endings, for he runs from the middle-game, the full play of experience that bequeathes a life-story. A structure of foreboding beginnings culminates in catastrophic ends. Held for too long in the grip of a possessive family, his attempt at autonomy only moves him into the protracted death of a failed birth. The history of Victor Frankenstein, with its sensationalism and abnormality, recounts gothic variations on Oedipal myth. It tells the story of one who pays debts to inner figures by forfeiting his life. After his energies come to an aborted end, he devotes them to the resistance of desire. Victor becomes *the figure of anti-desire*, while yet transmitting desire to the rejected Son recounting its tragic tale.

Beginning his story, the Creature foregrounds the importance of narrative and, by implication, his own narrational talents: "Hear my tale; it is long and strange" (10:101). The tale alters the tone of the novel by its painstaking work of differentiation. The Creature describes individuation where Victor describes interfusion: perfect solitude counters total merger. Their respective tales exemplify the contrast between an idyllic childhood pervaded by benevolence and an exilic childhood pervaded by malevolence. It is interesting that exile leads to better writing.

A creation myth recast as an autobiographical romance, a genesis of an individual sensibility, the Creature's tale describes the birth of consciousness. In romantic style, the early development of awareness occurs simultaneously in inner and outer spheres:

> It is with considerable difficulty that I remember the original era of my being. . . . A strange multiplicity of sensations seized me . . . it was . . . a long time before I learned to distinguish between the operations of my various senses. . . . I remember, a stronger light pressed upon my nerves, so that I was obliged to shut my eyes. Darkness then came over me, and troubled me . . . opening my eyes . . . the light poured in upon me again. (11:102)

The Creature takes possession of his being by defining a psychic presence. Beginning with the perception of light, his retrospective narrative parallels the discovery of the world with the discovery of the self. The double movement of perception provides a depth of focus, a precision in the work of narration and identification. His early tale describes a luminous surround. Reclaiming the nature absent from Victor's narrative, his story describes the kind of romantic origins that are enchanted by reality.

He gazes with "wonder" at the moon lacking a word for its "radiant form," enacting the unmediated experience of sensory innocence. Discovering nature before feeling translates into language, his magical perceptions precede the words that express them. His earliest being—pace Lacan—consists of affects not words. These birth sequences, paralleling the early childhood passages from Wordsworth's *Prelude*, introduce an unmediated vision of nature; the lack of mediation in the Creature's tale assumes special significance in *a text where everything else is mediated.*

Thus, after the vague synesthesia of first impressions, the received "multiplicity of sensations," he separates the capacities of the self from the characteristics of nature. Finding beauty in distinction, he establishes a certain balance between knowledge and love:

> I began to distinguish my sensations from each other. . . . I was delighted when I first discovered that a pleasant sound, which often saluted my ears, proceeded from the throats of the little winged animals who had often intercepted the light from my eyes. I began also to observe, with greater accuracy, the forms that surrounded me, and to perceive the boundaries of the radiant roof of life which canopied me. Sometimes I tried to imitate the pleasant songs of the birds, but was unable. (11:103–4).

Delight leads to clarity as he confronts his elemental difference from the world of song and light. Perceived separation intensifies strength of feeling. The spontaneous emotions extend to the realm of the human: "How miraculous did [the village] appear! the huts, the neater cottages, and stately houses, engaged my admiration by turns" (11:106). The Creature's tone recalls the early Wordsworth, for he finds himself in a luminous world that he recognizes, but cannot possess. In his natural love, the Creature achieves the secret recovery motivating Victor's project. Fulfilling Victor's unconscious desire for life, he regains nature's lost reality; the Creature recaptures the radiant world his creator abandons.

If nature teaches of separateness-through-love, the human reimposes brutal exile, an attack by villagers leaving the Creature "grievously bruised" (11:106). Taking refuge from human hostility, he conceals himself in a rude hovel. The cottagers' sequence commences. The center-within-the-center of the narrative, this section of the novel is almost silent, silent as a Coleridgean reality-dream. For, while the cottagers are not silent, the Creature observes them from his inaudible self-concealment. Observed from a rude chink in the wall, the pastoral life of the cottagers recalls the glorified life of the Frankensteins. But the Creature views the objects of his wonder with a clarity that maintains their separateness.

The Creature takes refuge in an act of disappearance. *His* disappearing game entails self-concealment; the withdrawal into protected space allows inward forces. Refuge from being observed is the prelude to the acquiring of language, as if the attainment of sexual/Symbolic autonomy *required* disappearance from the familial scene. A voyeur of language, he stares hungrily at the feast of words from the outside, lacking the path to the inside.

His need for others intensifies as he remembers his rejection by the world of men. The mystery of his exclusion is solved in an agonizing self-encounter:

> I had admired the perfect forms of my cottagers—their grace, beauty, and delicate complexions: but how was I terrified, when I viewed myself in a transparent pool! At first I started back, unable to believe it was indeed I who was reflected in the mirror. (12:114)

In a moment of negative mythology, the Creature confronts himself as a dark Narcissus, his self-rejection an inverted mirror of narcissistic self-embrace.[22] His self-confrontation in the mirror negates Narcissus. Thus, he looks at himself with horror rather than terror (terror is an emotional response, connected to the fearful, where horror is an aesthetic response, connected to the hideous). The drowning of Narcissus is a psychoanalytic parable, an elegant description of self-love as a fall into nothingness, a descent into the trans/parent depths of death. To fall in love with the self is to drown in the inner psyche, to return to the object of original desire blocking the object of life-desire. Because the self's original object is inseparable from the self, there is no other in the place of the original Other. When we fall into the water of our own beauty, searching for love in the mirror-image, we fall deep into the abyss of nothingness. There is no love object behind the beauty of the mirror image. Narcissus is doomed.

Retreating from the watery image, the Creature withdraws from Narcissistic death. If the seductive self-love that draws the viewer into the mirror—the watery depths of self-love—begins with Motherlove, the Creature's ugliness has to do with Mother-lack, the *béance* of maternal absence. The Creature is created to efface the Mother or be effaced by her: he fills the abortive space of the un/Mothered. He is not Narcissus negated (for that would leave Narcissus intact) but Narcissus annihilated. With no Mother-love to enforce a sense of the beautiful, the Creature is something far less imaginable than the ugly. The maternal abyss means the absence of a face and the absence of an eye. The history of the abyss is found in the love/hatred of the Imaginary out of which the Creature is created. His creation is Victor's grotesque construction for autonomy and against merger, a hideous incarnation of Tancred's liberating sword.

The ugliness is precisely the problem here, because Victor creates out of anti-Imaginary excessiveness, and it is just this *excess* that shows his debilitating ambivalence toward the Mother. Victor did not really want to escape Caroline Frankenstein, and the Creature's consequent ugliness could only redeem the Imaginary in Victor's eyes. Hence, the Creature is only *almost* redeemed by the replacement of the Imaginary by the Symbolic, only *almost* makes his ruthless transition. His failure comes about even if his turn from narcissistic self-love indicates his own capacity for love of the other. Indeed, his narrative is about object-love as Victor's narrative is about narcissism (creating the Creature could have been a refutation of narcissism by the making of an *imageless image*, could have been, if Victor had not fled from the shattered mirror).

It is left to the Creature to attempt to shift narrative focus to Symbolic images, to verbal rather than visual figures, to voices rather than faces. His distanced experience with the cottagers thus concerns itself with language-texts, story and journal, literature and song. He is an omnivorous consumer of texts, a genius who rapidly masters *The Sorrows of Werther*, *Plutarch's Lives*, and, above all, *Paradise Lost* to comprehend the individual, political, and cosmic levels of human experience and expression. His prodigious intellect absorbs the microcosm of feeling in *Werther*, the body politic of reason in *Plutarch,* and the macrocosm of the imagination in *Paradise Lost*.

His reading of Milton is particularly acute as he recognizes that the difference between Adam and Satan inheres in the denial of love. Like other romantic figures, he encounters the Judeo-Christian God to reject him; this rejection is redoubled when the Creature reads the fourth and most crushing of his discovered texts: Victor's journal. He encounters emotional catastrophe when emotional need displaces mental power, and, despite the evidence of his Father's unexpungable hatred for him, he turns to another Father figure. In perhaps the most haunting sequence in the novel, he focuses on the aged father of the cottagers, a blind old singer recalling the legendary Homer. The old man condenses language, literature, and music, all Symbolic systems, into a playing and singing that is communicative, aesthetic, sightless. The Creature devises his plan, admirable yet hopeless, to approach the father of voice and song, an old man who lives in acoustical creativity to fill a visual vacuum:

> Safie, Agatha, and Felix departed on a long country walk, and the old man, at his own desire, was left alone in the cottage. When his children had departed, he took up his guitar, and played several mournful but sweet airs, more sweet and mournful than I had ever heard him play before. (15:132)

In this atmosphere, sound compensates for sight to establish conditions where he might be accepted into the human community. The Creature makes his anguished approach to another being. The pace of the dialogue quickens as he speaks of his need for "the protection of some friends," for to fail with them is to be "an outcast in the world for ever" (16:133–34). The old man is generally but not personally sympathetic, for he notably avoids—deliberately or not—connecting himself and the other cottagers with the sought "friends." Insofar as there is an approach to the old man himself, the desired direct "protection" of the Father, every advance increases the distance. At one point there is a tantalizing hint of success: "I am blind, and cannot judge of your countenance," says the father, "but there is something in your words, which persuades me that you are sincere" (16:134). This inspires the Creature to make his agonized appeal:

> "How can I thank you, my best and only benefactor? From your lips first have I heard the voice of kindness directed towards me; I shall be for ever grateful; and your present humanity assures me of success with those friends whom I am on the point of meeting."
>
> "May I know the names and residence of those friends?"
>
> I paused. This, I thought, was the moment of decision, which was to rob me of, or bestow happiness on me for ever. I struggled vainly for firmness sufficient to answer him, but the effort destroyed all my remaining strength; I sank on the chair, and sobbed aloud. At that moment I heard the steps of my younger protectors. I had not a moment to lose; but, seizing the hand of the old man I cried, "now is the time!—save and protect me! You and your family are the friends whom I seek. Do not you desert me in the hour of trial!"
>
> "Great God!" exclaimed the old man, "who are you?" (16:135)

The old man's exclamation dooms the Creature's efforts even before the younger cottagers, sighted but blind in the old tragic paradox, reimpose in fury a visual curse. The Creature's tragedy occurs in the piteous expression of need, for the pitiful comes from the abyss of the absent Imaginary. Yet nothing he could have done would have permitted the old man to confer his favor, to transmit the Symbolic order from Father to Son. Part of the significance of the scene is found in the way Symbolic and Imaginary remain fused—the parent needs to be charmed by the Imaginary child before consenting to form him into the Symbolic man. The larger significance of the scene is as a *mise-en-âbyme*, the appeal to a (physically) blind father, the aged cottager, within an appeal to a (spiritually) blind father, Victor Frankenstein. Indeed the *mise-en-âbyme*, the totalizing miniature image within a greater image that reflects and expands it, is an aesthetic key to the reading of a novel filled with significant portraits and employing the *matrushka* structure of figures within figures.

After his agonizing rejection by the blind father, the Creature will become, as Heathcliff becomes, a figure of revenge. If he begins like Jane Eyre, watching the familial perfection played out beyond a circle of exclusion, he ends as Heathcliff and destroys those same arenas of perfection. Revenge should be understood as a composite of two of the death-romance paradigms. Revenge turns on the point where the-play-of-substitution, the repeated wounding of the subject, is reversed to the-romance-of-death, the repeated wounding of the object—in the-romance-of-death the subject controls the destructive series instead of being controlled by it.

In the the-play-of-substitution the narcissistic self is persecuted or seduced by projections of inseparable inner objects. At its most fundamental level the-play-of-substitution is a drama directed by the ego (the ego *is* the demon). Basing myself on the metapsychological speculations of *Beyond the Pleasure Principle*, I take the ego as that part of being that masters the self under the movement toward death and the exclusion of the sexual other. In the world of the ego, death colonizes love. The narcissistic self, and this is exemplified by the early position of Victor, is driven by desire that remains within the self, directed at internal figures. This is an intermediate position that can go forward to the desire for the other, its energy called *Eros*, or backward toward death, death being the final anti-desire, of the isolated self, its energy called *Thanatos*. Facing (unfacing) the blind Father and the cottagers the Creature endures the-play-of-substitution; in that passive situation fate is the demon. Thereafter the Creature turns the drama on its axis, and returns to Imaginary figures not as a faceless victim but, wresting the demonic from fate, as a ferocious devil. He becomes a murderer, and the murders direct themselves, not coincidentally, against maternal love and facial beauty. Revenge changes the-play-of-substitution to the-romance-of-death.

The handsome child, William, Victor's younger brother, wears a locket with a portrait of his beautiful mother, "her dark eyes, fringed by deep lashes, and her lovely lips" (16:143). The maternal image achieves a special luster as both the subject and the object of the gaze, the eyes regarding the regard of the other, possessive in their seduction. The child who wears the locket models his inner world, containing on his heart the mother who contains him. But the possessed child, William, is murdered by the abandoned child, the Creature, now transformed, truly, to a Monster. The Monster has an uncanny relationship to the Mother, replacing her in narcissistic symbiosis with Victor. He murders an image of the Mother as if to eliminate a rival. Significantly, he plants the locket with her portrait in the folds of the dress of the sleeping servant-girl, Justine. Modeling Mother within Mother, he punishes the girl, who adores and "imitates" Caroline, for her resemblance to a prior figure: "The crime had its source in her: be hers the punishment" (16:144).

Hence, we encounter the Creature in stages. First we observe the mute pathos of his desire for relationship, his hideous newborn smile seeking parental love, the intimacy of the Imaginary. Then we see him going through and beyond the Imaginary in his relationship to nature. The lovely union at the beginning soon develops into the work of separation, a sort of preparation for the Symbolic. Accordingly, the story describes separation as a lyrical, Romantic self-discovery. If the early stages are about the losing of the Imaginary and the acquiring of the Symbolic, the later stages concern the outbreak of the Real, with its assertion of autonomy through violence.

Fire, as a natural representation of the Real, is the Creature's element, as ice, as a natural representation of the Imaginary, is Victor's element. The movement from Symbolic to Real for the Creature is a movement between two uses of fire. Fire accompanies his acquisition of language; words, like small domestic fires, construct a cultural environment; the Creature provides firewood for the cottagers while he learns "Godlike" words through them. He himself is the principle of energy behind their flourishing. This suggests the potential power of the Father within him. Indeed, fire is identified with the Creature throughout: "One day, when I was oppressed by cold, I found a fire which had been left by some into the live embers, but quickly drew it out again with a cry of pain. How strange I thought, that the same cause should produce such opposite effects" (11:104). The burning element condenses his own creative and destructive powers. As a force that consumes and changes the surrounding world, a separate element transforming material objects into its own energies, *fire resembles language*. The Creature is master of fire as he is master of language. This would make fire the very principle behind his signifying capacities, his Symbolic force: fire is the signifier of all his signifiers, his Phallus.[23] Controlled fire refers to the Symbolic, but uncontrolled fire is despair redeemed as hatred, a transformative devouring where the Real consumes the Symbolic.

The Creature's genius for revenge manifests itself in relation to other elements: he employs Victor's own destructive element, ice, as a medium of punishment. Similarly, his inimical relationship to the moon reflects his feelings about women, taking the moon as a traditional feminine representation. Inflicting revenge on the cottagers he waits for the moon to set, only setting their house alight as the moon touches the horizon. After the murder of Elizabeth, the direct collision of the monstrous and the maternal is manifested by a yellow moon, as though the Monster had transfused its luster to his own sickly hue. But his language of destruction speaks most forcefully in the connections between fire, language, and sexuality: "The wind fanned the fire, and the cottage was quickly enveloped by the flames, which clung to it, and licked it with their forked and destroying tongues" (16:139). The key signifier is the freighted word *tongue*, for he ends the possibility of relationship, despairs of his hopes for a non-Imaginary connection, and replaces the relational tongues of words and the bodily tongues of sensuality with the incinerating tongues of conflagration.

Coming to the end of his searing presentation, he requests the creation of a female other, a partner with whom he may "interchange . . . those sympathies necessary for [his] being" (17:144). He wants to retreat from the chaotic Real back to the Eros of the Symbolic. (The signifying play of language makes a space for the erotic other at the same time as it loses the pure fusion with the original Other.) He recognizes that the gift of Eros is bestowed through the favor of the Father. Symbolic creativity occurs in the medium of language but is driven by the energy of desire. The energy of desire intersects with the desire of the other, and requires the interlocking of sexuality. Desire is sanctioned by the-Name-of-the-Father but Victor will never willingly confer his name on his misshapen son. (Yet our culture, intuiting the strength of the Frankenstein myth, attaches the name to the Monster and lets the scientist share it.) Still, as the Creature represents his renounced passions, Victor undertakes an obligation against his deepest impulses. In an unsustainable gesture he agrees to create a female Monster. Thus, he accepts Godhood, creates Adam and Eve in malformation, and configures the fulfillment of desire.[24]

The Romance of Revenge

The Creature withdraws to leave Victor in characterizing surroundings: "dark pines . . . a broken tree. . . . stars and clouds, and winds" (148–49), the glorified and empty landscapes of the Imaginary. The narrative loses its fire in the long denouement of Victor's tale. A dull travelogue relates his self-distancing from sexuality, femininity, and the female body: he abandons Elizabeth as he revokes his willingness to provide a mate for the Creature.

Yet he submits to the marriage-decree of his father. His bride discusses their prospects in compliant language: "You well know, Victor, that our union had been the favourite plan of your parents ever since our infancy" (22:187). A sentimental haze surrounds Elizabeth throughout: she fades into other feminine objects in a continuum of narcissistic merger. The haze derives from the presentation of characters as psychic images, the diffusion of the body. Voice, gaze, and name are haunting fragments of the beloved which exist primarily in fantasy. Diaphanous Elizabeth contrasts with the Creature's overweighted body, his shapeless mass. (Gerard Depardieu projects the phallic sexuality of such an ungainly body in contemporary film.) The solidity of his body distinguishes the Creature from Victor's lack-of-body, and is essential to the dichotomy of their *doubling-in-negation*—the way they encompass a complete idea when taken together.

Similarly, the female Creature in her fragmentation doubles as the negative of Victor's bride (she is a physical fragment where Elizabeth is a psychic fragment). Her body shows the physical actuality lacking from female figures in the novel. Victor's encounter with evisceration stimulates; moreover, a rare intimacy with physicality; he dismembers her in a kind of penetration: "I thought with a sensation of madness on my promise of creating another like to him, and trembling with passion, tore to pieces the thing on which I was engaged" (20:166). Her physicality is the more actual for being violated: *the torn body reveals the real/Real body*. "The remains of the half-finished creature, whom I had destroyed, lay scattered on the floor, and I almost felt as if I had mangled the living flesh of a human being" (20:170). He dominates the physical in his antagonism to the element Slavoj Žižek describes as "skinless, raw flesh

. . . the indestructible life-substance, the pure embodiment of enjoyment."[25] Aggression enables connection, passion releases itself in the sadistic paradigm of love subordinated to death. The excitements of destruction involve, moreover, the return to the early fantasy of the *fragmented body*. In Lacan's notion of *le corps morcelé,* the Real/ity of the pre-Imaginary repeats the infant's corporeal disintegrity, its self-perception, previous to the sight of visual integrity in the mirror, as a being in "bits and pieces."

Aside from the Creature, an abomination, there are no substantive bodies, no *bodies-of-desire*, in *Frankenstein*. The Mother goes from the hall of mirrors, fantasy duplications, to the graveyard dream. The narrative's one feminine body is murdered by medical instruments. Victor's bisection of the female body emulates and parodies the sexual act. Violence is both protection and aggression against sexuality; by means of verbal (Symbolic) or physical (Imaginary) violence, the death-ego vanquishes the desiring-self.

Strikingly, the act Victor performs on the Creature's mate in murderous transfiguration is performed on Elizabeth with astonishing literalness. After the destruction of his partner, the Creature threatens appropriate revenge, a woman for a woman: "but remember, I shall be with you on your wedding-night" (20:168). Victor looks to his wedding with foreboding only, for he is in dread of death, or of sex, or of both: "Oh! Peace, peace, my love . . . this night is dreadful, very dreadful" (23:194). Out of concern for himself, he abandons Elizabeth. In a murderous oversight he leaves her to her fate—a death to which he is more than an accessory:

> She left me. . . . suddenly I heard a shrill and dreadful scream. It came from the room into which Elizabeth had retired. As I heard it, the whole truth rushed into my mind, my arms dropped, the motion of every muscle and fibre was suspended; I could feel the blood trickling in my veins, and tingling in the extremities of my limbs. . . . Great God! Why did I not then expire! Why am I here to relate the destruction of the best hope, and the purest Creature of earth? She was there, lifeless and inanimate, thrown across the bed, her head hanging down, and her pale and distorted features half covered by her hair. Every where I turn I see the same figure—her bloodless arms and relaxed form flung by the murderer on its bridal bier. Could I behold this, and live? . . . She had been moved from the posture in which I had first beheld her; and now, as she lay, her head upon her arm, and a handkerchief thrown across her face and neck, I might have supposed her asleep. I rushed toward her, and embraced her with ardour; but the deadly languor and coldness of the limbs told me, that what I now held in my arms had ceased to be the Elizabeth whom I had loved and cherished. (23:196)

The climactic scene supplements Victor's earlier dream: post-wedding murder parallels post-creation vision, the two vignettes merging in displacements and condensations. In the later scene, Elizabeth receives two embraces: first, the Creature inflicts a death that is paradoxically vital when expressed on a living body—her scream is like an orgasm of expiration; second, Victor's embrace of the dead beloved, her visage veiled by a kerchief, constitutes the only act of love-making he will ever know. The faceless beloved, as in a painting by René Magritte, conjures psychic fantasy and is his only possible sexual object.

The act describes a ghoulish lovemaking *à trois*, with the Creature the massive copula uniting Victor and Elizabeth, and murder subtending the inter/course of three disparate figures. Thus the blood tingles in the extremities of *Victor's* limbs at the moment his Creature evokes the consummating scream from Elizabeth, her cry of connubial passion elicited in a ghoulish parody. If the killing of the beloved arouses an uncharacteristic tumescence, Elizabeth's limp body is a comment on the impotence of fantasy-love, her splayed position spelling revenge for a devitalized life.

Following the killing of the beloved with the embrace of the beloved, Victor returns to fantasy-love. The enfolded adored corpse of Elizabeth inherits Caroline's maternal shroud. To kiss Elizabeth in her blankness is to return to the original beauty of the dead Mother. Thus, the substitutions of Frankenstein return to the romance paradigms of *Beyond the Pleasure Principle*. Tancred destroys the series of Symbols to approach the underlying Image. The infernal myth of mechanical-Imaginary repetition can yield only death. Withholding the acceptance of the Father, Victor arranges the return of the Imaginary. Murdering out of the refusal of desire, he is his own final victim.

In a fundamental difference, the Monster is driven by passionate hatred while his maker is driven by hatred of passion. The Monster provokes a reciprocal pursuit to *revive* his relationship to the other, his hatred a transformation rather than an obliteration of love. The Creature's revenge-hatred is inverted desire still desiring, a vital force reversed. He is a force of annihilation that still recognizes the objects of annihilation. Victor generally neither hates nor loves, no other exists in the serial fantasies of the Imaginary. He is moved toward real feeling in relation to one figure only; all his feelings converge in the space of a colossal denial.

Consigning himself to fantasies that preclude desire, Victor detests his Creature, his inescapable creation, *the form of denied desire*. The narrative culminates in an Agonistic struggle, but with a fundamental difference between the antagonists. While the Creator concentrates on the destruction of his Creature, the Creature is focused no less on the salvation of his Creator: "you have determined to live and I am satisfied." Understanding that *revenge perpetuates relationship,* the Creature finds connection in Symbolic codes, food and other traces of his presence appear on the glacial-plane, the world where Victor lives. Victor embodies the anti-desire that destroys its object to destroy itself, but the Creature is sworn to the continued vitality of active hatred. He directs an ongoing chase, with waves of delay before the goal is reached; he extends relationship by elaborating a death-pursuit along glacial surfaces; etching life in the landscapes of death, he constructs a Father-Son death-romance from revenge. The Creature extends his romantic end-game out of a continuing desire for desire, but is defeated by the Father's continuing irreparable abhorrence for the Son. Desire can reverse itself to violence, but is perplexed by immovable hatred: "if yet, in some mode unknown to me, thou hadst not ceased to think and feel, thou wouldst not desire against me a vengeance greater than that which I feel" (24:223).

Anti-desire eludes the comprehension of desire, as evil eludes the comprehension of good. The Creature's remorseful self-eulogy is filled with baffled love. He vows to extinguish himself on the alien ice in a burst of fire: death is the protracted but inevitable end for an unhappy Creature, no longer a Monster, whose frozen-hearted Father is his last object of desire.

Return or Advance

The irresolution at the novel's close focuses on the destiny of Walton. Walton, walled in the closed town of his obtuseness, mediates between the text and its readers. Representing our own trepidations before otherworldly texts, he parallels his counterpart, Lockwood, locked in the wood of his self-protecting mind, or the prototype of both characters, Coleridge's fatuous guest at the wedding. The outside speaker holds the fate of romance in irresolute hands.

The struggle for Walton becomes intense and contradictory at the novel's end. Reversing his cautionary stance, Victor reasserts the grandeur of ceaseless quest. Throughout, Victor maintains an ambivalent discourse with Walton. But the younger man reads the main subtext, intuits the anguish of Creation, and withdraws homeward. To return, however, is to return to Mrs. Saville; *Sa-*

ville, her-city; he comes home to be possessed. He decides not to risk himself further because of the threat to her: "Oh! my beloved sister, the sickening failing of your heart-felt expectations is . . . more terrible to me than my own death" (24:213). Mirroring the relationship between Victor and Elizabeth, Walton's beloved Margaret is a "more than sister." After Victor dies, irradiated for the sentimental Walton by "a gentle smile" (24:218), the younger man prepares to retreat: "I journey toward England, and I may there find consolation" (24:218). Nor does Victor die without cautioning Walton against the open-hearted receiving of the Creature's words: "He is eloquent and persuasive; and once his words had even power over my heart: but trust him not. His soul is as hellish as his form" (209). Yet it is "hellish" for Victor to reduce the complex turmoil of the hidden self (his *own* hidden self) to its criminal form, despite its fearful actions.

We never observe Robert Walton's return, for more than being overshadowed by "a face of loathsome yet appalling hideousness" (24:218–19), Walton's homecoming is interrupted by the Creature's voice of unearthly eloquence. While Victor's regret remains stilted because of an underlying falseness, the Creature expresses his repentance in a valedictory that overcomes the stylistic limitations of the novel.

> I shall die. . . . I shall no longer see the sun or stars, or feel the winds play on my cheeks. Light, feeling, and sense will pass away. . . . when the images which this world affords first opened upon me, when I felt the cheering warmth of summer, and heard the rustling of the leaves and the warbling of the birds and these were all to me, I should have wept to die; now it is my only consolation. Polluted by crimes, and torn by the bitterest remorse, where can I find rest but in death. . . . I shall ascend my funeral pile triumphantly. . . . The light of the conflagration will fade away; my ashes will be swept into the sea by the winds. My spirit will sleep in peace; or if it thinks, it will not surely think thus. (221–23)

He presents the opposed yet related aspects of himself ("the series" of his being); the nature worship that Victor professes but that betrays his artificial conventionality takes on the precision of natural interplay in the Creature's words. Perceiving the reality of nature he also experiences the reality of the self; love of song and sunlight resolve in the knowledge of anger and guilt, the relationship to living Creatures indicating—as in *The Ancient Mariner*—inner life. The language of the Creature remains faithful to the course of his natural emotions. Mary Shelley recovers her own inhibited resources of feeling and language through the spurned Creature.

Walton, at last, is speechless, his final actions unknowable, unless we judge him by our own susceptibility to a Creature descending from dark distance, our astonishment at the figure fated to become the most widely disseminated image in world Romanticism. Hardly swept by the wind into the sea, Shelley's Creature, blown to the four corners of the earth, projects poetry from the ashes of fire and allows her to trumpet a prophecy of her own.

5

From Demonic Romance to Satanic Myth: *Wuthering Heights*

CENTRALLY CONCERNED WITH THE TEMPORAL ORDERING OF LITERATURE, Russian formalism and French structuralism make an overall distinction between *story* and *text*. The *story* refers to the tale as it exists (or would exist) in chronological order outside the fiction. The *text* follows narratological rather than chronological order and subordinates time-scheme to the dramatic necessities of narrative scheme.

In the romantic temporality of *Wuthering Heights*, Emily Brontë employs temporal categories to transcend them (constructing to deconstruct), for she *surrounds story by text*, placing an outer narrative, Lockwood's-text-in-the-present, around an inner narrative, Nelly Dean's-story-of-the-past. Existing both within and before Nelly's story, Catherine's and Heathcliff's myth-out-of-time adds eternity to temporal order. Lockwood's story-surrounding text is itself encircled, moreover, by Emily Brontë's demonic romance, the outermost fiction that encircles orders of temporality in an organization of desire.

In four circles of narrative, *Wuthering Heights* brings forward the genres of story, myth, and romance, adducing a series of narratives from the realistic text. The spatial, as opposed to temporal, order of

---

Theoretical Forenote : the role of the germinal narrative fragments becomes intricate in a novel disposed over not only four narrational levels but four literary genres. On the realistic first level, Lockwood intrudes on Heathcliff in a play-of-substitution; this occurs not only in the narrative present but, more strongly, in a timelessness of dream, a dream-of-the-wound where Lockwood enters the mythic world in the novel. Heathcliff and Catherine find/create the Father in their mythic union, but, lacking merger with Catherine, Heathcliff plays the-game-of-disappearance and comes back empowered. In a powerful rendering of the-romance-of-death, Heathcliff's destructiveness reaches its apex in relation to Isabel, the second Cathy, and Catherine Earnshaw herself.

the four narratives would be myth, story, text, romance. Myth refers to events out-of-time, story refers to past-time, text refers to present-time, and romance is the total organization of the whole narrative. In their full and alluring form the stories trace elusive tales, their absences unfilled by memory, the wholly recovered story protected by lost time. In French the untellable story is a *histoire;* ironically, factual history is the most unattainable of narratives, the Russian term, *fabula*, affirming such histories-before-the-story as the most fabulous of fables. Emily Brontë employs narrative frames to separate the texts we have from the stories we want, her inserted stories receding amid surrounding texts in infinite intensification of *literary desire*.[1]

Text and Dream

Despite the formalistic enclosure of story by text, Lockwood cannot subsume the hidden worlds of *Wuthering Heights*. Using the realistic diary genre, Lockwood locates his experience in "1801," and describes a social environment in a narrative of appearances. His self-conscious discourse remains on the surface of things.

Hence he initially places his reclusive landlord, Heathcliff, within vocational and geographic categories even as his brusque host escapes economic classification. "Mr. Heathcliff forms a singular contrast to his abode and style of living. He is a dark-skinned gypsy in aspect, in dress and manners a gentleman."[2] Lockwood subordinates Heathcliff's black foreignness to the more familiar image of a provincial landowner. He seeks similar reassurance in nomenclature, the polite "Mr." softening the challenge in an astounding name. Yet the name *Heath/cliff* already evokes a treacherous abyss, an aporia of falling space within the illusion of a secure field. Heathcliff's name predicts the experience of *Wuthering Heights* with all the condensed power of a nominal *mise-en-âbyme*.

Moreover, as an outsider curious about a strangely designated figure who inhabits a rudely unfamiliar structure, *Wuthering Heights*/"*Wuthering Heights*" (the novel named for a place is itself a place), Lockwood becomes reader-representative. The opening narration remains defamiliarized just as the narrator's name, Lockwood, suggests one who is restricted to the material world. Nevertheless, the limitation of Lockwood's comprehension to superficial appearances conceals his attraction to hidden forces. The existence of violent depths within surface civilization, suggested by

Heathcliff, also reflects on Lockwood himself, for his modulated sociability hides unexpected destructiveness.

He, is, indeed, one who violates that which attracts him; his timid self-distancing oddly accompanies disruptive intrusion. He proves himself an invasive visitor as, earlier, he had been a deceptive lover. With complacent "shame," he recalls his defensive flirtation in a brief non-affair. He had been fascinated by a woman who he had maintained in a remote realm where love is received, but not reciprocated. When her erotic recognition had demanded the return of the gaze, Lockwood had insisted on a one-directional glance, thus reducing his object to a fantasy-image. Lockwood is one who limply retreats from generative interaction, his glorification of the object entailing a withholding of the subject.[3] Thus his name suggests the being *locked out of the wood*, precluded from erotic entrance. In contrast to *Beyond the Pleasure Principle,* if Freud's Tancred destroys his objects of desire in the dark wood representing unknown areas of the psyche, Lockwood protects himself by seeking eros without risk and avoiding desire itself.

Lockwood's style of interaction vacillates between voyeurism and provocation, he prefers—as in his teasing of the Heights' untamed dogs—to remove himself as if unimplicated from the scenes he precipitates. Making foolish faces at the animals, he causes Earnshaw's "ruffianly bitch" to break "into a fury" at the visual indignity, for she reacts in proud assertion of her own instinctual otherness. Hardly the only female in *Wuthering Heights* to battle underestimation, she violently opposes Lockwood's solipsistic actions.

Such brief vignettes between Lockwood and the denied-female-other reveal the hostility behind his evasions. Indeed, Brontë raises general issues of sexual and textual voyeurism through Lockwood's agency. For a self-protective Lockwood-like perusal of an object protects the oberving/reading self, preventing a full encounter with the narrative. In textual voyeurism a reader may remain a literary *demi-vierge*, unendangered by the risk of exposure, of being *found out*. Merely a "text," a weave completed and done, the book remains a "locked" text like a closed wood, its words lacking the power to return the readerly gaze. Yet *Wuthering Heights* violates our psychic protection, for it also penetrates *us*, and raises the question of *the gaze of the text.* The *bitch of otherness* makes no haphazard appearance when Brontë's text bites.

In Lockwood's second excursion to the Heights, repressed emotions are reflected by metaphorical landscapes. Having suffered in a rude parlor with churlish inhabitants, Lockwood invites himself, with brazen fatuity, for a return visit. "[Heathcliff] evidently wished no repetition of my intrusion. I shall go, notwithstanding. It is astonishing how sociable I feel myself compared with him" (1:7). Returning to the source of harshness, Lockwood reveals the perverse desires beneath his conventional sentiments, for he performs an act of *destructive repetition*. Despite "the misty and cold" afternoon Lockwood walks (or disorientedly circulates) the steep distance between Thrushcross Grange and *Wuthering Heights*. Brontë describes nature in figurative weather-images, while Lockwood places himself near the perilous edge of self-loss: "A sorrowful sight I saw: dark night coming down prematurely, and sky and hill mingled in one *bitter* wh*irl of wind and suffocating snow*" (2:12, my emphasis). The annihilating snow-whirl, a cold self-enclosure, is a key trope in the novel, for the Brontëan presentation of regressive return reveals itself—repeatedly—in a white formlessness.

Lockwood enters with difficulty a house where the threatening storm finds linguistic echoes. When Joseph, Heathcliff's ancient and "vinegar-faced" servant, directs barely comprehensible vituperations at Cathy Earnshaw, Lockwood confuses himself with their maligned object: "'Aw woonder hagh yah can faishion tuh stand their i' idleness un war, when all on 'em's goan aght! But yah're a *nowt*, and it's no use talking. . . .' I imagined, for a moment, that this piece of eloquence was addressed to me" (2:12, my emphasis). Joseph's favored denomination is "nowt," used with malicious philosophical import to suggest a being so worthless as to be nonexistent. Lockwood enters the ontological space Joseph destroys to take the attack on himself.

The early encounters with Joseph, combined with the manservant's oppressive role in Catherine's diary, inspire Lockwood's first dream.

> I began to dream. . . . I had set out on my way home, with Joseph for a guide. The snow lay yards deep in our road; and as we floundered on, my companion wearied me with constant reproaches that I had not brought a pilgrim's staff, telling me I could never get into the house without one, and boastfully flourishing a heavy-headed cudgel. . . .(3:18)

The dream begins with exile to the enveloping snow, reifying the threatening conditions at the Heights. He seeks a guide through the snowdrifts in a landscape of entrapment. Brontë's snow assumes elemental force, its dangers those of sinking-in or submergence: Lockwood's manifest motive is to stay on secure surfaces but his latent motive may be, indeed, to drown. He finds a counterforce in the guide-stick that forges through enveloping frost; the image undergoes a reversal from an ecclesiastical staff to a "heavy-headed (and earthly) "cudgel." Thus, the dream conflates masculine authority and Puritanical repression: when an ascetic God takes a virile servant all the power of denied sexuality accrues to the one with the strength to deny it. Punitive authority attracts the man of uncertain masculinity: his dream is about a perverse attraction to oppressive Patriarchy.

The dream begins accordingly over a volume of sermons by Jabes Branderham, the North Country hellfire preacher. The discussion is of "Seventy Times Seven, and the First of the Seventy-First," a phrase referring to how many sins may be sinned before divine grace is exceeded. Christians suspend mercy with the sin against the father, the denial of paternal omniscience, but acknowledgement of the Father permits the unlimited proliferation of sins (and sermons). Lockwood's dream begins in some obscure individual analogue to doctrinal sin; it is as though he needed to expiate some distant sin against the Father.

Yet, if guilt brings punishment, punishment still provides access to authority. Lockwood seeks paternal strength as represented by Joseph's club; moreover, the servant, the manifest form of Joseph, serves the master the latent form of Heathcliff. In other words, the harsh inhabitants of the heights attract Lockwood because of his unconscious drive toward reprimand and rejection. Lockwood desires, finally, a battering or, in the rustically metaphysical term, "Wuthering," from Heathcliff. His need would be shared by readers excited to enter the domain of a master rough "as a saw-edge, and hard as whinstone." The temptations of *Wuthering Heights* encompass exposure to masculine ferocity with a sexual—homoerotic—element. The attraction to the authoritative father, with the intimate corollary of paternal punishment, clarifies Lockwood's incessant and infuriating *provocations*, his continuous playing with emotional hellfire is understandable as an incitement to Heathcliff's violence.[4]

The first dream closes, accordingly, with a mass attack on the dreamer:

> "Thou art the Man!" cried Jabes, after a solemn pause. . . . "Brethren, execute upon him the judgment written! . . ." With that concluding word, the whole assembly, exalting their pilgrim's staves, rushed round me in a body, and I, having no weapon to raise in self-defence, commenced grappling with Joseph, my nearest and most ferocious assailant, for his. (2:18–19)

The dream is based on the guilty desire for union with a punishing father. More precisely, the manifest dream reveals the latent wish for a punishment that is itself constitutive of guilty pleasure. Providing indirect intimacy with Heathcliff, the dream grasps at his strength as though punishment were an empowering conferral of the absent masculinity represented by the missing staff. The dream cruelly initiates the dreamer into the ferocious fellowship of Heathcliff and his world. It projects the search for a weapon as part of the desire for a wound. On one level it describes Lockwood's fantasy of being raped by Heathcliff. Screening the experience of abuse and the lack of a weapon, reminding us that Lockwood's relationship to Heathcliff involves reciprocal penetrations, the first of Lockwood's night-visions is *a dream-of-the-desired-wound*.

To inflict the wound is to create feminine identity, to reveal a homoerotic desire for the female sexual role, but the power desired is also verbal. Lockwood wants, as well, to penetrate the magic club of rhetoricians and enjoy a masculine strength of language by being part of the furious speech of accusers. With his admittance to the group of aggressive speakers, the dream-masters, Jabes, Joseph, Heathcliff, would speak to Lockwood and say: "Thou art the Man."

The entire introductory narrative may contain an oblique element of autobiography. Emily Brontë spent her otherwise isolated life in proximity of a distant and difficult father. We may speculate that Brontë's representation of Lockwood has something in common with the little girl in Freud's essay on "A Child Is Being Beaten."[5] In such fantasies the figures are always displaced, the one who punishes never being the father, while the one punished is never the fantasizing child, but a substituted other, usually with a change of gender. Brontës presentation of violent dream-figures shows parallels with the fantasizing girl in Freud's essay. Brontë draws close to her father in a reversed-gender fantasy where the Father, Heathcliff/Patrick Brontë, punishes a younger figure, a victim, Lockwood/Emily Brontë, who receives his/her chastisements with rich ambivalence. Lockwood is the medium for Emily Brontë's intimate punishment fantasies—beyond the closeness in pain, she wants to possess/join the father's magic club. *Her* rhetorical gain, at any rate, was enormous, and she embedded this fantasy in her rich text.

Myth and Dream

Lockwood's dreams take place in an inner chamber, for Catherine Earnshaw's bedroom is concealed deep within the Heights. The violation of this forbidden sanctum by Zillah, an interfering housekeeper who anticipates Nelly Dean, serves to undermine Heathcliff's authority. Zillah guides Lockwood toward a closed room that contains a further enclosure, an "old-fashioned couch" protected by "a large oak case, with squares cut out near the top, resembling coach windows" (3:15). The private room-within-a-room is fashioned as a kind of conveyance, a carriage for stationary journeys.

Inside, Lockwood finds a window ledge covered with variations on a name; in his fatigue the ghostly letters seem loosed from their written contexts: "Catherine Earnshaw—Heathcliff—Linton, till my eyes closed; but they had not rested five minutes when a glare of white letters started from the dark, as vivid as spectres—the air swarmed with Catherines" (3:15). In their white dissolution the tumultuous letters recall the "whirl" of snow that earlier covers and confuses Lockwood; Catherine like Lockwood seems to disappear in a ghostly disintegration in white.

The dissolution of words follows the earlier dissolution in nature. The many names circle into a kind of namelessness; Catherine's history is of one named so many times as to be unnamed. Beginning with her father, and continuing with those who echo him, all of Catherine's links to male figures dissolve into nothingness. The dissolution of a name is the dissolution of a bond. Lockwood observes the negating power of language, a force of *unnaming* in a reversal of the capacities of words. The "air swarm[s] with Catherines" to anticipate later scenes where flurries of whiteness dissolve into formless nonbeing. Such whiteness describes Imaginary connections, as of one who remains prone-to-dissolution, for Catherine had never found full connection to nor full separation from her father, had never acquired, thus, the Name-of-the-Father. The Imaginary Catherine recedes as Lockwood encounters her one attempt at Symbolic self-expression, as he unearths her amazing secret books:

> [First there] was a Testament, in lean type, and smelling dreadfully musty: a fly-leaf bore the inscription—"Catherine Earnshaw, her book". . . . Catherine's library was select, and its state of dilapidation proved it to have been well used, though not altogether for a legitimate purpose; scarcely one chapter had escaped a pen and ink commentary. . . . (3:16).

The marginal commentary takes the form of a journal found in Catherine's annotations to a volume of Jabes Branderham's sermons. Its rebellious glosses may be taken as a Catherine's own Counter-Testament, her "Bible of Hell."[6]

Understanding Catherine's *demonic* vision requires an act of interpretation, and Lockwood represents the reader's own baffled involvement with her quest:

> An immediate interest kindled within me for the unknown Catherine, and I began, forthwith, to decypher her faded hieroglyphics. "An awful Sunday. . . . I wish my father were back again. Hindley is a detestable substitute—his conduct to Heathcliff is atrocious—H and I are going to rebel—we took our initiatory step this evening." (3:16).

The lines he "decyphers" reverberate throughout as *the thematic core of the novel*, describing the thoughts and feelings lying behind its action.

The timeless union of Catherine and Heathcliff fills the space left by the absence of a father. They wish to reconstitute missing paternal—and maternal—figures in Symbolic actions, creating a relationship that recuperates the father. The journal begins under the weight of a fatherless seventh day. The wish for the return of the father motivates Catherine's writing (cf. Freud: "*Writing was in its origin the voice of an absent person,*" *SE* 21:91—my emphasis). Catherine's despair of Hindley continues the wish, for her brother's treatment of Heathcliff is merely vindictive and envious—satanic. Hindley not only abuses Heathcliff but blocks the path to the father. Catherine reopens that path by recording, and participating in, a rebellion conducting *toward* the paternal. The events of the reported evening (Sunday, 19 November 1777) initiate a kind of revolutionary way.

As Heathcliff later recounts, the promises of their rebellious escape go unfulfilled (6:37–40). The journal is a fragment recollecting the desires and visions of the past. The written reflection of the "initiatory step" inscribes revisionary conviction, demonic also in a traditional-religious sense. The subversive quality attached to Catherine Heathcliff invokes the role of the father in *Wuthering Heights*. Earnshaw inspires the energy of rebellion without restricting its contours. Catherine's vision begins with her rebellious father, the discovery of his unknown, demonic past.

What Lockwood reads in the closet, then, is a fragment of a romance. The relationship between Catherine and Heathcliff is creatively original, a supernatural combination of merger and freedom. They plan to run away under the dairy-woman's cloak, an image of activity within maternal space, a security of union that empowers a play of exploration. They play at vanishing in a game-of-disappearance; and as in *Beyond the Pleasure Principle*, creative entrances into the Imaginary are made in search of—designed to move toward—the Symbolic.

The Symbolic game reflects itself in the Symbolic text, the retrospection of writing. Opposing the standard texts of their culture, the devilish children kick Joseph's hellfire-and-brimstone pamphlets aside. Catherine's marginalia amounts to a kind of "newer Testament." Her text indicates the direction of her thoughts and actions: toward the recuperation of the paternal (the father refound and internalized). The demonic child is an adversary of hypocritical Christian culture, yet he inherits more of the father's strength than the submissively accepting child. (Heathcliff and Catherine are closer to the elder Earnshaw than Hindley is.)

Yet, the second part of Lockwood's dream is an ironic anti-climax to the journal. The dream-fragment combines with the diary fragment to show that the glorious quest of Catherine and Heathcliff will turn, somehow, to a tragic exile. Catherine appeals to Lockwood from the a cold abandoned realm:

> "Let me in—let me in!" . . . As it spoke, I discerned, obscurely, a child's face looking through the window. Terror made me cruel; and, finding it useless to attempt shaking the creature off, I pulled its wrist on to the broken pane, and rubbed it to and fro till the blood ran down and soaked the bed-clothes: still it wailed, "Let me in!" and maintained its tenacious gripe, almost maddening me with fear. (3:20)

Lockwood is the dreamer, yet the dream belongs not to the creator of the dream but its protagonist. Not a dreamer, she is the dream itself, one who exists outside time in dream-space. Her child's face completes the pathos of a child's cry, pleading for entrance to the space recapturing her union with Heathcliff. Presenting the amorphous realm of exile and dissolution, the snow-dream shows the agonizing unreality of her isolation. The child pleads from within the hovering remnant of an uncompleted journey. Left adrift by an interrupted rebellion, she cries from some strange disrupted area where text was destroyed into dream. Trapped in an interrupted quest, she is, like Hamlet's father, a ghost in the limbo of an uncompleted narrative.

The relationship between dream and mythic fragment is suggested by the ghost's self-described exile of "20 years." Considering that Lockwood dreams in 1801, we may take this as a number falling between 1777, the year that Catherine and Heathcliff undertook their revolutionary excursion, and 1784, the year of Catherine's death.[7] The twenty years condense death and bereavement, her own passing and her grief for her father. It is as though—the mad scenes support such a reading—she had returned to childhood in death, becoming a ghost-child to complete her interrupted rebellion.

Her return is triggered by Lockwood's violation of her most private chambers; he comes into her territory in actuality but also in his imagination, the novel allowing no absolute separation between the two. Thus she is enabled to cross over to the vital realm. Catherine's window, like Heathcliff's gate, affords spatial entrance to the atemporality of mythic worlds. Lockwood, however, is helpless in timelessness. The narrow limits of his vision refer to his role as a representative of the reader, while the hand extended from a space of twenty years recalls the "childish hand" that writes Catherine's marginalia. To accept her hand is to accept its writing, to receive her ghostly fragments as scattered clues to *Wuthering Heights*. It is as though Lockwood were the last reader, or the last man, the one who might reach her in imaginative empathy, might understand her enough to confer a name upon her. Lockwood attacks Catherine's hands to reveal the limits of his being.

Lockwood's in/cursion culminates in an ex/cursion, a discovery of an "outside" only reachable from the "inside" (the scene takes place actually in the air outside the bedroom). Having intruded into a secret room, he resists a reversed crossing *from* the tumultuous snow-world, locus of denied death-desire, the place where the destruction he is attracted to has actually occurred to others, *toward himself*. What is necessary is to recognize the mythic crossing of the other, a communication across crossings, to allow death to cross to him as a locus of life. For Lockwood, by reading a broken romance and restoring it in his dream, has set a scene which could allow the ghost-child, the mythic Catherine, to complete her journey, reverse her exile and come home to a continuing story. To return to the room where she lived with Heathcliff as a child, and to return to the world-within-a-world of her unfinished journal, is to be enabled *to complete the narrative and turn a disrupted myth to a completed romance*. To acknowledge the mythic death-world is to potentially release it into the reality of action. Lockwood's failure to do so is a failure of literary, no less than emotional, reception.

Story and Dream

Heathcliff arouses desire for such knowledge as only narrative provides. Lockwood turns to the "matronly" Nelly Dean for the story of local history, although remaining uncertain whether he desires to be aroused to "animation" or "lulled" asleep. Presenting Lockwood with a story, she adds to concurrent ministrations as nurse and cook, the initial relationship between Lockwood and Nelly resembling that of feverish child and comforting mother. Indeed, Lockwood—the part of Lockwood that seeks rather than avoids entrance—turns to Nelly for a restoring (re/story/ing) narrative. He wants a completed memory of the past to repair the fragmented experience of the present; with the windowpanes shattered *before* Nelly's recitation, her story soothes mythic disruption.

In response to Lockwood's childlike need, Nelly begins with the natural rhythm of a folk-tale: "One fine summer morning—it was the beginning of harvest, I remember—Mr. Earnshaw, the old master, came downstairs, dressed for a journey" (4:28). The story begins in the timeless negation of paternal absence. Old Earnshaw's unexplained departure leaves behind a space of abandonment, a disappearing father gone for three long days in a journey of sixty miles each way. The Earnshaw children run continuously to the *empty gate*, a gate that *spatializes* entrances and exits to changing spheres of narrative. When Old Earnshaw returns, he brings a ragged gypsy orphan, its unexplained relation to the father evoking an untold *story-before-the-story*.

A play-on-words introduces the fabula of the novel. The father's *presents* compensate for missed *presence*, for the paternal gift is designed to re/present the lost father. But the children are abandoned again, twice deprived. Hindley loses the "fiddle," harmonious gift to the son, while Catherine misses the "whip," authoritative gift to the daughter. Nor does Nelly receive her apples and pears, reminders of burgeoning sensuality (her sexuality never knows fruition). Rather, the master, like a gothic wizard, returns with the capacious coat containing a replacing presence.

Earnshaw produces a son to produce a new image of himself, for he never explains Heathcliff's origins, so the dark son gives birth to a dark father. The unknown son moves the remote father into the unknown, his implacable charge *the gateway to the paternal*. Thus Heathcliff's outsider-status begins not as a rebellion-against but an extension-of Earnshaw; in a wicked inversion of *King Lear, Wuthering Heights* legitimates bastardy. The elder Earnshaw is placed as implicit patron of adversarial values, the wildness of the Heights beginning with its recusant-patriarch.

Catherine joins the Earnshaw-Heathcliff world by her seductive freedom within the world of desire: "A wild, wicked slip she was—but she had the bonniest eye, and sweetest smile, and lightest foot in the parish'' (5:33). Fiercely imaginative, rather than creating airy fantasies she engages in vital actuality, her mode of visionary energy most strongly realized in connection with Heathcliff. As one who leads and is led into a visionary-energy-world, she echoes the fairy-like form and motion of another romantic heroine, her description bearing an unmistakable similarity to the (in)corporeal characterization of Keats's *Belle Dame*.

Catherine, Heathcliff, and Earnshaw share the primary oneness of a heretical Eden, their unity captured in the somber triptych (a rough folk-*Pieta*) depicting Earnshaw's death: "she leant against her father's knee, and Heathcliff was lying on the floor with his head in her lap. . . . she kissed [Earnshaw's] hand, and said she would sing him to sleep. She began singing very low, till his fingers dropped from hers, and his head sank on his breast'' (5:33–34). The unconventional nature of the Earnshaws, their Protest/ant insistence on a personal interpretation of spiritual law, passes from Earnshaw to Catherine to the Heathcliff-outsider (a radical trinity of father, daughter, and unholy spirit). Catherine's death-accompanying song recalls the artistic-imaginative quality of her devotion. The lyric's intimate connection to the dying father reflects the journal, as does Catherine's and Heathcliff's consoling vision: "The little souls were comforting each other with better thoughts than I could have hit on; no parson in the world ever pictured heaven so beautifully as they did'' (5:34).

The restorative dream recreates a "heavenly'' fantasy of paternal resurrection. Alongside the hell-centered theology disseminated by Joseph, such millenarian joy is itself heretical. Moreover, the dutiful Nelly may conventionalize childlike visions more daring than she recognizes, for shortly thereafter, as Joseph and Hindley make a hell of heaven and a heaven of hell, Catherine's diary expresses shocking heterodoxy. The imaginative world of Catherine and Heathcliff recreates lost unity in paradoxical restoration, a dark redemption in revolutionary romance.

But its powers are vitiated on that same "Awful Sunday.'' Encountering Thrushcross Grange, the hellish heaven of the Earnshaws is replaced by the heavenly hell of the Lintons. Outside another window, Catherine and Heathcliff gaze from an exuberant nature into an extravagant culture. The Linton salon of shining crystals and crimson carpets appears both resplendent and threatening. The acquirements of cultivation exact a price in emotional scope, the instinctual cost of cultural acquisition diminishing the primary energies of (super)natural childhood. The bored futility between Edgar and Isabella dramatically contrasts with the inexhaustible intensity between Catherine and Heathcliff.

A mocking canine representation demonstrates the attenuation of the instincts in the Linton household. The "little dog" over which Edgar and Isabella strive, struggling for a trace of animal warmth, stands for the "petted" Edgar Linton, just as the violent watchdog, Skulker, parallels Heathcliff brooding at the edge of domestic boundaries. But Heathcliff's derision for the Lintons evolves more from their limited emotions than their feeble instincts. The notion of a *contest* between brother and sister astonishes him in its assertion of bounded selves; merged in tumultuous drives, Catherine and Heathcliff unify in the realm of infinite desire.

The connection between the reduction of instinct and the separation into singleness influences the play of genres in the novel. Mythic origins unify Catherine and Heathcliff, while a fairy-tale sequence foregrounds Catherine alone. The developmental plot of the fairy tale follows the entrance of the protagonist into separate identity. (Nelly Dean's entire narrative follows a fairy-tale structure, with the second Catherine as its heroine; going from one Catherine to the other, Nelly manages to transform herself from wicked stepmother to fairy godmother.) Still, the going over to the fairy-tale mode entails a falling-off of imaginative force. If Catherine moves from myth to romance at this juncture, the fairy tale remains a childlike form of romance.

At Thrushcross Grange, Catherine enjoys a magical transformation:

> Mrs. Linton took off the grey cloak of the dairy maid. . . . Then the woman servant brought a basin of warm water, and washed her feet. . . . Afterwards, they dried and combed her beautiful hair, and gave her a pair of enormous slippers, and wheeled her to the fire. . . .(6:40)

Cinderella, the most widely disseminated of folk legends, describes the cleansing of the heroine from the traces (cinders) of a childish nondifferentiation. In *Wuthering Heights*, the fairy tale mediates between myth and realist novel, the Lintons providing a bridge to the actuality of the here and now. With the maternal dairy-cloak removed, the foot-washing ritual suggests preparation for social movement, an integration into the attractive refinements of culture. Thus, Catherine drinks a magic potion (which appears to reverse the *mana* of *La Belle Dame*) and becomes a socialized girl. Her foot will not, however, be "light" when protected by "enormous slippers." With her hair shining like a narcissistic emblem, the passage hints at both lustrous acculturation and indulgent self-weakening.

Heathcliff returns to the status of isolated outsider as Catherine is wrested away by the forces of social advancement. Her singleness of fairy-tale advance is paid for by the forfeiting of the romantic transfiguration shared with Heathcliff. Diverted from the deeper path (with its potential and danger), she finds a family but loses a soulmate, for she breaks the fusionary bond with Heathcliff, her foster brother, her demon-lover, her Father-found-again. Alone, Catherine goes toward the fairy tale's cycle of normal development, but with Heathcliff she moves to the imaginative refiguration of authority. In their natural wildness, Heathcliff and Catherine could have found their "dark Father" in a rebellious and incipiently erotic relationship. Thus the fairy tale, the simpler form of romance, diverts Catherine from the more complex demonic romance awaiting completion *within* her relationship with Heathcliff.

With her "escape" Heathcliff is forced into satanic isolation. He moves into the *destructive mode of being* that replaces the *creative mode of being* shared with Catherine. He becomes a satanic rather than a demonic figure. The demonic refers to the transformative powers of the unconscious, the unconscious other which can move us into the literary otherness of the *imaginative*. The satanic refers back to the negative phase of the demonic, trapped in with primary, regressive images. The demonic relates to the Symbolic, referring to the creation of images as well as narratives. The satanic remains close to the Imaginary, violently opposing the state-of-being that holds it. After the loss of Catherine, Heathcliff becomes an aggressive prisoner of the Imaginary. The satanic vents its hatred against an Imaginary it cannot escape. The satanic is associated with myth and the death drive, as the demonic may reach romance and the life-drive.

I take the mythic as the narrative expression of fundamental psychic drives. The mythic is compressed and essential, tending to express the archaic psyche in its early or regressive patterns. In such fundamental mythologems as that of Demeter/Hades/Persephone, a forward movement, a progressive, developmental phase, *closes* the myth—once Demeter is appeased the myth is over. Myth is a rudimentary life-and-death struggle ending in a primitive defeat or triumph. Had the relationship of Hades and Persephone continued in flexible unpredictability, they would have entered the world of romance. I am positing that romance like myth begins with fundamental psychic patterns but that romance is about literary elaboration, including the supplementarity of extra and unpredictable development, so that an excess or bounty of material is woven around the psychic core.

To attain a clearer idea of the difference between myth and romance, I wish to turn to Daniel Rubey's provocative analysis of the mythic elements (most tellingly the Oedipus legend) in the narratives of French medieval poetry. Romance

> combined tales of adventure with the courtly love poetry of southern France to form a new literature of sexual desire, a written literature based on oral sources but explicitly concerned with interpretation and textuality. . . . [romance may be distinguished] from its oral sources by the skillfulness and beauty of its *conjointure*, a term which . . . means both narrative structure and the interpretations and commentary built into the work. Romances are infused with a new reflexivity, a new sense of themselves as texts to be read and interpreted. (my emphasis)[9]

Rubey's evocative notion of "conjointure" presents romance as the literary elaboration of myth, the transformative release of mythic structures—Oedipus and its variants, incest and its discontents—into romance by an exploration of narrative possibility. In *Wuthering Heights*, as elsewhere, the mythic pertains to an indwelling arche/myth, a return to the cave of original memory. We could, arguably, view myth as the more restrictive rendering of fantasy into narrative. Myth, then, might retell in narrative *fantasies already unconsciously bound* in the psyche, while romance would find the way to release those bonds*; myth as narrative repetition, romance as narrative transformation*.

Romance in the novel comes in various forms when the interrupted romance of Catherine Earnshaw empowers the completed romance of Emily Brontë. All of Catherine's attempts at romance disintegrate into fragments; yet a totalized narrative—Emily Brontë's complete romance, *Wuthering Heights* itself—emerges beyond the traces of Catherine's interrupted romance. Emily Brontë, who may be connected in this respect to Keats and Lawrence, presents a form of the *creative-demonic*. By the creative-demonic I refer to the use of the oppositional or uncanny figures in the unconscious for subversive and creative ends. This is a mysterious process, a poetic magic, the examination of which takes us back, again, to Plato. One point here—and this brings us to an area where paraphrase is heretical and we need to return to the poetry or poetic prose itself—is that the force within that takes us out of our conscious selves, which can undermine all the clarity of the sought-after daylight self, creates as well as destroys and brings us into areas where love and death cannot be neatly separated no matter how much we seek that clarity. The adversarial self within, which Freud wrote about eloquently but comprehended, on the explicit level at least, only negatively, can, in some mysterious and difficult way, go beyond the backward moving force, the retreating power that betrays us and, by some unconscious alchemy, become the advancing power that redeems us.

Heathcliff, like Mary Shelley's Creature, embodies neither the power of love nor the power of death but the power of love/death. The power he becomes is determined by how he is received. Once he is rejected the power he incarnates and the narrative he engenders are reduced, simplified; the rejection of Heathcliff stills the transformations of romance. Once disrupted, the story of Catherine and Heathcliff is reduced to *myth*, with its return to *need*, a falling-off from the higher vision of *romance*, with its elaborations of *desire*. Their aborted *romance of union* diverges into separate *myths of separation*. Catherine is reduced to her mythic fairy tale (little is said about Catherine and Edgar because there is little to say, the mini-romance of the fairy story *ends* with a "happy marriage"). Her marriage is the positive resolution of her separate fate, the fulfillment of her single self. Yet in an ironic comment on conventional marriage, there is no indissoluble bond, no union with an intrinsic completing other.

At the stage when he loses Catherine, Heathcliff's story undergoes a kind of generic reduction to the simpler order in the diminishment from the demonic to the satanic. The satanic takes the mysterious powers of the demonic repetition, with its connection to sources in the Father, and reduces them to the vengeance of the isolated subject. *Conscious, deliberate, vengeful, the aggressions of the satanic reveal its subjected status as the conquered demonic.*

Story and Dream II

In the important confession scene, Catherine turns to Nelly as she hums Hareton, Hindley's infant son, a plangent lullaby:

> It was far in the night, and the bairnies grat
> The mither beneath the mools heard that
> [It was deep in the night and the babies cried,
> the mother beneath the earth heard that]
>
> (9:59)

Nelly's song to the young child accompanies Catherine's confession to her older friend-servant-sister; the two recitals combine to make the dead mother the scene's hidden auditor. The appeal to the hidden mother is echoed by Catherine's plea for listening.

Listening to Catherine's description of her opposing suitors, Heathcliff and Edgar Linton, Nelly discusses insightfully Catherine's comparatively shallow feelings for her wealthy neighbor. While Catherine recognizes Edgar's social graces and natural gifts, Nelly demands a more lasting kind of vital connection. Accordingly, a generation later she affirms the forward-moving connection, the sexuality in the actual world, that characterizes the relationship between Hareton and Cathy. If gentility and grace, the quality of light, renders Edgar an over-rarified love-object, Cathy and Hareton show a this-worldly strength that will inherit the earth.

But if Nelly sees through the above-the-world position and comprehends the benefits of the continuing world, her emotional limitations emerge toward hidden forces beneath-the-world. Wary of subversive powers not already known, Nelly is out of her depth in a dream-narrative, and regards with suspicion stories that evoke unknown worlds. For, judging by her preamble, Catherine's dreams subvert reality to offer an alternative vision:

> "I've dreamt in my life dreams that have stayed with me ever after, and changed my ideas; they've gone through and through me, like wine through water, and altered the colour of my mind. And this one—I'm going to tell it—but take care not to smile at any part of it."
>
> "Oh! don't, Miss Catherine!" I cried. "We're dismal enough without conjuring up ghosts, and visions to perplex us. . . ."
>
> "However, Nelly, I shall oblige you to listen—it's not long; and I've no power to be merry to-night."
>
> "I won't hear it, I won't hear it!" I repeated, hastily. (9:61–62)

Catherine's sacramental language suggests that her dream will tran/substantiate the material world. Her dream-vision, had Nelly allowed it to be articulated, would have had an oppositional force likely to have been demonic in nature (opposing, thus, the angelic scene that *is* recited). But Nelly, in a strident repetition, spurns Catherine's need-to-be-heard; the older woman's auditory denial is assertive, almost desperate, yet beyond appeal. Nelly's refusal to *hear* the dream parallels Lockwood's refusal to *participate* in the dream; Nelly *refuses* an episode from the same dream-series that Lockwood *violates*.

Indeed, in a related denying based on fear of the imagination,

Lockwood nearly burns Catherine's book before he reads it. Both of the narrators of *Wuthering Heights* resist the deeper, more subversive order of romance-narrations, opposing the fragments—torn journal, denied dream, mad-vision—of her disrupted romance, the shattered narrative of her life. Returning to the dream, it is clear that, like the journal, it involved a narrative about an unconscious bond with Heathcliff, containing regressive, even incestuous, elements. The dream-story, however, would have subjected (how much of *Wuthering Heights* takes place in conditional tenses?) such dimensions of feeling and drive to narrative and commentary, to perhaps remake, or unmake, the relationship into a different form. But Nelly forcibly prevents the elaborations of the dream-story from taking place. No life-affirming romance will ever be woven before such an audience; no talking cure will ever occur before such an interlocutor.

Consequently, the mother who was never part of Catherine's life eludes her again, for the scene is pervaded by auditory emptiness, by the echo of nonrecognition in *the repetition of an absence.* (The death of Mrs. Earnshaw is barely remarked; like the passing of Emily Brontë's own mother, Maria Branwell Brontë, it happens too early to be marked as anything but generalized absence.) While in the situation that calls for a listening (m)other, Nelly keeps from Catherine the maternal/sororal/human solace she provides, in bitter contrast, for Hareton. *Nelly is the ironic double of the absent mother.* Furthermore, had Catherine been allowed (for, yes, she is prohibited) to render the incestuous beloved in language, had she subjected him to romance elaboration, Rubey's conjointure being a way of describing the Symbolic order, he might have become available as a "true" erotic object. This subjecting of Heathcliff to the Symbolic is what Catherine Earnshaw (the inside narrator of an aborted romance who remains in the Imaginary) fails to do. Yet the larger elaboration of the Symbolic order in the narrative as a whole, the demonic romance called *Wuthering Heights* is precisely that which Emily Brontë, the outside narrator of a completed romance, succeeds in doing.

The recuperative way, the path from the *incestuous-Imaginary* to the *erotic-Symbolic*, would be rendered through a transfiguration of the paternal—what is wanted is a reworking of the father's *ideas* that maintains his *energies*. The continuation of Catherine's desired-demonic romance is twice aborted by the novel's narrators. (Emily Brontë can complete *her* romance by minimizing the interfering narrators in an ironic presentation.) Catherine yields to Nelly's obdurate non-listening, exchanging her undesired (by Nelly) "queer dream" for an innocuous dream of heaven. Catherine yields the search for Symbolic articulation, but as she fails, Emily Brontë, in a counter-doubling with her protagonist, succeeds. *Emily Brontë presages Lacan by recognizing that desire creates presence within absence in the continuing act of desiring.* The reader completes Catherine's and Heathcliff's unrealized romance (reduced in action to rudimentary myth by social opposition) in his or her desiring imagination. The unwritten erotic romance exists in our passionate experience of *Wuthering Heights*.

It is in the play of temporality and genre within the novel as a whole—the larger organizing demonic romance called *Wuthering Heights*—that we have the surfacings of a lost Symbolic story. The absent story underlies the present narrative; it is repeatedly refused but extant in its traces, finally recuperated and recognizable at the end of the novel, when we consider it in toto. Yet, it often regresses within the experience of the protagonists, to the simpler genre of Imaginary myth. The traced fragments of Catherine's lost romance suggest a creative vision—compressed, radical, figurative—that would have been precisely indicated by a dream of hell. The distinguishing quality of the Catherine and Heathcliff "world" would concern a salvational yet threatening Eros, Catherine's unpictured vision suggesting in absentia *the passionate transformation of childhood merger to demonic love*. This abandoned content suggests itself when the absence in *Wuthering Heights*, that which drives Heathcliff toward agonistic frustration, is the *denied fulfillment of desire* or, precisely that which determines the difference between Symbolic and Imaginary.

Indeed, Nelly's trepidation about the reciting of dark dreams, her feared evil prophecy, becomes actualized, ironically, because the dream is *not recited*. For Heathcliff disappears precisely as Catherine describes his degradation, the disappearance initiated because Catherine's dream, with its vision of union between Catherine and Heathcliff, remains *undescribed*. Nelly precipitates disaster by refusing rather than receiving the dream. Never hearing Catherine's dream of demonic marriage, the ferocity of Heathcliff's consequent revenge fills a narrational vacuum. *Denied the romance of demonic marriage, he is relegated to the myth of satanic revenge*. Nelly plays an anti-auditing role as a non-listener (a sardonic counterpart to a listening mother) negating the creative prophecies of dream-description.

Heathcliff leaves because Nelly compels a change in the mode of Catherine's discourse. Denied Nelly's interlocution, Catherine substitutes abstract for imaginative language; beginning with the social introspection—"it would degrade me to marry Heathcliff now"—that drives Heathcliff away, she goes on to metaphysical speculation. Her famous lines, needing no rehearsal here, describe the other-in-the-self, the other who completes the self by continuing it, to create wholeness in male-female union. Her experience of Heathcliff as self-continuation recalls the way Heathcliff contrasts the passionate unity of the Earnshaws with the tepid *autonomy* (a negative concept in *Wuthering Heights*) of the Lintons. After Heathcliff's disappearance Catherine's "wandering to and fro" the empty gate repeats the experience of being left by the father. The open gate like an abandoned self swings ungrounded without the male other.

The withdrawal of the male other estranges universal nature, for the nature Catherine describes is starkly dualistic. Her love for Edgar Linton, "like the foliage in the woods," expresses the organic life of nature, the seasonal flowering of generative desire between individual lovers. This is the lovely ephemeral face of nature. "The rocks beneath" suggest a cave of death, an ending and an origin, a bond beyond "pleasure," forged not in sensation but in being. The foundation of being refers to the earliest self, the instinctive child formed with the father and his replacing dark twin, the other half of natural (androgynous) completion.

Edgar Linton incarnates the otherness of *emotional erotic* connection (the stronger *sexual erotic* identified with Hareton and Cathy), while Heathcliff returns her to the sameness of pre-organic beginnings, the undifferentiated oneness of the beginning, or the *deathly erotic*. (Catherine and Edgar create the irrepressible Cathy Linton; Heathcliff's single biological creation, from a loveless marriage, is the enfeebled Linton Heathcliff.) Where vitality would reside with Edgar Linton, the stony depths are reservoirs of energy, Catherine and Heathcliff intimate with the self-continuing universe. Catherine attempts to recover her untold dream by transcendent oration, bringing forward the higher romantic conception that would locate the love within death. At the same time, the metaphysics of mythic love-death *valorize inorganic universal energies over organic biological energies*.

Thus, Catherine describes a deathly-Imaginary mode of being. The rhapsodic speech has a static quality, presenting repetition, return, and the relegation to origins. The formulation of the myth of Catherine and Heathcliff in philosophical terms is a concession, a yielding to the necessity of unsympathetic conditions. For the achievement of vision in romance, or of subjective truth in originally formulated language, requires more than the persevering courage of the speaking subject. It *requires the completion of a speaking reality by the inclusion of the listening (m)other*, the releasing of self-creative speech by auditory affirmation, the expansion of utterance in creative communication. Impatient with Catherine's "folly," Nelly quells the vision of the dream to repel the story-romance and return Catherine to the philosophy of the myth. The irony is that the abstract presentation is only a secondary statement, strong enough but displacing something stronger still.

The author of the larger narrative, Emily Brontë, inscribed rather than implied in the book as a whole, projects a reader capable of the reception Lockwood and Nelly reject. Nelly oversees the double separation of Catherine from the essential figures of Heathcliff and Nelly herself; disrupting Catherine's romantic confession in a dooming gesture, Brontë retrieves the elisions of myth in a potential romantic recuperation based on the reader's abiding dream of the love between Catherine and Heathcliff. What Catherine Earnshaw loses in tragic fragments, Emily Brontë gains in the silent work of totalization, a painful building of romance. Nelly's rejections occur within a larger frame. The context of the narrative makes Nelly's refusals ironic as it restores Catherine's losses. In the end we have the romantic telling of a "queer dream" called *Wuthering Heights*.

Hallucination and Vision

Nelly's story climaxes in Catherine's mad hallucinations, a descent into delirium initiated by Heathcliff's reappearance. His long absence repeats earlier abandonment; the beloved's three-year vanishing in the experience of a young woman repeats the father's three-day disappearance in the experience of a child: "and yet, cruel Heathcliff! you don't deserve this welcome. To be absent and silent for three years" (10:75). After the happy marriage of Catherine and Edgar, the novel finds genealogical symmetry between Earnshaw and Linton because of Isabella's attraction to Heathcliff. But, using Isabella to take revenge on the Lintons, Heathcliff threatens Catherine's own perilously balanced position.

Initially, because she not only *knows* but *is* Heathcliff, she confronts his ominous manipulations. Her canniness about their uncanny bond restrains his retributive design: "Quarrel with Edgar . . . and deceive his sister; you'll hit on exactly the most efficient method of revenging yourself on me." Catherine restricts the force of Heathcliff's revenge by sharing the heresy of his passion: "I never say to him, 'Let this or that enemy alone, because it would be ungenerous or cruel to harm them'; I say, Let them alone, because *I* should hate them to be wronged" (10:78–79). She comprehends Heathcliff's oppositional self, his opposed-yet-connected need to merge with the object of his love and destroy the object of his hatred. Hence she evokes his "fierce, pitiless, wolfish" nature in an admonitory speech to Isabella. Nelly assents to Catherine's prescient warnings, "Mrs. Linton spoke strongly, and yet I can't contradict her." Still, she interferes deliberately with Catherine's positive strategy.

By her provocations Nelly begins an (unconscious?) unraveling process; she clumsily (or deftly) intrudes Edgar into the scene of Catherine disarming Heathcliff: "Mrs. Linton . . . was scolding with renewed vigor; Heathcliff had moved to the window, and hung his head, somewhat cowed by her violent rating apparently" (11:88). Interrupting this pacification, Nelly elicits the worst traits of all the characters, arousing Heathcliff's menace, Edgar's propriety, and Catherine's frenzy. Changing the style of her hostility from indifference to interference, Nelly arranges a *second separation* of Catherine from Heathcliff. Divided from Heathcliff again, Catherine enters a state of hysteria.

The fall into madness derives from Catherine's misreading of the older woman. In a violent mirroring, Catherine's complete trust is reflected by Nelly's complete untrustworthiness. Always certain of the other's concerned love, Catherine is the victim of lingering narcissistic innocence. The urgent appeal for recognition from a mis/recognized other dedicated to non/recognition of her own self, imperils Catherine's sanity: "I'm nearly distracted Nelly. . . . And, Nelly, say to Edgar, if you see him again to-night, that I'm in danger of being seriously ill. . . . Will you do so, my good Nelly?" (11:90–91). Catherine's innocence entails a naïve trust based on total lack of competitive envy; it derives, perhaps, from the higher passions of her nature, but her passion-of-feeling makes her helpless against Nelly's power-of-will. Thus Nelly responds to need with deceit, informing Edgar, who is shocked to see Catherine with "blood upon her lips," that "nothing in the world [is] the matter."

Nelly's withheld empathy in the confessional scenes intensifies to active malice in the mad scenes. Having avoided Catherine's earlier recitation of unity, she withdraws from her present reality of isolation. If the confessional scenes explain Catherine's oneness with Heathcliff, the mad scenes illustrate her fragmentation without him: the one scene follows the other, refusing to listen to a story leads to refusing to listen to a plea for support. Catherine's shattering madness follows her frustrated confession. Yet she remains incapable of recognizing Nelly's hostility. Compelled by the need to *repress* Nelly's betrayal, Catherine expresses herself somatically. She abuses herself in a self-starvation, her wasted body an icon of abandonment, her "anorexia" a protest against neglect, a plea for nurture.[10]

Yet her disorientation contains vision; her illusory images are retrieved insights that correct misperceptions. Catherine enters into a discourse of madness; her poetic explorations recall Felman's identification of the language of madness with the intuitions of literature.[11] In a series of vignettes—a lapwing allegory, visions of Nelly-as-witch, an encounter in the mirror, and the nostalgia for the Heights—Catherine hallucinates figurative realities.

The lapwing sequence begins with aggression against soft Linton civilization; in "feverish bewilderment [increased] to madness" she tears open her pillow with her teeth. Regressing from culture to nature, Catherine finds, in Nelly's words, "childish diversion in pulling the feathers from the rents . . . and ranging them on the sheet according to their different species" (12:95). Nelly dismisses Catherine's sorting as "childish," yet it attempts an essential organization, a tracing of a deeper, integral order of the mind, to replace the imposed scheme of the world. In the course of her categorizing, she recalls the fatal memory of the lap-wing:

> "Bonny bird; wheeling over our heads in the middle of the moor. It wanted to get to its nest, for the clouds touched the swells, and it felt rain coming. . . . Heathcliff set a trap over it, and the old ones dare not come. I made him promise he'd never shoot a lapwing after that, and he didn't. . . ."
>
> Give over with that baby-work! . . . There's a mess! The down is flying about like snow!" (12:94)

From the disorder of the scene, the whirl in her mind reflecting the storm of the past, Catherine traces the significance of her relationship with Heathcliff. The passage may depict Heathcliff's intrinsic "sadism," for his release of destructive powers accords with Brontë's view of the natural order.[12] Taken further, the trap motif shows Heathcliff displacing the parental bird to nullify natural process. In a premonition of his mythic-revenge self; he prevents normal development, stifling her with his possessiveness in an elaborate snare.

But, Catherine's dream yields another interpretation; blocking the bird's return, Heathcliff protects as well as destroys. Preventing the exposure to the elements that being bound to the nest would cause, he forces the bird to fly out of the nest, to go beyond the return to origins, to fly into greater nature. The allegory separates the full-fledged creature from its fledgling beginnings; Heathcliff replaces the natural parent in a substitution readable as either destructive or creative. Catherine may be the child stifled without her parent, or the adult liberated from her beginnings, free to wheel out toward the sky; the lapwing is literally abandoned or figuratively released.

Thereafter, in the extremity of disarray, Catherine figuratively renames Nelly: "I see in you, Nelly . . . an aged woman—you have grey hair, and bent shoulders"(12:95). Perceiving the latent image of "elf-bolts" under the manifest "locks of wool," Catherine finds in Nelly a destructive maternal figure, the Imaginary Mother in her hostile power. Critics like Philip Wion have discussed the importance of the "absent mother" in *Wuthering Heights*,[13] but the damage is performed by aggression rather than nonparticipation. This is not the absent mother but the terrible witch. Hence from the *Imaginary-unconscious*—consistently invoked by "the fairy cave under Penistone Crag"—comes the repressed image of Nelly as the hexing witch, and Catherine self-represented as the object of the spell: in her pregnancy Catherine herself becomes the "heifer," the vulnerable beginning-to-reproduce female body.

The scene reconfigures the mother to the mode of the murderous maternal.[14] Rather than vacating a space of absence Nelly intrudes herself as an instrument of force, flattening Catherine to unreality. Nelly herself is the "black press" fantasized in place of Catherine's mirror. In psychoanalytic terms, the mirror is brought to an extreme of anti-mirroring that coincides with Nelly's anti-mothering. The unrecognizable image in the mirror arouses the starved death-harbinger, Freudian-deathly and Lacanian-Imaginary in its uncanniness. Catherine's black mirror is specular death, the ironic reflection of the unreflected self. Catherine returns to the nothing before something, the non-mothering that preceded bad fathering, the maternal abyss. Hence the terror of isolation with her own rejected self; Nelly's assuagements, first occluding the mirror with a shawl, then reassuring her that "There's nobody here. . . . It was *yourself*," are catastrophic ironies.

The rejection of a self in extremity leads first to a dramatic speech and then to a dramatic return: "I was enclosed in the oak-panelled bed at home. . . . the whole last seven years of my life grew a blank! . . . I was a child; my father was just buried, and my misery arose from the separation that Hindley had ordered between me and Heathcliff" (12:97). Like Lockwood's second dream, Catherine's hallucinatory delirium describes a return to a scene of separation. But if the dream was an attempted reparation, returning to the scene of separation in order to alter it, the hallucination seems to consecrate the separation itself as something final, not to be circumvented. It is as though Brontë were demonstrating the genesis of the Lacanian Imaginary, the repetitive doubling structure of Imaginary scenes, while adumbrating, also, their inevitable relationship to the death drive. The original object, the Father, disappears into death—death at the end of disappearance—and Heathcliff substitutes for the Father in a further absence. The condensing of absences in the past and in the present also combines with Nelly who in her "utter blackness," her aggressive erasure of the Mother, precedes the double-loss of the Father and Heathcliff.

The sequence accords with the theory of repetition, bringing forward the emotions that accompany the compulsion to repeat. For that which disturbs Freud is the return of the subject to *unpleasure*, the inexplicable return. In Freud the source is the mysterious inner com/pulsion toward pain, the beyond of the death drive. Yet in Brontë the refusal of the (M)other to receive the words, or the suffering of the self, *the denial of listening,* relegates the speaker to the pain of repetition. Thus, in *Wuthering Heights* the compulsion to repeat has its source in the outside, in an absent or hostile object. Nelly is the inimical listener, saying and doing precisely that which unravels Catherine's progress in language and action. *The hostile listener triggers the compulsion to repeat* because s/he refuses the support that underlies the forward motion of the self.

Returning to Freud after reading Brontë, we may reconsider the necessity "to speak severely [to patients] and treat them coldly" (*BPP,* 3:21), a necessity expressed after Freud had shown extraordinary empathy toward his patients. The question becomes one of cause and effect—at which point does the subject regress, and at which point does the listener withdraw sympathy. In the case of Nelly it is clear that she interferes precisely at the point of reparative creativity; Nelly, and perhaps Freud, dismantles the fledgling beginnings of *Symbolic* words and gestures.

Yet the Freudian and Brontëan romances diverge fundamentally on the theme of death. In Brontëan romance, the destruction of life is not the end of being. The difference between Freud and Brontë is represented by the relationship between the black mirror and the open window. Rather than being destroyed by the lack of psychic mirroring, the denial of forward movement by the unresponsive other, Catherine regresses (or progresses) to unifying empathy with

Heathcliff; she moves toward the winter wind outside the window, as if reinforcing Freud's conviction that the repetition compulsion culminates in death. But if for Freud death is the entropic end of biochemical process, a "*returning to inorganic existence*" (*BPP*, 5:39, my emphasis), for Brontë death is the energic end of spatial and temporal restrictions, *a transcending of organic existence*. To formulate the distinction as that which obtains between biologism and mysticism is to simplify, for what is at issue is the empowering relationship between texts, the mutual enrichment of intertexts. Brontë, that is, gives us a way *to read beyond the pleasure principle*, to open imaginative worlds. For Freud, death ends the literal dimension wherein we realize our psychical/biological being, yet his clash between Eros and Thanatos presents a conflict of *preternatural forces*. If Freud provides a text that *alternates* between death-romance and love-romance, Brontë's death-romance *is* a love-romance. Unified with Heathcliff in the spirit/psyche, Catherine goes through the open window of the Grange to perceive the invisible windows of the Heights; past times and earlier relationships converge in the condensed and inclusive reality of memory-vision:

> But Heathcliff, if I dare you now, will you venture? If you do, I'll keep you. I'll not lie there by myself; they may bury me twelve feet deep, and throw the church down over me, but I won't rest till you are with me. I never will! (12:98)

From the moment of exposure to "the frosty air that cut about her shoulders as keen as a knife," Catherine submits herself to death. She returns not to the experience but to the imagination of death, to the point where psychic-unison-in-the-father dissolves the barriers between self and other, past and present, existence and annihilation. As Heathcliff rejoins her the separation from the death-world falls away like a daylight illusion, material hindrances thrown back like a cover of burying earth. Catherine's mad-vision unlocks the gate that holds them in place, in history, in materiality.

After Heathcliff violates Catherine's chamber, vision returns in the death-grip of their *Liebestod*: "[my Heathcliff is] in my soul . . . the thing that irks me most is this shattered prison. . . . I'm tired, tired of being enclosed here" (15:124). Catherine dies from a final effort to translate Imaginary experience into Symbolic narrative. All the strains of a broken tale take their toll. The narrative design of what might have been *between* them and what is in the greater story *beyond* them is fulfilled in the later Heathcliff-dominated sequences. His passionate narrative, which begins as a myth-of-revenge, transfigures to the higher meanings of a romance-of-death.

Satanic Plot and Demonic Vision

The dialectic of *Wuthering Heights* proceeds in three stages. The rejected love of the *early romance* becomes, first, pitiless hatred in the *central myth*, and then completes itself in the cosmic love of the *later romance*. Heathcliff, who dominates the *plot* of the novel (as Catherine dominates its *theme* and Nelly dominates its *narration)*, begins as a wounded boy, transforms to a tyrannical man, and redeems himself as a kind of transcendental demon. Changes within him—deep transitions in his psychic being—alter the generic substance of the novel "like wine through water." In the second half of *Wuthering Heights*, he dedicates himself to *the revenge that reverses rejection* and, subsequently, *to the desire that reverses revenge*. The transfigurations of revenge end in self-dissolution—in metaphysical adoration of the universally-disseminated beloved.

His cycle of restorative action originates in acts of disappearance, and parallels the boy's *fort/da* game. Like young Ernst, Heathcliff inverts the relations of power that follow the disappearance of a beloved object. From being the *slave* of disappearance, the one who *suffers* in the space of emptiness, he becomes the *master* of disappearance, the one who *creates* a space of emptiness. Like the boy, Heathcliff exploits the disappearing game to strengthen himself, to stage a *disappearing and reappearing self*, to become *someone else*. (The reader may remember that where Freud sees the boy's reel as symbolizing the mother or *disappearing object*, my own reading takes the reel as representing the boy himself or *disappearing subject*.) In both cases disappearance permits transformation and the powerless victim reappears as a powerful author/ity.

Heathcliff's transformation parallels the boy's remaking, the ability of the self to change loss through artistry. As the boy stages a completely altered scene by imaginative mastery, so Heathcliff returns from his disappearance in a scene of magic-romance; thus, he appears under "a score of glittering moons" in a new soldierly form though obscured by darkness. He sends Nelly as a sort of reconnecting reel, for she is the bearer of a word whose purpose is to remake relationship. But, she betrays him as she betrays Catherine; it appears that the true object of her hostility is transformative, or demonic, romance itself. Edgar's disruption of the reunion of Catherine and Heathcliff, on Nelly's instigation, finalizes the dominance of Heathcliff's revenge; again denied romantic connection, he turns to a *mythic* plot of regression and return.

Heathcliff's return takes the circuitous form of revenge which he initiates by appropriating material wealth, acquiring the property whose lack had disempowered him. Reconstructing the social and economic relationships between the Grange and the Heights, he takes control of a microcosmic world, and eventually controls the place of previous humiliation. His revenge play, like a Jacobean fantasy of compensation, takes possession of the scene of dispossession. But if Heathcliff evokes a Renaissance revenger, he is no tragic hero—no flawed victim of fate—for his soul-usurping love dominates his full personality. Since *revenge achieves control of repetition* (Hamlet is a tragic hero but a failure at revenge), Heathcliff returns to power rather than powerlessness, and is in apparent command of his fate.[15]

In the revenge mode, Heathcliff becomes a patriarchal tyrant. First exacting retribution from the Earnshaws, Heathcliff displaces Hindley as receiver of the familial inheritance. He contemptuously appropriates the Earnshaw wealth and birthright, his obliteration—and possible murder—of the legitimate brother showing biblical and Shakespearean force. Hindley's unforgivable crime was to separate Heathcliff from Catherine; similarly, Heathcliff's limitless abhorrence of the Lintons derives from their perceived theft and murder of Catherine. His terrible endeavor, the plot of revenge, is to add further damage to already irreparable damage.

To separate Heathcliff from Catherine is to nullify him in a way, but erotic nullity leads to revenge. If the first nullification by Nelly led to the game-of-disappearance, the second nullification also by Nelly is compensated by a reconfiguring of the romance-of-death. The use of a substitute object reverses the relations of power. Heathcliff, having been rejected by an original figure, Catherine, proceeds to abuse the recapturing figures of Isabella, Hindley, Cathy, and Edgar. Ironically, Heathcliff's vengeance is powerless against both the murderer according to *his* perceptions, Catherine herself, "I love *my* murderer—but *yours*! How can I?" (15:125) and the murderer according to *our* perceptions, the Nelly whose guilt evades Heathcliff's searching gaze.

As revenger Heathcliff is an omnipotent creator of claustrophobic atmospheres, an imprisoning and battering presence (he who was *nothing* becomes *everything*). His inseparable connection to Catherine has its dark reflection in unbound hostility to other women, indeed to femininity itself. (Catherine transcends gender as the completing other in an androgynous union.) Heathcliff reduces Isabella and Cathy to *abject* figures in the Kristevan sense where the male diminishes the female to a worthless object.[16]

Thus Isabella's introduction to *Wuthering Heights* exposes her to a dismissal of Lintonesque civilization, her refinement regarding food, language, and the arrangement of domestic interiors mocked out of existence by Joseph. Hareton's "slavering into the jug of milk," defying Isabella's preference for neatly apportioned bowls, concerns lack of autonomy as well as lack of manners. Such communal and even corrupted taking of food indicates deindividuation, with more than a hint of primary process.

Accordingly, Joseph employs both his preferred epithet, "ye marred, wearisome nowt," and mocks her linguistic and architectural niceties in maliciously pointed exclamations: "*Parlour*! . . . Nay, we've noa *parlours*. . . . *Bed-rume* . . . . Yah's see all t' *bed-rumes* thear is" (13:110, italics original). Brontë italicizes the words whose right to exist Joseph contests. His denial of linguistic legitimacy extends to both the sound and the sense of words whose function it is to indicate separateness and civilization. His own language, he refers to his "*rahm,*" strings together guttural expletives in self-congratulatory combinations of piety and derision. The goal is to shatter Isabella to the condition of a "nowt." Indeed the exasperated Isabella flings her dinner tray to the floor and falls to pieces with its broken crockery. At that point, in a slip surprising from an elder whose malignity keeps his wits sharp, Joseph reveals his true object: "Weel done, Miss *Cathy*! Weel done, Miss *Cathy*! (13:112, italics mine). Taking Joseph as Heathcliff's troll-like servant, or a Pharisaical Sancho Panza, we realize that Catherine's ghost hovers behind Isabella's beleaguered figure.

For the *abject* is the object reduced to will-less dis-integrity. Heathcliff sets himself against Isabella's civilized being, destroying the autonomy that seduced Catherine. He intends to disintegrate Isabella's superfluous cultivation. Heathcliff aims his reductive energies, equally, at Hindley. In her first encounter with Hindley, Isabella is shocked by the self-neglect of "a tall, gaunt man, without neckerchief, and otherwise extremely slovenly; his features . . . lost in masses of shaggy hair that hung on his shoulders; and his eyes, too, were like a ghostly Catherine's with all their beauty annihilated" (13:107). Perhaps the most devastating aspect of the portrait of Hindley in his despair pertains to the annihilation of the gaze. The extinguished glance refers not only to the Earnshaw expression but to the regard of the loved Catherine. More than her beauty, Heathcliff annihilates the being in the eyes of the beloved and her mirroring substitutes. Oppressing Hindley, Heathcliff extinguishes the self evoked by Catherine's look. As Heathcliff's love and hatred both spring from his incomplete ego, the gaze of the enemy still reifies Imaginary merger. To kill Hindley is both to unify with and destroy Catherine. In pursuit of his goal, Heathcliff batters Isabella psychically and *mutilates* Hindley physically.[17] After Hindley's aborted retributive attack on Heathcliff, when his gun with its hidden knife goes off uselessly, we observe a fierce scene:

> The charge exploded, and the knife, in springing back, closed into its owner's wrist. Heathcliff pulled it away by main force, slitting up the flesh as it passed on, and thrust it dripping into his pocket. He then took a stone, struck down the division between two windows, and sprung in. His adversary had fallen senseless with excessive pain and the flow of blood that gushed from an artery, or a large vein. The ruffian kicked and trampled on him, and dashed his head repeatedly against the flags. (17:137)

The beating of Hindley finds a collateral action in the breaking down of fenestral separation. We recall the importance of windows in the dreams and deaths of *Wuthering Heights*, with the window, like the gate, a transitional boundary, a medium for the violation of borders. Heathcliff's violence is always in search of a metaphysical goal. Breaking the window boundary is turning two into one, a figurative anticipation of Catherine's return, while beating Hindley senseless advances the same end, the violence against a visible body pursuing a hidden soul.

Thus, the "slitting" open of Hindley's wrist provides the scene's most penetrating moment. Heathcliff's indifference to the dripping blood evokes images of vampirism, the blood-connection deeper than sex. Pertinent to *the opening of Hindley's body* is Lacan's description of invaded and invasive body images, his finding in the paintings of Hieronymous Bosch an Imaginary index of incendiary intention. For Lacan the images of the fragmented body are specular illustrations of the destructive drives.[18]

Heathcliff's motive is the destruction of a series of signifiers that return, like a signifying circle around a signified center, to the same original figure. The resemblance to a metaphysical conceit is not haphazard, the juxtaposition of Freud and Brontë achieves a kind of metapsychological conceit. Hence, Heathcliff transforms *the one center*, Catherine, to *changing circumferences*, while the old triangle of Edgar, Isabella, and Hindley, is replaced by the new triangle of Linton, Cathy, and Hareton. The self dependent on love strives to become the will omnipotent in power. Yet in the paradox of such transformations, the will can become both dependent and impotent.

The limits of Heathcliff's power emerge in a scene associating Brontë's character with the beleaguered hero of Tasso's poem as presented in *Beyond the Pleasure Principle*. We recall that in his agonized confusion, lost in the magic forest, Tancred "slashes with his sword at a tall tree . . . blood streams from the cut . . . he has wounded his beloved once again" (*BPP*, 3:22). In an amazing textual parallel, Heathcliff also encounters the tragedy of bereavement in the difficult trope, the catachresis, of *the bleeding tree*. Nelly watches Heathcliff's violent mourning in the Grange park; his grief combines self-aggression and aggression against nature, battering through surfaces to reach hidden elements: "He dashed his head against the knotted trunk. . . . I observed several splashes of blood about the bark of the tree, and his hand and forehead were both stained" (16:129).

In this sanguinary variation on the pastoral genre, Heathcliff produces a violent elegy, a blood-parody of the traditional sympathy between man and nature in mourning. Although the scene takes place on Good Friday, there is no transubstantiation; the blood reveals no spirit, the parody being on both Christian faith and vengeful energy.

Moreover, the scene shows the relationship between the two texts, that of Tasso-in-Freud and of Brontë, to be both parallel and opposed. Heathcliff and Tancred each encounter the beloved in her changing forms, but in the supernatural encounter Tancred suffers from the *presence* of Clorinda precisely to the degree that Heathcliff suffers from the *absence* of Catherine. For Tancred all figures of injury return to the original object of hostility, the maternal-in-other-form, figures that reinflict the narcissistic scar. For Heathcliff the objects of hostility are those mythic figures—forced into one-dimensional meaning by revenge-reversal—who recall Catherine without containing her. Catherine herself only consents to meet Heathcliff, as she longed to meet Lockwood, in the dream, within the world of romance. My point here is that so long as Heathcliff pursues mythic revenge he will never meet Catherine, for she awaits his transcendence. To put this another way, Tancred violates the Symbolic world that pursues him, while Heathcliff violates the Imaginary world that he pursues. Both men are driven figures who wound in order not to be wounded.

Heathcliff's natural mode is vengeance; fury motivates his actions at the end even toward Catherine herself. His wildness emerges at the scene of their last meeting, an encounter out of German Romanticism; in speeches resonant with Wagnerian depths, love-death (*Liebestod*) is strained to love-murder (*Liebesmord*). While Catherine is restored to Heathcliff in Imaginary-vision, staring at the world to come like a disoriented demon, Heathcliff remains alone, the momentary reunion serving to infuriate until he "foamed like a mad dog," as savage as Satan.

The dying Catherine recognizes the inferiority of the revenger-Heathcliff to the romantic-Heathcliff: "That is not *my* Heathcliff. I shall love mine yet; and take him with me—he's in my soul," (15:124, original italics). She looks outward to the soul or psyche, but Heathcliff is too wild for spiritual merger. His unforgivingness encompasses Catherine herself: "don't let me see your eyes!" Hence, the grand expansion of their dual-aria at the close is countered by the compression of a suffocating embrace; their grasp leaves locks of Heathcliff's hair in Catherine's hands and his bruised finger-marks on her fragile skin.

Heathcliff figuratively repeats the suffocating embrace, years later, with the second Cathy. The sense of claustrophobic entrapment reflects Heathcliff's withdrawal into his isolate ego, the satanic will an expression of the ego's quest for omnipotence, and of what Milton meant when he wrote of the self as hell. Heathcliff becomes a prisoner of the ego, and we know that death is the goal of the ego. Yet the drive toward the death of the self is externalized as the drive toward the death of the Other.

Thus Heathcliff appears as the novel's patriarchal tyrant, an overbearing presence, who, in a major sequence, locks the gates on Cathy and aggressively withholds the key. When he fiendishly prevents its retrieval despite her determined courage, he unites varied tropes of liberation and imprisonment:

> Heathcliff had the key in his hand and that remained on the table. He looked up, seized with a sort of surprise at her boldness, *or, possibly, reminded by her voice and glance, of the person from whom she inherited it* . . . he seized her with the liberated hand, and, pulling her on his knee, administered with the other a shower of terrific slaps on both sides of the head, each sufficient to have [knocked her down] had she been able to fall. (27:204–6, italics mine)

The juxtaposition of the key with Cathy's "voice and glance" intensifies the significance of the scene's objects. Cathy demands the key to the house, but provides the key to his fury: for Heathcliff, whose enclosures are inward not outward, the key to freedom is in the voice and glance of the beloved. His violent response takes as its target a beautiful face with an uncanny resemblance to the original Catherine. His desires aim for the destruction of a countenance and the deconstruction of a signifier. The murder of cultivated speech and an engaging regard, beauty and depth, is an aggression of profound enormity, its motivations to destroy *the covering signifier (Cathy)* and *the covered signified (Catherine)*. Aggression is the inversion of love, the profanation of desire. Yet after seeing Catherine in Cathy's face something essential changes.

Henceforth Heathcliff devotes himself to dis/covering the disintegrated and disembodied forms of Catherine, her spirit, voice, corpse, dust. He exhumes her body, bribing the sexton to arrange their mutual dissolution. Despite satanic indifference to death and its physiological consequences Heathcliff forbears from removing the coffin lid, prevented by her ghost from defiling her corpse. The taboo against the dead body of the beloved, even with such an inveterate iconoclast as Heathcliff, remains potent. Indeed the damaged, dying, or dead body of beloved objects or would-be objects carries a central valence in all the novels examined in the present study. I think of Elizabeth and the destroyed female Creature in *Frankenstein*, of Catherine and her parallel/opposite, the disabled Rochester, and of Mrs. Morel before the fire (perhaps of the damaged Baxter Dawes) in *Sons and Lovers*. I am reminded again of the connection Lacan and the Lacanian critic Slavoj Žižek make between the Real on the one hand, and, on the other, physical dissolution in all its felt actuality. The dissolution of a loved body threatens to unveil the unbearable signified the Real.

On another level, Heathcliff's satanic isolation precludes demonic union with Catherine; even as he feels her ghost's breath she eludes his hostile-substitutive mode, for the capacity to embrace her necessitates an inner transformation. It finally occurs as Heathcliff sees Catherine and himself in the rebellion of Hareton and Cathy, two outsiders he himself desenfranchises. They revitalize the Heights by replacing its black currant trees with flowers from the Grange. Most significantly, however, Cathy and Hareton find their connection in words, in a romance of the book. The Blakean term Hareton reads to Cathy, as he acquires language with her encouragement, is "Con-*trary*" (32:233). The word refers to progressions of disparate union, and suggests a language that empowers sexuality. Hareton's championship of Cathy takes on special resonance as, while Nelly watches, he defends Cathy from Heathcliff's characteristic brutality: "He had his hand in her hair. . . . when of a sudden, his fingers relaxed, he shifted his grasp from her head to her arm, and gazed intently in her face (33:243).

Hareton's rescue reconceives the romantic child—the child as father to the man—in Lacanian terms, the son liberating the father from his Imaginary obsession. We have a startling reversal in the no/name-of-the-son, *Non/Nom du Fils*. Hareton (heir/town, Herr/town, the true lord) reconquers his name through actions which say: "*do not strike your daughter, the reflection of the love you cannot love, for I have your name and she is my wife*." The intercession of the son, a self-progression for Hareton, also causes the father to look into eyes that encounter rather than reflect. Relinquishing the obsessive inwardness of revenge, he returns to outward vision.

Thereafter Heathcliff's perceptions take universal form. The beloved becomes an encompassing emanation disseminated through cosmic endlessness; the bringing together of Brontëan fiction and Lacanian theory enables a visionary-psychoanalytic synthesis, a transfiguration of the *Fractured Imaginary* (deathly dependency) through the *Violent Imaginary* (aggressive destruction) to the *Higher Imaginary* (a vision both ironic and transcendent):

> Nelly, there is a strange change approaching—I'm in its shadow at present. . . . what does not recall her? I cannot look down to this floor, but her features are shaped on the flags. . . . filling the air at night, and caught by glimpses in every object by day, I am surrounded with her image. (33:244).

Death is not a return but a turn, not inward but outward. The replacement of the mythic by the romantic occurs as egocentricity advances to universalization. The altering of the beloved to a cosmic force is less a transformation, the movement to other signifiers, than an expansion, the conceiving of all perception in terms of the original signified. Heathcliff never moves from the Imaginary to the Symbolic, from death to life, but rather achieves a conceptualization in a greater Imaginary, its existence enabled—one recognizes a similar process in *Jane Eyre*—by the intrusion of the Real. (I think of Heathcliff's unclosable eyes and sharp teeth, the terror Nelly feels at his dead countenance and the malevolent joy of wicked Joseph.) The visionary-spiritual passion between Catherine and Heathcliff is Real in its erotic ferocity and Imaginary in its relentless invasion of the self. The lovers are inscribed each in the psychic perception, the *soul's eye,* of the other. Brontë's Higher Imaginary overrides the Symbolic.

Coincidental with Hareton's and Cathy's inscription into the Symbolic order, Heathcliff's vision of Catherine takes its significant turn. Catherine moves outward into all perception; her presence in the perceptual surround valorizes the beloved, while leaving the larger worlds of nature and society unredeemed. Heathcliff's end perplexes Nelly as the strange "dark thing" perplexed her at the beginning; she is unable to respectably

> close his eyes—to extinguish . . . that frightful, life-like gaze of exultation. . . . They would not shut; they seemed to sneer at my attempts, and his parted lips and sharp, white teeth sneered too! (34:254)

Finally, Heathcliff looks out at the world with a sardonic death-gaze. He dies completed by a universal beloved, yet in mocking disregard of the surrounding world. The universal idea values the idea and devalues the universe. Transfiguring the perceptual surround into the form of the beloved while yet dismissing all that is not the beloved, achieving an erotic connection to an object that may be encountered only as Imaginary fantasy, Heathcliff brings the novel to closure in the Brontëan mode of Higher or Universal Imaginary; the cosmos take the form of the beloved to absorb the subject-lover. Achieving such expansive visionary power Brontë succeeds in creating the rare genre of true *Imaginary Romance*, the image of the lover as not only a universal value, but a transvaluation of values. The reader strains to understand a gesture of rare artistry.

6

From Child of the Imaginary to the Real Life of a Woman: *Jane Eyre*

The Winter of the Imaginary

THE IMAGINARY IMAGE DEFIES THE WORD. IN LITERATURE (IT WOULD BE defined differently in visual representations) the Imaginary picture reveals itself by its resistance to the frame of language. Imaginary representations leave us anxious and *silent* by arousing feelings that go beyond thought. We recall that, according to the Lacanian reading of the mirror-stage, our earliest experiences of mirror-reflections assert themselves before our verbal powers are developed. The preverbal genesis of the Lacanian Imaginary, the conditions that determine the development of the specular, leaves its trace in the silencing power of later visual experience. As it begins in the eerie specular world of the mirror, the experience of visuality can annihilate language. The special authority of the mirror is found in its silence.

The silence of the mirror-image emerges from the paradox of a complete visual portrait reflecting an incomplete ontological subject. The feeling of being incomplete derives from not having been born into language, from the absence of a completing system of

---

Theoretical Forenote: Jane Eyre *begins with games-of-disappearance as the child-protagonist vanishes first into the literary images in Bewick's* History *and later into her own reflection in the mirror. Thereafter, Jane tries to unplay the games that close her within herself. She escapes the patterns of substitution in the acquisition of language; the Mother no longer needs to be reproduced when the self is achieved, and the image of the Father may be shattered by the creation of a lover. Unplaying the death-games means living the romance-of-life. Jane's story is about the movement from the death-ego to the vital self. At the end of the novel, a striking union fuses the Lacanian Real with the achievement of sexual and spiritual intimacy. Jane's romance-of-life depends on the shattering of the narcissistic forms that give shape to the Imaginary.*

thought; the Imaginary, always about lack, is something surrounded by nothing. Hence the finished picture of an unfinished self provides a *reflection-in-opposition*. The reflection projects the strength the observer desires, but remains completely Other. (The Other in the mirror is the Other that cannot be reached.) The paradox is that the self is negated by an affirmation experienced as unreal. Each glance *in* the mirror redoubles the gap between the subject *and* the mirror.

While the Imaginary begins with mirror-images, finished pictures of unfinished selves appear in other natural and cultural contexts. In romantic literature we find the Imaginary in remote visual expanses, in dark, frozen landscapes that loom over conceptualized understanding. Vast natural panoramas in writings by Wordsworth and Coleridge, by Percy and Mary Shelley, by D. H. Lawrence and Thomas Mann, present scenes of the romantic sublime. Indeed, the romantic sublime recalls the Lacanian Imaginary, for each is an abstract idea recognizing the limitations of language.[1] When we describe a depiction as Imaginary or sublime we recognize that a full verbal elaboration is not available; each of these abstract conceptions refers to a *visual field* that eludes verbal consciousness. Indebted to the Imaginary, the fear in sublime representations coincides with the impression of their muteness. Sublime terror arises from icons of incomprehensibility disposed on an infinite plane. (One thinks of the paintings of John Martin or Caspar David Friedrich.) Thus the power of the representation refers to the powerlessness of the observer, while the feelings evoked by such scenes refer to death and the inconceivable.

In vistas of the romantic sublime, the transformation of ice into other elements can suggest the dissolution of frozen landscapes—whether inner or outer. Furthermore, the imagistic transformation points toward a verbal transliteration. I use the term *transliteration* for the translation of image into word, and refer in particular to the *release* of the frozen Imaginary into the organic or fluid Symbolic, to Imaginary ice melting into the generating waters of language.

Jane Eyre begins with a child's helplessness in a forbidding nature, its somber clouds and penetrating rain precluding her from "taking a walk that day."[2] Jane is surrounded by an impenetrable nature that refuses to establish a physical or imaginative relationship with her. The novel's initial scene subverts Wordsworthian myths of interfusion between self and nature: nature in *Jane Eyre* (*throughout Jane Eyre*) denies such connection. Yet the novel's protagonist, its isolated child, is "glad" to be excluded from nature. Jane has learned to keep her distance from a surround composed of bare "leafless shrubbery," and illumined by harsh "raw twilight." Indeed, the scene is "raw" because not susceptible to reconsideration: the visual expanse resists being entered, or negotiated with, or refigured, and the novel begins in an ironic mode where nature defeats expectations of solace or comfort.[3]

The rejections of nature (with its overtones of mother-nature) are redoubled as Jane is spurned by her social mother (she has no natural mother), her guardian, Mrs. Reed. Mrs. Reed, whose name indicates the insecure support she offers, confronts Jane with the great paradox of parental withholding—she *denies* love to the child from whom she *demands* love:

> . . . until she heard . . . I was endeavouring in good earnest to acquire a more sociable and childlike disposition, a more attractive and sprightly manner . . . she really must exclude me from privileges intended only for contented, happy, little children. (1:5)

Her emotional frigidity matched by an indifference to sequential logic, Mrs. Reed insists on enjoying the effect of parental support while declining to provide its cause; desiring a "happy" child, she disdains the empathetic effort that would produce her.

Twice deprived by her actual environment, Jane withdraws to read in a secluded window-seat with its glassed-in view of nature. She disappears into an imaginative kingdom: closed in by "scarlet drapery" on the right hand, to her left

> were the clear panes of glass, protecting, but not separating me from the drear November day. . . . At intervals, while turning over the leaves of my book, I studied the aspect of that winter afternoon. Afar, it offered a pale blank of mist and cloud. (1:5)

To return to deprivation is to envision loss. Jane observes a wintry setting from protective distance, creating a scene of the imagination by combining distanced nature with the illustrated (and interpreted) nature in her book, *Bewick's History of British Birds*.[4]

Englassed, she is both inside and outside a comfortless environment. This wintry scene consists of a series of impressions-within-impressions, for it inscribes 1) winter itself, 2) the illustrated book *imitating* winter, and 3) the impressionable mind *receiving* winter. Jane passes through a series of impressions; the young girl separates comprehensible images from images eluding her comprehension. Beginning as metaphor for the coldness of her treatment, the scene continues with visual and verbal reflections transforming sensory experience into imaginative experience:

> There were those [pages] which treat of the haunts of sea-fowl; of "the solitary rocks and promontories" by them only inhabited. . . . Nor could I pass unnoticed . . . "those forlorn regions of dreary space—that reservoir of frost and snow, where firm fields of ice . . . surround the pole, and concentre the multiplied rigors of extreme cold." Of these death-white realms I formed an idea of my own: shadowy, like all the half-comprehended notions that float dim through children's brains, but strangely impressive. The words in these introductory pages connected themselves with the succeeding vignettes, and gave significance to the rock standing up alone in a sea of billow and spray . . . to the cold and ghastly moon glancing through bars of cloud at a wreck just sinking. . . . The fiend pinning down the thief's back behind him I passed over quickly: it was an object of terror. So was the black, horned thing seated aloof on a rock, surveying a distant crown surrounding a gallows. (1:6)

The distant vistas are encompassed partially; located somewhere between the familiar and the defamiliar, they open a space in which the self can locate itself. This occurs through the mediations of explanatory language, a verbal bridging to frigid expanses affected by the transliteration of image into word. Jane's capacity to place herself within a frozen landscape shows her childlike Negative Capability. She situates herself in landscape by suspending her judgment while remaining open to a variety of aroused feelings. In a paradox of Imaginary experience the frozen self begins to unfreeze precisely as it sees itself frozen. The visualization of the negative is the beginning rather than the end of a process.

Yet there are areas that transliteration cannot reach. These are the particularly dark self-images, the Imaginary reflections found in the picture-book. Jane in the window-seat is in the position of one who finds a Symbolic expression for her surroundings yet confronts the continuing darkness of the Imaginary self. The scenes concern themselves most deeply with Jane's self-projection as a heartless thing of death and destruction. Her eerily insentient self-images turn predatory nature to surrealistic tropes outside nature; a seabird becomes a "black horned thing" turned to "an object of terror." Haunted by the supernatural "fiend," Jane experiences a terror of silence. It is in her uncanny ability to see herself as not integrated into life, as an alien thing on the borders of death, that Jane reveals her Keatsian depths. For like Keats she brings forward death's romantic pleasure. She knows not only the pain but the pleasures of *isolation*, of, so to say, *isolation / ice-elation,* familiar from Coleridge and Mary Shelley, a state of being that locates joy in icy withdrawal and exaltation in snowy desolation. *Isolation / ice-*

elation includes the cold desire to abandon all objects and achieve ecstasy in death's surroundings. Thus, Jane's fearful landscapes affirm the death drive underlying the experience of the Imaginary, the frigidity of merely visual perception.

Jane's alterations of pleasure and terror refer to the negations of desire. Opposed desires include one another to proliferate into aporetic forms. The representational benefit is gained from the creative immersion in death, the pleasurable unpleasure of the death drive. Her full encounter with deathly feeling mitigates the absoluteness of the icy plane to suggest the beginnings of change. This romantic paradox delineates an opposition to romantic irony, for it affords a kind of provision. (I take the ironical as suggesting *subtraction*, irony being a use of language where the signified takes something away from the signifier; the *provisional*, with its dual meaning, offers a positive counterpart to the ironical by suggesting *addition*). Such a trope of romantic provision is inherent in Jane's articulation of death; for the continuity of articulation *is* life, it is a life-through-death, and the energy of verbal exploration is a path toward vitality. Hence in Bewick each

> . . . picture told a story: mysterious often to my undeveloped understanding and imperfect feelings, yet ever profoundly interesting: as interesting as the tales Bessie sometimes narrated on winter evenings, when she chanced to be in good humour; and when . . . she . . . fed our eager attention with passages of love and adventure taken from fairy tales and older ballads: or . . . from the pages of "Pamela" and "Henry, Earl of Moreland." (1:6–7)

The capacity to turn image into story is connected to a maternal figure, a Good Mother who allows the child escape from a world of multiple reflections. Hence the importance of Bessie, the kind servant, playful and conversable; the memory of Bessie's recitations affords the imaginative and emotional strength necessary to the work of transliteration. The romantic immersion in ice is exhilarating, but hopefulness comes from the brighter, freer alteration of cold reproduction to aesthetic exploration "as interesting as the tales Bessie sometimes narrated on winter evenings." Bessie is the good object, the Mother of the Good Word; the flexibility of language, the word which offers both abstract comprehension and emotional closeness, releases the grip of ice. Bessie's good influence allows the book of commentary and drawing, *Bewick's History*, to become a bridge between picture and story. Hence, the introductory window-seat sequence indicates the movement of the novel. Jane will move from Imaginary death (the being locked in the self), to Symbolic life (finding the way toward the other), through mediating forms. Such passage is enabled by a psychic object that incarnates an otherness within him or herself.

In her early experience Jane moves between the annihilating extremes inherent in the play of fire and ice. After her experience in the window-seat, Jane responds with fierce courage to the bullying of her cousin, John Reed. In their altercation he uses a book as a weapon, a missile, but she reverses the power-relations between them because she knows the contents of the book and understands its words; she turns the brute violence of John Reed to metaphor by comparing him to a Roman emperor. Exemplifying the social—the metaphysical—injustice that pervades the novel, Jane, the victim of the incident, is treated as its perpetrator. It is Jane who is banished to the portentous red room, the parental chamber abandoned after the death of her uncle, Mr. Reed.

The red-room assaults Jane with intrusive visual representations; banishment to the charged chamber seems *designed* to bring on hysteria. The furnishings of the room condense denied sexuality and revered death, the linked cultural constants of the Victorians. The hidden chamber, "very seldom slept in," contains "A bed supported on massive pillars of mahogany, hung with curtains of deep red damask . . . like a tabernacle in the center" (2:10). By means of the red room Charlotte Brontë introduces laden gothic motifs—deathly histories, hidden chambers, and secret practices—into her narrative.

Brontë's Victorian gothicism is prurient with psychoanalytic (and pornographic) suggestion as it inscribes the repression of sex in the expression of death.[5] God the father is embedded in the "tabernacle" of the parental four-poster, its grandeur a sign of sexual-ecclesiastical condensation. Indeed, the colors of the room rage like a Primal Scene without parents, the aura of parental sexuality strengthened by the immense *size* of the furnishings, the "massive pillars" of the bed and "ample . . . easy-chair . . . like a pale throne." Jane's recollection of Mrs. Reed's occasional visits to the room, "to review the contents of her . . . jewel case," outlines a child's vague sense of sexual rhythms.[6] The massiveness of the scarlet setting communicates prohibited sensuality, and arouses feelings of inferiority and fear in the child-Jane.

The gross representations in the parental bedroom create an excess of sensation, a destructive overstimulation that assaults her senses to the point where she feels her personality obliterated.

Thus it is not surprising that one of the dramatic vignettes in the red room presents an experience of specular annihilation.

> All looked colder and darker in that visionary hollow than in reality: and the strange little figure there gazing at me, with a white face and arms specking the gloom, and glittering eyes of fear moving where all else was still, had the effect of a real spirit: I thought it like one of the tiny phantoms, half fairy, half imp, Bessie's evening stories represented as coming out of lone, ferny dells in moors. (2:11).

Jane's self-disappearance in the mirror suggests a connection between a surfeit of oedipally-derived feeling and the periodic reappearance of the Imaginary. Her experience of self-insignificance (her *tininess*) takes form as a fantasy—a phantasm of emptiness—in the mirror.[7] Jane encounters herself as an alienated specular image in an encounter that reinforces the Lacanian reading of the mirror. Yet the "visionary hollow" unfolds in a manner that belies Lacanian theory. In *Jane Eyre*, as opposed to Lacan's Mirror Stage, the observer and her reflection are not antithetic but congruent: in the mirror Jane sees what she is rather than what she is not. Jane confronts *an image of a negative state in an accurate replication of its affective reality*. She is one not yet born into a sense of bodily reality. The unreal image in Jane's mirror is close to her inner conviction while the real image in Lacan's mirror opposes the observer's lack of affective reality. Moreover, Jane does not so much view the reflection as narrate it, placing an alienated visual image within the context of a familiarizing story. The capacity for transliteration, learned from the provisioning Mother-figure, Bessie, suggests that the emptiness Jane confronts can be ameliorated. Through language, which gives the later Jane a way to *frame* the images of the earlier Jane, the paradoxes she faces are resolvable and the injuries she suffers are, ultimately, reparable.

Still, the red-room contains overwhelming sensations. They begin with the repressed paternal image who brings, at the same time, terror and redemption. The Father in Jane's fantasy condenses the two mythic figures of the Freudian object who arouses desire and the Lacanian lawgiver who takes vengeance. The Father conflates sexuality and authority.[8] Mr. Reed makes his appearance in a passage where Jane confronts the reality of her own isolated suspicious nature. She recognizes herself as a hostile outcast, perceived by others as inimical to the social context. Lacking the means for establishing human connection, she longs, nevertheless, for deliverance from exile:

> I wiped my tears . . . fearful lest any sign of violent grief might waken a preternatural voice to comfort me, or elicit from the gloom some haloed face, bending over me with strange pity. This idea, consolatory in theory, I felt would be terrible if realised. (2:12–13).

The "strange pity" on the paternal countenance indicates more than supernatural consolation. The complexity of the bond with the fantasy-Father develops from conflated desires, with latent longing inseparable from manifest isolation, and the need for recognition no less motivating than the need for love. The narrative describes her inwardly "disturbed mind like a dark deposit in a turbid well." The corrupted self-perception is sustained by her self-designation as a "noxious thing," unnamed and unseen ("thing" being a nondescriptive term devoid of linguistic nuance, a formless but dark apprehension encouraging horror and in that sense an *Imaginary word*).

Jane, startled by a vagrant gleam of light, hallucinates the return of the Father from death. Her fantasy-Father, a dual Patriarch returning in an act of vindication, combines repressed sexuality and redeeming law. The duality of the Father places him as the simultaneous obstacle and path to civilization, for he represents both the object of unlawful desire and the desire for lawful order. The complex representations of the Father place unbearable strain on Jane's relations, including fantasy relations, with men throughout the novel. The later relationship with Edward Rochester continues to show the tension inherent in Jane's conflicting needs from a male figure.

Jane contends with the simultaneous need for a Father of Desire and a Father of the Law by perceptual division; in a childlike manner, she splits adults into figures of benevolence or malevolence. The child's perception, expressed in the divided characterizations of fairy tales, or novels with fairy-tale elements,[9] informs Jane's encounters with Mr. Lloyd, the apothecary, and Mr. Brocklehurst the educator. Mr. Lloyd concretizes the Father of Desire by drawing close to her in intimate visual encounters. He considers her "at leisure" from his "hard-featured yet good-natured looking face": sympathetic recognition allows eventual freedom and advance. Through Mr. Lloyd, she goes to the Lowood School, and begins her successful career in the outside world.

Like a pilgrim in an allegory, she continues to encounter obstacles to desire. The black figure of Brocklehurst, the Evangelical minister who directs Lowood, represents the Father as (Proscriptive) Law. Despite the change of color, his dimensions recall Jane's experience in the red room: "a black pillar! . . . the straight, narrow, sable-clad shape standing erect on the rug" (4:26). His formidable figure simultaneously inscribes guilt and incarnates sexuality. Brocklehurst is a minister of the gospel bound to a demonic identity, a self-righteous devil foregrounding sin. He is, moreover, a force of nonrecognition. He knows Jane by Calvinistic preconceptions that decree the Original Sin of the Human Child (particularly if she is impoverished), while the mendacious testimony of Mrs. Reed adds further prejudgments to his view. Observed by witnesses with malevolent intentions, Jane's being is always under assault.

As Lloyd and Brocklehurst represent two different perceptions (or projections) of men, Jane has similarly divided experiences of women. The division operates in relation to the two woman servants. In a narrative vision (sustained evenly throughout the novel) lying somewhere between perception and imagination, blending the epistemologies of novel and romance, Jane counterposes empathetic Bessie with judgmental Abbot (allegorized by her churchy name). Overhearing the servants' speech, Jane listens to her own early history, and in hearing the story of her origins she begins the process of self-understanding. In *Great Expectations* Pip undergoes the same process in a more elaborate fashion. Like Pip, Jane learns about the long-ago fabula-before-the-sujet, the chronological events before the narrated fiction, in story fragments that spin off from crises in the sujet: in both novels a function (perhaps *the* function) of plot is revelation.

As the two servants speak, they show their contrasting natures in a dialogic interchange:

> . . . "Poor Miss Jane is to be pitied, too, Abbot."
>
> "Yes . . . if she were a nice, pretty child, one might compassionate her forlornness; but one really cannot care for such a little toad as that." (3:21)

Hearing the voices in pretended sleep, the dialogue occurs as if between maternal images in Jane's mind. The difference between the sympathetic and antipathetic mother depends on the capacity for aural reception, the readiness to enter into Jane's story. Bessie arrives at compassion, going *beyond* surface appearance through knowledge. Abbot forecloses her verdict, her hostility is confirmed by the appearance of its object. She comes to her conclusions in an area located *before* verbal appeal. The division between the two servants can be formulated in terms of the Imaginary and Symbolic orders. Bessie listens to the story and the narrative places a context around the "rawness" of Jane's aggression. Abbot, who tells the story without being affected by it, simplifies the child by reducing her to the visual immediacy of the image. To relegate Jane to the position of "a little toad" (or horror) is to restrict her to a mythic image (related to the Calvinist myth of original guilt). The mythic image is created by translating the appearance of the other to a cultural stereotype, in this case the unassimilated, less-than-human child. The superficial perception scapegoats the Other.

Opposed to the mythic image we have the romantic story, which draws from the clarifying knowledge of the past to illumine the benighted confusion of the present. If Bessie is a gateway to self-discovery, Abbot is the gate to despair. Indeed, she stands in for Mrs. Reed, and it is the repelled censure of the Mother, her speech which refuses further speech, and not the supernatural appearance of the Father, which causes the fainting spell concluding the chapter. While Jane calls out at the appearance of the illusionary paternal light, she faints and loses consciousness after being repelled by Mrs. Reed. Her aunt is a figure of maternal dread who stands at the beginning and end of the red-room experience. It is Mrs. Reed who consigns Jane to the world of ghosts and refuses to grant her any reprieve. In a later expression of detestation, Mrs. Reed clarifies her fundamental rejection of Jane: "I hated it the first time I set my eyes on it—a sickly, whining, pining thing" (21:203). Herein are the roots of Jane's feeling of being not only unlovable but less than human. Her perception of herself as detestable, "thing-like," derives from the way she is perceived by Mrs. Reed, the detesting mother. Indirectly, Mrs. Reed relegates her adopted child to isolation and death.

The visual experience of the child inside the mirror shows an intrinsic relation to the voice of the mother outside the mirror. The unreal image in the glass is experienced by the child denied maternal reinforcement and identification. Maternal denial precedes, indeed, melodramatic events in the red room.[10] Mrs. Reed's imperative, "Silence! This violence is most repulsive," culminates in the loss of breath that anticipates an early dying.

Jane's belated response takes place after Mrs. Reed falsely accuses her, in front of Brocklehurst, of having a tendency toward "deceit." Jane's verbal counter-assault, leveled after the hypocritical cleric leaves the drawing room, is designed to destroy its object. Her attack occurs in a full confrontation with the older woman's visual and vocal powers. The young girl finds her tongue in a frenzied self-assertion, her destructive articulations uttered in a wild struggle for survival. With a kind of final violence, Jane asserts her deep truth: that since falseness is the last thing she, a girl of unpolitic honesty, could be accused of, to charge her with deceit is itself deceit. In the deadly struggle between Mother and Daughter, Jane's furious speech erases the gaze and extinguishes the voice of Mrs. Reed; she blinds and stills—castrates—her older rival. Her words destroy the image of the accuser and redeem the image of the accused. Her verbal attack takes imagistic form in destructive fire.

> A ridge of lighted heath, alive, glancing, devouring, would have been a meet emblem of my mind when I accused and menaced Mrs. Reed: the same ridge, black and blasted after the flames are dead, would have represented . . . my subsequent condition [and] . . . the dreariness of my hatred and hating position. (4:32)

Lacan connects fire to the transformative annihilation of the Real,[11] for fire at once alters and eliminates that which it grasps. The trope of burning appears when the Imaginary, which is at once hypnotic and illusory, falls away, yet the creative and analytic powers of the Symbolic are only partially available, and thus prove themselves treacherous in turn. The third way of apprehending experience then emerges, and an energy of destruction is achieved in the Real. The Real is a desperate resolution of the Imaginary so incendiary as to leave the subject more scarred than its object. What occurs between Jane and Mrs. Reed at this point, and not only at this point, is primitive, tribal, a feminine version of the devour or be-devoured state portrayed in Freud's *Totem and Taboo*.[12]

Between the two women a primordial blood-hatred is aroused that suggests nothing less than a feminine-oedipal-rivalry unto the very death. In its terrifying dimension, which Brontë portrays so successfully, the relationship between Mother and Daughter is as basic as it is murderous: the necessity for each partner in the rivalry is to destroy the gaze, voice, and image of the Other.[13] The signifying actions between Mother and Daughter, on this level of connection, remain Imaginary or semiotic in the Kristevan sense, evoking actions and interactions of prelinguistic valence, for the Symbolic is unattainable within such relationships. The semiotic terrors of the Mother/Daughter relationship in *Jane Eyre* culminate in Bertha Rochester's flaming destruction of Thornfield.[14]

Yet fiery destruction yields deferred benefits. Violence settles a formidable enemy, Mrs. Reed, while releasing the constraints on Jane's relationship with Bessie. Only after Jane violently *explodes* her isolation can Bessie *describe* her isolation: "You are a strange child, Miss Jane . . . a little, roving, solitary thing. . . . a queer, frightened, shy little thing" (4:33). Violence breaches the closed walls of the self. Bessie designates Jane as a "thing," affectionately altering a word that had hitherto indicated the isolated and unnamable aspect of her being; Bessie allows Jane to emerge from her "thing-like" identity (the human "thing" is a conception as foreboding in Brontë as it is humorous in Dickens). The adjectives describing the veiled "thing" become, in Bessie's formulation, milder, relational, capable of connection with the other. Bessie shows compassion, condensing Jane's history in the ballad of the "Poor Orphan Child," but treats the real child with sympathetic playfulness. She expresses acceptance by recognition: Jane says, "I shall soon have another set of people to dread." Bessie's response is, "If you dread them, they'll dislike you" (4:34).

Fracturing Jane's brooding isolation, Bessie's speech enables communication between the two women. Bessie looks ahead to the later feminine figures—Miss Temple and Helen Burns, Diana and Mary Rivers—who advance Jane's self-development by embodying the culture of speech.[15]

Hunger at Lowood

The carriage of Brontë's narrative drives over the breadth of England. Its restless movement traces allegorical place names, its houses (Thornfield, Moor House, Ferndean) and spaces (Whitcross) charting Jane's geography of being. On the map of romance, *Gateshead* focuses on beginnings: Jane's first home is where *visual* fantasies begin. *Lowood,* her only formal school, begins with the *visceral,* the *physical* self. In this place of scant provision, the reader shares Jane's agonies of hunger and nausea. We note the way the one turns into the other when a famished child faces "rancid fat. . . . the mess . . . of indifferent potatoes and strange shreds of rusty meat." We share, with corresponding relief, Jane's rare moments of repletion.

Sickened by her miserable fare: "the first edge of hunger blunted, I perceived I had got in hand a nauseous mess" (5:38), Jane's brooding on hunger suggests, at the same time, a return to prior emptiness. For if her concern with food foregrounds the material deprivations of the orphan, the lack of physical sustenance remains inseparable from the lack of psychic sustenance. Inadequate nourishing concretizes inadequate mothering. The dual meaning of hunger is condensed usefully in the Kleinian synecdoche of the "bad breast," an image that refers to the frustrating maternal body. The bad breast provides little yet intrudes itself into experience with negative force.[16] Klein's image accords with the experience of impoverished nutrition.

Indeed, negative female images—repellent Mrs. Reed, coarse Abbot, narcissistic Georgiana, anal-obsessive Eliza—invade the child-Jane from her beginnings, starting at the point of origin. She is inhabited by female images she will not internalize as part of herself. Hence she is both nauseated by and starved for the presence of feminine figures. Negative objects evoking disgust and lack are part of her Imaginary experience. In this connection, we recognize that the bad breast is a Kleinian trope of Lacanian suggestiveness; the juxtaposition of Klein and Lacan places food, related to our earliest human sensations, in the visual field, and connects the experience of eating to the Imaginary order.

Yet at Lowood Jane encounters admirable women, feminine images who serve as positive objects of identification.[17] Two figures, Miss Temple, the headmistress, and Helen Burns, an older student, contribute to Jane's cultural development. Each is distinguished by the nuanced grace of her speech. The feminine figures Jane idealizes also recognize Jane's own separateness; with insightful sympathy, they perceive her in her otherness. Miss Temple and Helen Burns are rehabilitating figures who enable Jane to acquire a voice of her own.

We encounter Miss Temple in opposition to the condemning harshness of Brocklehurst's religion. For her aura recalls Hellenic learning rather than Christian piety. Her family name evokes the mythic prototype of Pallas Athena, while her physical description accords with a pagan rather than a Christian house of worship.

> . . . she looked tall, fair, and shapely; brown eyes, with a benignant light . . . relieved the whiteness of her large front . . . hair . . . very dark brown, was clustered in round curls . . . a gold watch . . . shone at her girdle. (5:40–41)

Miss Temple's appearance expresses enlightened intelligence while suggesting a time-conscious existence in the changing world. Thus her image contrasts with Brocklehurst's guilty Puritanism, the dark transcendentalism of his doctrines. Brocklehurst, a figure of accusation arousing dread, affirms the foreboding power of external forces; men like Brocklehurst, dark ecclesiastics like Emily Brontë's Joseph, reduce the importance of history when Satan's plots transpire *outside* temporal events. The minister's epistemological focus thus extends past the place of actuality; he examines (or postures as one who examines) black depths readable by privileged—male—interpreters. Yet, Miss Temple exemplifies a fearless standing *inside* the scene of experience. The Grecian description evokes her *feminist humanism,* her representative role as a secular woman cultivating the moral intellect. She is connected to the Wollstonecraftian values of feminine independence through education, and upholds challenging ideas in a society beset with religious reaction. The Miss Temple model affirms the potential in Jane's own participatory nature, the young girl's capacity to enter into the scene of things. (Catherine in *Wuthering Heights,* lacking this talent, leaves the scene of things, abandoning Heathcliff and life-intensity to find herself *elsewhere*, in the otherworldly place where she fails her life.)

If Miss Temple provides the this-worldly ideal Jane will eventually follow, Helen Burns represents a world-rejecting mystical position. Miss Temple and Helen diverge in relation to their fundamental motives; their differing paths to fulfillment exemplify different trajectories of desire. Jane shows her own preference for living within the immediate scene of events—an epistemology defined by experience—in philosophical clashes with Helen Burns. Jane and Helen base their beliefs on differing premises, their conflicts encompassing the difference between historical and visionary approaches to human existence. Jane's being-in-the-world is grounded in sensory, emotional, and imaginative perception; she determines reality by direct apprehension. Contrarily, Helen takes a transcendent position, for her endurance of humiliation is predicated on the *unreality* of historical events: "her sight seems turned in, gone down into her heart" (5:45).

Helen dislodges Jane from her isolation even as Helen herself remains spiritually isolated. In a psychological critique with rhetorical implications Helen counsels Jane against brooding on collected injuries; the older girl moderates Jane's enclosure in a beleaguered self. Indeed, a backlog of hostility underlies the fierce egocentricity of Jane's narrative. In an exceptionally *accosting* narrative, Jane intrudes her intense subjectivity—sometimes attractive, sometimes not—on her readers.

Helen's breed of spiritual-yet-rational Romanticism comprehends the stern necessities of the world it surmounts. Understanding issues of hierarchy and power, Helen's dreaming imagination takes precedence, nevertheless, over her clarifying reason. She bows to authority by a double consciousness that allows her to submit physically to powers from which she withdraws spiritually. Helen's deeply Wordsworthian sensibility drifts toward the imagined sound of waters, and lingers on adored paternal figures like King Charles I, or her own distant father, or God Himself. What she calls the "impalpable principle of life" (7:51) takes her backward toward an eternal home; it will show its true face as a principle of death.

In her double consciousness Helen describes Jane's place within the world Helen herself forsakes. She intercedes silently after Brocklehurst humiliates Jane before the assembled students. Adding false verdict to Mrs. Reed's false witness, Brocklehurt bases his findings on *a priori* beliefs, already-concluded conclusions; his biased ideas allow him to arrive at a verdict without testimony from the accused. Miss Temple witnesses Brocklehurst's performance and becomes increasingly grim as hypocrisy grows to vilification. Simultaneously, the shadow of Jane's shame is dispelled by the "strange light" from Helen's eyes; Helen's gaze "imparts strength" (7:58) as she finds a pretext to pass by the younger girl.

Similar imagery surrounds the later entrance of Miss Temple; she comes forward luminously as "some heavy clouds, swept from the sky by a rising wind, had left the moon bare" (8:61). The feminine moon, a central trope in the novel, assumes its particular significance as an unobtrusive light allowing an independent clarity of perception; beneath the sympathetic beauty of its surface, the moon represents feminine being as cool, remote, and self-integral. Miss Temple invites her students to her room; Jane and Helen follow her light "to thread some intricate passages, and mount a staircase before [they reach] her apartment" (8:61).

Miss Temple offers Jane the opportunity for advantageous self-presentation (a better offer than mercy, with its suggestions of Patriarchal benevolence):

> "Well, now, Jane . . . when a criminal is accused, he is always allowed to speak in his own defence. . . . defend yourself to me as well as you can. Say whatever your memory suggests as true; but add nothing and exaggerate nothing." . . . having reflected a few minutes . . . I told her all the story of my sad childhood. . . . my language was more subdued than it generally was . . . mindful of Helen's warnings against the indulgence of resentment. . . . restrained and simplified, it sounded more credible: I felt as I went on that Miss Temple believed me. (8:61–62)

Miss Temple, like Helen, serves as a model because of the poised control of her objectified language. Her demand is for a clear and acceptable reflection between words and the emotional-historical reality they apprehend. Her goal is language as a recognizable bridge to recognizable thoughts and events, a language enlightening and comprehensible to the partners in its exchange. A diminishment of the subjectivity of Jane's discourse is encouraged. Generally, Jane distorts the surface of reality by an excessive immersion in the self; she shows the abused child's understandable, but other-canceling, concentration on/in the self. Jane's speech, less burdened by brooding self-involvement, proves persuasive and gives voice to a formed self suited to a cultivated setting. Description less freighted by guilt and blame is empowered by the sympathetic other. (Catherine Earnshaw never enjoys such reception from a feminine figure.) An unostentatious emotional bonding, as if to a mother and a sister on a higher level—Symbolic not Imaginary figures who enlist her into language—releases Jane and precedes the freedom underlying a wide-ranging interchange.

An evening of gifts transpires where Jane's deprivations are compensated morally, in the absolving dissolution of guilt, and intellectually, in the opening of a path to creative knowledge. Nor is the physical dimension of satisfaction disregarded: bestowing a "good-sized seedcake" tasting like "nectar and ambrosia" on her famished charges, Miss Temple stills pressing hungers while finding a metaphor for the process of growth, a metonymy for the fulfillment of desire. Strengthened, Helen Burns engages Miss Temple in the border-crossings of brilliant discussion:

> They conversed of things I had never heard of: of nations and times past; of countries far away: of secrets of nature . . . of books: how many they had read! What stores of knowledge they possessed! . . . French names and French authors: but my amazement reached its climax when Miss Temple asked Helen if she . . . recall[ed] the Latin her father had taught her . . . [Helen] construe[d] a page of "Virgil." (9:64)

In the striking contrast between Miss Temple's "cheerful" room (with its "good fire") and Mrs. Reed's threatening red room, the claustrophobic interior at Gateshead alters to a revelatory apart/ment at Lowood. The place-name of the school suggests an escape from the psychic imprisonment of "Gateshead" to the natural environment of "Lowood;" nor is the prefix "Lo" negative, for Jane descends from the high-wood cross of spiritual sacrifice.

Decoding a page written in a foreign language, a pagan text in Latin, Helen experiences a personal Renaissance by rediscovering the language of the Father. Helen performs such a return because of "the presence and kindness of her beloved instructress." Miss Temple's active concern brings out Helen's "beauty . . . of radiance." Without her teacher's presence, the foundation of Helen's knowledge would have remained the dead language of an absent father.

The relief from guilt releases, similarly, Jane's creative powers. Jane's experiences with Miss Temple and Helen Burns liberate her capacities for making and self-making:

> Thus relieved of a grievous load, I from that hour set to work afresh, resolved to pioneer my way through every difficulty; I toiled hard, and my success was proportionate to my efforts; my memory, not naturally tenacious, improved with practice: exercise sharpened my wits; in a few weeks I was promoted to a higher class; in less than two months I was allowed to commence French and drawing. I learned the first two tenses of the verb *Être*, and sketched my first cottage (whose walls, by-the-by, outrivalled in slope those of the leaning tower of Pisa). (9:25)

The process of internalization is painstakingly detailed. We observe Jane's struggle for being in the work of doing. The novel provides both the process and product of creative struggle, for it presents structures-within-structures. In her own masterful writing, Brontë creates models for a child's developing self; the narrating Jane captures the experiencing Jane for Jane Eyre as she exists at two different stages is presented in the skilled words framing unskilled pictures. Learning the first two tenses of *Être*—past and present, the temporalities she begins to understand—suggests that the child's mastery of language is rudimentary and that her future remains unknown. It also hints at the relationship between time and language. The past is the temporal-dimension of the Imaginary, for the past is the final goal of repetition, while the future, insofar as it is not to be a mere repetition of the past, requires the Symbolic, the flexible reformulation of new thoughts in new languages. If the narrative of *Jane Eyre* plunges forward, the narrator still presents a child contending with the power of the past. Similarly, the ramshackle amateurishness of her sketched cottage shows that Jane is not home yet.

The Lowood section, like the novel as a whole, affirms life yet culminates in death. Humility before sacrifice informs a narrative that rejects sacrifice. The meaning of the relationship between Jane and Helen Burns (her name describing martyrdom) clarifies with Helen's death. At the time of Helen's dying a "mighty, universal Parent" replaces her actual father; the unresponsive real father hardly regrets her passing (only Jane visits her grave). Helen's "long . . . last home" compensates her, affording a homecoming to the novel's second orphan; but unlike Jane, she submits to her decreed fate. Helen, the orphan, struggles for life because death seems inscribed in her very birth. Mortal illness delivers Helen from her own indifferent relation to living, her less-grand detour from the higher goal of her existence. Her own return to the Father, while valorized by religion as transcendence, entails a self-extinction that may be read otherwise. Turning to heavenly authority in self-subordination, Helen desires dissolution into nature's universal scene. The return to God-the-Father enacts the death-drive in religious form. The play-of-substitution turns the unloving father to the all-embracing Father.

The poignant final scene between Jane and Helen is both sentimental and surrealistic. The younger girl, an infant again, falls asleep in Helen's sickbed, which is miraculously transformed to "a little crib." Jane is found by Miss Temple with her arms around a lifeless Helen. In a reversion to infancy, Jane seeks maternal consolation desiring a gentle antidote for primary rejection. Yet if the tablet over Helen's grave is marked *Resurgam* ("I will rise again"), it is Jane who will rise from a momentary fusion, verging on self-annihilation. Like David Copperfield after the death of his infant brother, his double,[18] Jane will be resurrected to life from death's discarded alternative.

Thornfield Wood: The Romance of the Father

Jane's ambitions begin in metaphors of landscape. Hence the elusive horizon signals her to leave Lowood: "My eye passed all other objects to rest on those most remote, the blue peaks: it was those I longed to surmount" (10:74). She abandons her present home because of a Romantic attraction to the unknown in nature. The seduction of panoramic vistas mark, similarly, her arrival at Thornfield. Climbing to the roof of the spacious manor, she looks "out afar over sequestered field and hill, and along [the] dim skyline" (12:95); her longings are defined by the natural surround yet they are not restricted to it. Indeed, Jane's aspirations anticipate those of the women in Lawrence's *Rainbow*, and are located beyond rather than within the landscape. The natural expanse serves as a metaphor for cultural and physical desire.

Thus (despite her later immersion in the fields of Whitcross), Jane's aspirations never remain within *actual* nature. The literal landscape serves, rather, as a goal of *male desire*; the man's longing to dissolve in nature is a particularly male impulse, a kind of transcendent regression, itself the paradoxical climax of romantic lyricism. Nor does the male passion for landscape stop at the landscape. The turn to the natural for the male poet entails a return to the feminine.[19] But the return to nature may have narcissistic or annihilating import for a female protagonist. Hence, Jane looks beyond the borders of the natural to express her cultural ambitions: "I longed for a power of vision which might overpass [the natural] limit; which might reach the busy world, towns, regions full of life" (12:95). Jane narrativizes romantic feeling into a story of feminine and feminist desire.[20] Climbing the parapets of Thornfield, Rochester's great manor house, she listens to "a tale my imagination created, and narrated continuously; quickened with all of incident, life, fire, feeling" (12:96). The natural surround represents her hidden goals, for her social aspirations are previewed in imagined stories, and her sexual desires are inscribed in distant scenes.

She encounters Rochester amid pictorial close-ups of a *massive* nature characterized by a strength of density. Wandering the grounds of Thornfield before her "master's" arrival, Jane perceives a nature where scenic virility displaces Romantic enchantment: "the solid mass of crag, or the rough boles of the great oak, drawn in dark and strong on the foreground, efface[d] the aerial distance of azure hill, sunny horizon, and blended clouds" (12:98). The sexualization of landscape projects erotic longing: nature assumes masculine form in massed "crags" and "rough boles" (the correlative of feminine chasms and abysses). Jane hears Rochester before seeing him, the auditory reception of horse and rider releasing the "fancies bright and dark [that] tenanted [her] mind." She anticipates the legendary "Gytrash,—a lion-like creature with long hair and a huge head" (12:98). Rochester's association with animal-figures adverts to fairy tales and Jung's elucidations of the *theriomorphic* in representations of libido;[21] Jung connects the animals in dreams to the appearance of desire in the dreamer.

The "Gytrash" derives from Bessie's tales and is depicted as the "North-of-England spirit . . . which, in the form of horse, mule, or large dog haunted solitary ways" (12:98). Combining the *animalistic* and the *animistic*, its creaturely spirituality presages the novel's resolution at Ferndean. The fairy-tale trope of the enchanted beast[22] refers to the imaginative style, at once corporeal and figurative, that characterizes *Jane Eyre* as a whole. The physicality of Jane's imaginative-sexual fantasy opposes the idealizations of romantic desire. (Heathcliff shows related but different qualities: dark not crude, he is demonic not creaturely.)

Thus, the description of the Gytrash approximates the Rochester who is himself characterized by his "massive head" and "the horizontal sweep of his black hair." Indeed, the narrative focuses with pleasurable interest on Rochester's cranium, a part of the body that assumes, subsequently, further significance: "He lifted up the sable waves of hair . . . and showed a solid enough mass of intellectual organs" (14:116). With characteristically thick brush-strokes, Brontë describes the contours of Rochester's forehead in her overladen yet effective Gothic style. If a certain discord, even catachresis, emerges from Brontë's erotic phrenology, the passage still captures the sexuality of mental intimacy.

In the actual incident a canine "with strange pretercanine eyes" and "a tall steed" enter Jane's field of vision. At first, their magical aura appears to substantiate the reality of legendary creatures, but "the human being, [breaks] the spell at once." Indeed, the scene ends in a bathetic fall that breaks the romantic spell. Brontë revises romantic narrative by antiromantic narrative, advancing a genre by negating it.[23] Falling from his horse in a "clattering tumble" Rochester evokes Don Quixote rather than Prince Valiant. Still, it is the figure of the Byronic hero that most applies to Rochester, a man of peremptory impatience, angry, mysterious, aristocratic. His outraged reference to "the deuce," moreover, pairs him with the Heathcliff whose first words, as imagined by Lockwood, also concern the "deuce" or devil. But in comparison to Heathcliff, the demonism of Rochester is closer to facade than ferocity. Rochester's entrance can empower Jane, while his clumsy dismounting places him as not much more than a demon in distress.

> "If you are hurt, and want help, sir, I can fetch some one. . . ." "Thank you; I shall do: I have no broken bones—only a sprain;" and again he stood up and tried his foot, but the result extorted an involuntary "Ugh!" Something of daylight still lingered, and the moon was waxing bright: I could see him plainly. . . . I traced the general points of middle height, and considerable breadth of chest. He had a dark face, with stern features and a heavy brow; his eyes and gathered eyebrows looked ireful and thwarted . . . he was past youth . . . he might be thirty-five. I felt no fear of him, and but little shyness. Had he been a handsome, heroic-looking young gentleman, I should not have dared to stand thus. . . . I had a theoretical reverence and homage for beauty, elegance . . . but . . . those qualities . . . could have [no] sympathy with anything in me, and [I] . . . *shunned them as one would fire, lightning, or anything else that is bright but antipathetic.* (12:99, italics mine)

Positioning the expletive "ugh" (among the ugliest of English syllables) at a strategic juncture, Brontë subverts romantic fantasy.

Her references to fiery brightness are ironic about splendid youths, the princes and knights of dreams and fairy tales. The "lightning" adverts to the disorienting light of the red room, with its latent threats of regressive possession. Brontë's language suggests that the idealized hero, recognizable as an Imaginary Lover, usurps the imaginative woman who encounters him. The Imaginary Lover satisfies the need for visual perfection. A narcissistic ideal, he brings the fantasy-image in the mirror to finished completion. The different gender would make him all the more unreal and perfect.

Jane builds an antivisionary vision on the resistance to idealization. In Rochester, however, she discovers not a shining knight but a wounded rider, his injury bringing him down to terra firma. The disruption of his pose damages the dignity of an overbearing hero. Rochester proves *not to be* the resplendent princely version of the dominating male. (The *resplendent male* appears in the text by negation, as an absent presence in Jane's self-threatening fantasy, and by affirmation, incarnate in St. John Rivers.) The break in Rochester's body is *a fortunate flaw*. Assaulting the Prince Charming version of the dominant male, it leaves a space of entrance for a partner. Indeed, the break in Rochester's self-enclosure advances toward an androgyny of altered forms—the injury as metaphorical entrance *feminizes* the male body.

Thus the manifestation of the wound, the limp, demands the presence of an accompanying other. Disruptions open a space for connection, fracturing a projection that begins as imposing and masculine. The combined shapes of Jane and the once-lofty stranger—"He laid a heavy hand on my shoulder, and leaning on me with some stress, limped to his horse"—create a merged form. Balanced intertwining shows erotic equality in disrupted male integrity. The ruptures of the body disrupt the forms of being to leave a space for the other.

The moonlight illumination of the scene is inescapable. The moon in *Jane Eyre*, distinguishable from the destructive antinomies of fire and ice, irradiates its visionary sequences. Traditional romantic nature tropes, moon and fire, sea and ice, operate in the novel with convention-transcending intensity. Fire ravages in *Jane Eyre* no less than in *Frankenstein*, while the moon, foregrounded as a center of contemplative feminine self-possession, takes its familiar place as the supreme feminist trope. Representing the integral female ego in its separateness, the moon in *Jane Eyre* anticipates the more threatening moon in *The Rainbow* and *Women in Love*.[24] Jane's moonlit viewing of Rochester's unidealized form subverts the masculinist ideal, for she rejects the man as a petty tyrant, a splendid Sun-King. The foreground action and background lighting render this a subversive scene.

After the incident, Jane's introspective thoughts are contradictory: assuring herself that "it *was* an incident of no moment, no romance," her statement illustrates Freudian negation—to interpret its meaning we omit the "no"s and mark the emphasis. For she continues by acknowledging the seriousness of the incident: "My help had been needed . . . I had given it," and admits to the memorableness of a "masculine . . . dark, strong, and stern" countenance. Indeed, rather than "no romance," this is a "new romance," diverging from the traditional genre. The conventional hero invokes *Imaginary romance*, a fantasy-adventure based on a narcissistic cultural ideal. Imaginary romance arouses negative feelings in Jane for it evokes the facial beauty arousing the kind of approving forgiveness that was always denied to her. Through Rochester, however, she breaks the mirror to find a dark exit from specularity. His torn ankle diminishes the power in his overbearing face, while the achieved *interaction* between them explains Jane's ensuing exaltation. Her excitement is expressed in the breathless *liminality* of its description:

> I lingered at the gates: I lingered on the lawn; I paced backwards and forwards on the pavement . . . both my eyes and spirit seemed drawn from the gloomy house . . . to that sky expanded before me . .. the moon . . . aspired to the zenith, midnight dark in its fathomless depth and measureless distance. (12:102)

Viewing romance as a creation derived from an open imaginative conception, not subject to strongly intruded meaning, we apprehend from this description its feminine dimension. As Parker has suggested, the romance genre is based not on the thrust toward finality, but on the widening of possibility, on dilation rather than penetration. Jane looks to the expanse of nature in imaginative freedom.

Yet our readings of *Beyond the Pleasure Principle* suggest another meaning where freedom is not desired only for the sake of freedom itself. Jane's experiences repeat yet alter the events in Freud's amazing *Zauberwald*, for it is as though not Tancred but Clorinda were lost in the uncanny, magic forest. In *Jane Eyre*, it is the female protagonist who always encounters the same dominating figure, the same threatening Tancred. The question of "who is Tancred" is perhaps no easier to answer than "who is Clorinda." Yet the *Imaginary Lover* of idealized romance is eclipsed in *Jane*

Eyre not by a dispelling realism but by an alternative romanticism. The middle-aged, thickly built hero replacing the *Imaginary Lover* remains a visual image, if a less idealized one. Brontë refutes the perfection of a timeless dream, as represented by medieval or Byronic heroes, yet the brilliant image denied yields to the dark image affirmed. Charlotte Brontë, seduced still by specular powers, replaces the beauty of *The Imaginary Lover* by the strength of *The Imaginary Father*.

Thornfield Manor: The Return of the Mother

Outside the manor house Jane feels exalted. Her anticipatory excitement locates itself in the border area between visionary forest and domestic manor, her "lingering" at the "gates" suggesting a liminal state. Jane hesitates before entering "the gloomy house," anticipating that the equality she had felt in the dream of nature will dissolve in the actuality of culture. Thornfield Manor, like Wuthering Heights, is a property belonging to an arbitrary and volatile owner. Its cultural interiors are stifling as natural expanses are liberating; within his own residence the moonlight stranger becomes a controlling master. (Rochester, like Heathcliff, is *different* in the freedom of the outer surround, but *Thornfield*, unlike *Wuthering Heights*, is a misnomer: *Thornhouse* and *Sweetfield* would have been more accurate.)

Thornfield Manor is an enclosed territory enforcing the economic relations between omnipotent employer and dependent governess.[25] Therein she is treated as a possession of the Master. He presents himself as gloomy, irate, and commanding, while she remains self-possessed and clever, holding her own verbally despite her social inferiority. In dialogical exchanges they still assert master-servant positions, but in a subversive manner: each looks for that in the other which challenges the rigid hierarchy formally maintained. Their verbal sparring, with its search for an equilibrium of power, alternates with theatrical presentations and rendered representations, their elaborate rhetorical relationship counterpointed by individual art and dreams. The early conversations between Jane and Rochester achieve Symbolic dialogue, a mutual enhancement in communicative speech, but dynamic interaction is opposed by the static self-representations in Jane's paintings. Therein, Symbolic relationships are juxtaposed with Imaginary expression, interaction counterpoised by intimate self-revelation. Jane assumes the positions of both artist and work of art, while Rochester takes the role —handled with skill—of the critic.

Showing Rochester her Lowood paintings, Jane exposes her soul in her art as she defends it in her words, while his critical stance always protects him. The arch self-control of her social persona is negated in a series of terrifying self-portraits—paintings like phantasmagorias of virginity, self-suppression, and death:[26]

> The first represented clouds low and vivid, rolling over a swollen sea. . . . One gleam of light lifted into relief a half-submerged mast, on which sat a cormorant, dark and large, with wings flecked with foam: its beak held a gold bracelet, set with gems. . . . Sinking below . . . a drowned corpse glanced through the green water; a fair arm was the only limb clearly visible, whence the bracelet had been washed or torn. (13:110)

A reading of the painting's surface reveals, first of all, Jane's fear of violation and her obsession with the idea of ravishment. The great bird-of-prey appropriates the "brilliant gems" of her bracelet, which may be taken as the invaluable circle of her femininity. We note that Jane is destroyed as her jewel is stolen. Yet what is destroyed? We recall the self-representation of Bewick's "black horned thing" and find other interpretations in the self-accusing painting. The fierce self-deprecation of the cormorant suggests Jane's hatred of her own lovelessness, as if she were appalled at her ugly rage for isolation and the sacrifices demanded. It is the holding on to the precious jewel of her virginity that consigns Jane's womanhood to destruction; the cormorant represents the aggression in Jane-the-virgin, one who drowns her own body in sinister purity. Or, in another reading of a suggestive image, the dark thing may be the figure of necessary violence, a symbol of Jane's own forbidden desire directing its energies *against* sexless sublimation. Without straying from the painting itself, we may find Jane-the-sexual-woman in the scene; she is the one who sinks into the waves of green water, with its pleasures of a "half-submerged mast," and dies from either ecstasy or guilt.

The next two paintings appear as variations on the theme of exaggerated mental intensity, mind cultivated at the expense of body:

> The second picture. . . . rising into the sky was a woman's shape to the bust. . . . The dim forehead was crowned with a star . . . the eyes shone dark and wild; the hair streamed shadowy, like a beamless cloud torn by storm or by electric travail. . . . The third showed the pinnacle of an iceberg piercing a polar winter sky. . . . rose, in the foreground . . . a colossal head. . . . a brow quite bloodless, white as bone, and an eye

> hollow and fixed, blank of meaning. . . . Above the temples . . . gleamed a ring of white flame . . . the shape which shape has none. (13:110–11)

The "second picture" employs electric metaphors in a Frankensteinian manner, adverting to the negative turmoil of excessive energy of the mind, the devitalizing process that Lawrence calls "mental-consciousness." Indeed, the copresence of head, upper body, and the "cloud torn by storm or electric travail," recalls Lawrentian hostility to idealistic light, anticipating his rejection of a life based on the perceptions of the ego and the demands of the will. Metaphors of light and lightning suggest Jane's repressed yet raging energies.

Thus the "colossal head" moves into virtual freakishness, the "bloodless . . . bone . . . hollow and fixed . . . blank . . . glassiness of despair" adducing the skeletal death underlying the exiled body. Despite the creative self-discoveries of Lowood, Jane brings forth, in her paintings, morbid imagery evoking the scenes in Bewick's *History*. Jane's art objectifies a sexual fear, a frigidity and isolation, yet its presentation or articulation in art suggests the possibility of change.

Jane uses her art (a subtle order of power) to resist Imaginary self-dissolution. In a kind of romantic paradox, Jane *overcomes* her self-isolation by, precisely, *depicting* it. The going from the mental to the artistic image is already a step from id to ego, or Imaginary to Symbolic. Jane brings forth, in her paintings, morbid imagery evoking the scenes in Bewick's *History*. Jane's painting objectifies sexual fear, frigidity, and isolation, yet its *presentation as art* suggests the possibility of change. To present the isolated ego in Imaginary images, to render the created and creating subject, is to go beyond subjective enclosure. *The depiction of Imaginary fantasy is already a de-fantasizing; the reality of art, always more than psychical reality, shows the beginning of Symbolic initiation*. It is depiction itself that frames the Imaginary by the Symbolic.

There is a similar attempt to go beyond Imaginary ice in the sharing of the paintings with Rochester. Showing them to her employer, or deferring to his insistence that she show them to him, Jane resists isolation. Indeed, Rochester and Jane achieve a remarkably full communication that includes his uncanny comprehension of her inner meaning: "you have secured the shadow of your thought. . . . what meaning is that in their solemn depth? And who taught you to paint wind?" (13:111). He correctly reads her intensity as the manner by which she *distances* herself from experience. Yet

Rochester and Jane share the fear that masks love for it is over her paintings that he falters: "put the drawings away."

Subsequently, Rochester describes his dissolute career to Jane. Her mocking reprimands dissimulate a secret pleasure in scandalous recitals. Moral like physical weakness provides her entrance point. After the adventures he recounts excite her mock disapproval, Rochester's own bed ignites in flames. Bertha Mason, his mad wife, hidden in the upper recesses of the house, sets the bed alight, while it is Jane who douses the blaze. A Victorian reading of the melodramatic punishment would justify its application to an adulterer and would-be bigamist. But contemporary interpretation returns to Mr. Reed's crimson four-poster: the burning bed belongs to the Father. Jane floods the bed in flame to create a biblical field of chaotic forces; contrasting waves of basic elements cleanse Rochester to purify him. The interpretive issue pertains to the nature of Rochester's crimes, for the Victorian sins of the flesh may be reinterpreted as our contemporary sins of power. Fire may be taken as representing a domineering paternal will. Bertha may have resorted to literal fire when silenced and deprived of the metaphorical fire of her woman's empowerment. Dousing the flaming bed, Jane signals her desire to move their relationship to another element altogether. Jane seeks not destruction but generation. Indeed, under his playful forbearance Rochester shows a force of domineering will. It is reinforced by the Byronic accoutrements of aristocratic privilege. In relation to Jane, the aristocrat-servant relationship is paralleled by father-daughter suggestion to project overwhelming male dominance. Rochester's complex personality combines rebellion and Patriarchalism in the overlooming figure of *the Father-rebel* (Heathcliff manifests the same duality). Social privilege combines with scandalous immorality and the oedipal metaphor to turn Rochester to both an oppressive Jupiter and a kind of colossal Prometheus, tyrannical *and* revolutionary. (Yet somewhere, and in opposition to the inhuman Heathcliff, there is a vulnerable Rochesterian underpinning.)

If Jane refuses Rochester's fire-of-passion, she remains endangered by watery depths. On the night that follows the bed-burning, Jane goes to bed but "never thought of sleep;" she is troubled by waking visions vivid as dreams (Mary Shelley hallucinates the beginning of *Frankenstein* in similar apparitions). The sleepless presentations disturb Jane in a play of elements:

> Till morning dawned I was tossed on a buoyant but unquiet sea, where billows of trouble rolled under surges of joy. I thought sometimes I saw

> beyond its wild waters a shore, sweet as the hills of Beulah [the Promised Land]; and now and then a freshening gale wakened by hope, bore my spirit triumphantly toward the bourne; but I could not reach it. (15:133)

In her struggle with Rochester, Jane discovers the waters of generation. Water may be interpreted as representing the depths of the isolated psyche. The danger is the drowning within the self even as fury and isolation are avoided. The land may be taken as that goal, that otherness, reached through the self yet beyond the self. Jane's vision discovers the dry land that may be reached *through* the water. The shore foreshadows, moreover, the concluding role of Ferndean in the novel.

Where Jane reveals her insecure hopes in reverie, she projects her anxious premonitions in dreams. As her relationship with Rochester progresses, she becomes less dissimulating even as he retreats further behind disguises. For example, masking himself as an omniscient gypsy, he is protected where she is exposed; similarly, he masks Blanche Ingram as the object of his love while, as her prenomen indicates, Blanche in herself signifies nothing. His blunt teasing constitutes an abuse of power, a master mocking his slave. After he requests a betrothal, revealing his love in high romantic fashion, "be my second self, and best earthly companion" (23:223), the plot abounds with forebodings, like the chestnut tree struck by lightning. Sensing in Rochester a fundamental falseness, a world of withheld truths, Jane complains that her master is "phantom-like . . . a mere dream." She feels, moreover, purchased and disguised—occluded—by extravagant gifts like a luxurious wedding-veil. In this mood, she recites her haunting dreams to him:

> On sleeping. . . . I continued . . . the wish to be with you, and experienced a strange, regretful consciousness of some barrier dividing us. . . . I was following the windings of an unknown road. . . . burdened with the charge of a little child . . . which shivered in my cold arms and wailed piteously in my ear. . . . you were on the road a long way before me; and I strained every nerve to overtake you . . . but my movements were fettered; and my voice still died away inarticulate . . . you . . . *withdrew farther and farther every moment*. (25:247–48, italics mine)

The dream is the first of three dream-apparitions, two of them sleeping and one in the waking state (the paintings appear in a similar cluster of three). The first dream condenses dreamer and child by suiting the feelings of the dream-protagonist to the situation of the child-image. Jane's longing for the disappearing Father, turns her into a pitiful child. (She uses the word "farther" instead of the more common and pronounceable "further" in an aural pun, "farther/father," thus continuing, like a patient in psychoanalysis, the dream-contents in the dream-recital.) Her own fears of abandonment accord perfectly with the image of child-misery, and the connection between dreamer and child is projected in the dramatized action of the dream. The physical fusion of dreamer and dream-figure appears in the meeting of the child's shivering body with Jane's "cold arms." In a later passage she describes her love itself as a "shivering child" (26:260). In the end her dreams cancel all empowerment; she resumes her dependent position as Rochester remounts his steed. The dreams asserts that *the child is her; she will be abandoned*.

If the first dream functions as self-revelation, the second combines vision, the dream as insight, with prediction, the dream as prophecy; it condenses present-emotional and future-actual realities. Thornfield Hall becomes "a dreary ruin" while Jane, the dream-protagonist, still carries "the unknown little child: I might not lay it down anywhere, however tired were my arms." Rochester, Father of the child who is Jane, now departs for a longer time and to a further place. She is in a position to be deserted because she has deserted herself completely to him, giving up all self-protecting images. She climbs a wall to observe him, "the child clung round my neck in terror, and almost strangled me. . . . I saw you like a speck on a white speck, lessening every moment." The white speck is a displacement, for while she describes him, it is herself that she depicts; she is the white speck obliterated by a withdrawing Father and an encumbering child. Indeed, she is the child abandoned by the Father who she allowed to make her into a child.

Her identification with the childlike continues in the abrupt fall into wakefulness.The awakening is the fall of an ending, a death *in* the dream and *of* the dream; to emerge from the dream is to return to life. The real struggle occurs in the scene of reality, or, *on the Brontëan plane of romance where psychic and physical reality merge*.[27] The spell of Jane's dream-narratives is merely "the preface . . . the tale is yet to come." The dramatic melodrama occurs after Jane awakens into "reality's dark dream."[28] It focuses on the large shadowy woman who appears in Jane's bedroom, takes the wedding veil, throws "it over her own head, and turn[s] to the mirror." The face in the mirror is distended, its color "purple: the lips . . . swelled and dark." She leaves the mirror, removes the veil, rends it into two parts, "and flinging both on the floor, trampled on them"

(25:250). The scene emphasizes the visage in the mirror, the lurid countenance Rochester insists on hearing described in detail:

> "Did you see the face?". . . . "I saw the reflection of the visage and feature quite distinctly in the dark oblong glass." "And how were they?" "Fearful and ghastly to me—oh, sir, I never saw a face like it! It was a discoloured face—it was a savage face. . . . the foul German spectre—the Vampyre." (25:249–50)

The engorged countenance denies the being of the observer, for its gross features project an Imaginary usurpation. Indeed the mirrored visage is a kind of maternal variation on the Lacanian reflection that both is and is not the self.

Sandra Gilbert takes the image in the mirror as Jane's double, the specular reflection of her "ferocious secret self." Rebelling against woman's "servitude" in patriarchal culture, the mirrored image repeats Jane's own "resentment" at Rochester's "manipulative" presumptions.[29] Jane's secret desire, thus, is to become a red fury of a woman. Yet we note that after Lowood Jane remains untempted by the fiery mode, that after Jane's childhood anger loses its dominion. The power of the mirror image inheres not in its release of a repressed self, but in its implicit demand that Jane return to the regressions of Gateshead and its fearsome red-room.

Regression and repression, while connected, refer to radically different modes of being: if the one is about moving back, the other is about holding in. In relation to Jane, in front of the mirror at this moment, regression is what the image-in-the-mirror demands but does not achieve, while repression is hardly a factor. The two scenes, the red room at Gateshead and the bedroom at Thornfield, remain inextricably connected because in each Jane is overwhelmed by presences both psychic and physical. In each encounter Jane faces an image, whether a quivering light or a discolored face. These uncanny images, formed between projection and perception, reside at the heart of Brontëan romance.

In each scene, the power of the imagistic figure obliterates Jane. She passes out in a fainting fit, an experience that suggests the devouring of consciousness by the unconscious. Each scene dramatizes the threat of annihilation Jane experiences in front of parental figures, specifically, of the annihilating Mother blocking the way to the saving Father. In the end, the *mirror-image represents not the appearance of a secret self, but the intrusion of the hostile Mother.* The return of the maternal figure perpetuates the alienation between observer and image, asserting with hatred the specular gap between the self and the Other. In Lacanian theory and Brontëan practice, the continuation of the specular gap in later life, the experience of alienation in the mirror, results from the impositions of the hostile Mother. Antagonistic maternal figures interfere with the achievement of self-continuity. The scenes of Jane's fainting concretize, therefore, *the annihilation inherent in the Imaginary order*. We note the ways in which Father and Mother play opposed roles in the Imaginary. The demand of the Imaginary Mother to the Imaginary Daughter is: admit that I dominate you and that *you have no self*, while the Imaginary Father communicates, somehow, *the possibility of acquiring the Self through the difficult (thorny) path to the Other* (who can then become an other with a small *o*). In *Jane Eyre* the-play-of-substitution is a passage through an annihilating mirror.

Gilbert's reading lacks the necessary dialectical link. The ferocious self, not essential but potential, is incited by the incendiary image. Within Jane ferocity emerges in relation to Mrs. Reed, the violent mother who engenders a violent daughter. Mrs. Reed is a mother out of a fairy tale, Cinderella's stepmother partly novelized, suited to the proportions of novelistic romance. Bertha Mason is sheer myth; her character ignites Primary Process like a Fire-Mother drying up the waters of birth. The fiery Mother appears, indeed, more terrifying than the fiery Father. Both are characters out of the Lacanian Real, for fire is its privileged trope. The Real is itself an elusive figure for the unbearable, an abstraction fused with the image of fiery light in a signifier/signified merger that evokes Plato. The figurations of the Real are formed in the space where language ignites.[30]

But judging from *Jane Eyre* and looking ahead to its use in *Sons and Lovers*, a distinction can be made in the gendering of the Real. The Real of the Father is on the far edge of the Symbolic: the post-Symbolic Real/Reel of the Father spins forward to take language beyond its scope. While the Real of the Mother antecedes the Imaginary: the pre-Imaginary Real/Reel whirls backward to a point before language. If Bertha performs actions and gestures of obliteration readable within the Symbolic, *her face precedes all codes*. If the Fiery Father comes after the end, the Fiery Mother comes before the beginning—she denies origins instead of extending possibilities.

The fury in Jane is that which would be aroused by a direct encounter, a death-struggle with the annihilating mother (Catherine Earnshaw approaches that confrontation and dies for it). To emulate such a figure is to yield to her being if not to her power. Bertha represents a kind of temptation towards flame. She rends Jane's veil to deny her womanhood, the aggression of the Mother unmasking the fear of the child. Then the great image draws close, facing Jane at the edge of a conflagration:

> . . . she thrust up her candle close to my face, and extinguished it under my eyes. I was aware her lurid visage flamed over mine, and I lost consciousness: for the second time in my life—only the second time—I became insensible from terror.

The first such loss-of-consciousness occurs in front of Mrs. Reed, Bertha's originating double. The second takes place as Bertha's admonitory drama affirms her as the true bride, *the full woman*. The corpulence of Mrs. Reed and Bertha arouses Jane's feelings of physical inferiority, maternal obesity reinforcing the daughter's self-perceived insignificance, as if she were a girl-child slight of being. Jane swoons when the intimate approach of the Father precipitates the violent intervention of the Mother. In its helplessness the-play-of-substitution occurs at a point where the Imaginary spins backward toward the Real. By the same token the-romance-of-death, with its beginnings of agency can create a momentum that crosses from the Imaginary to the Symbolic. Hence Heathcliff's abuse of women leads him to a higher or Symbolized Imaginary, a communion with Catherine at last.

In this connection, the description of Bertha is luridly phallic, the phallic quality in *Jane Eyre* being aggressive in an assertive way rather than sexual in a connective way. The child's red room and the governess's bed room present complementary scenes, for the girl-child returning to a Father confronts a hostile Mother again. Bertha assumes a psycho/physical position as an admonition in the mirror, an *Imaginary Mother*. Destroying the evidences of Jane's entrance into womanhood, the nightmare affirms herself as Rochester's wife. The Mother terrifies her daughter; invasive images destroy sexual independence.

But the fainting is also an escape from the scene, *a refusal to repeat*. Jane's repetitions are not driven from the inside, but imposed from the outside by the malevolent characters in her personal history. She accomplishes the necessary withdrawal from Bertha's proximity instinctually, in styles of escape, but will liberate herself from regressive figures in the end by the courage of her vision and the freedom of her action. She resists the impositions of regression in an inner struggle, its meanings discovered retrospectively in her fictional autobiography. A war of psychic elements drives the plot of the novel. Ultimately, rather than a compulsion to repeat, Jane shows a desire to advance.

After the mirror-vision Jane discovers horrifying truths. The dramas in and before the glass signal Rochester's marriage to their contained spectre, the Monster in the mirror. With the exposure of Bertha, Rochester's paternal dominance becomes satanic aggression. Fiery bed and negating glass demolish the earlier equalities of word and action painstakingly achieved within their relationship. Jane discovers, momentously, that her betrothed is married to a madwoman hidden from the world; yet Rochester resists her leave-taking with overbearing arrogance: "Jane! will you hear reason? . . . because if you won't, I'll try violence." Her insistence merely strengthens his overbearing will: "He seemed to devour me with his flaming glance" (27:279).

The "fiery glance" expresses unbearable demand, moral oppression doubled by a subtly incestuous connection. Jane had hitherto avoided the abyss of incest by the strength of her speech, her rhetoric of equality. After the revelation of Bertha, Rochester replaces the intricacy of argument with the brutality of power. As a balance against unrestrained male force, Jane turns to lunar apparitions, "not a moon, but a white human form shone in the azure" (27:281). The projection of feminine power provides an essential reinforcement. Recalling Miss Temple's Hellenism, the Moon-Goddess supplies the maternal gaze and restores feminine sovereignty. Empowered by the mystic moon, Jane remembers an obscure path out of Thornfield: "beyond the fields . . . a road I had never travelled, but often noticed and wondered where it led" (27:282). The road evades tyranny but exits toward isolation. Rushing and falling, "delirious" on an unknown path, Jane yields herself up to fortune. The game-of-disappearance is her only chance for a romance-of-life.

White Crosses, More Houses

The narrative of *Jane Eyre* shows a pattern of pull and counter-pull; the going forward and backward illustrates the dialectical struggle between inner drives. The novel is based on a journey structure, with long excursions on slow coaches, yet the prospect of return always underlies the voyage out. We may place the grim excursion to Gateshead from Thornfield, which includes Mrs. Reed's death, and the desolating rediscovery of Thornfield after Moor House, which includes Bertha's death, in the dialectic between repeating again and advancing ahead. Thus, Moor House, nearly at journey's end, also returns to the beginning, to the home of Jane's natural father. Jane's story begins with the death of parents; the originating point of the fabula is complete emptiness. The journey plot may head toward the point beyond return. In *Jane Eyre* every going forward contains an undertow, a drifting backward whose meaning Jane already understands in the window-seat.

After leaving Thornfield, Jane behaves with a fatalistic lack of direction hiding unconscious choices; it is as if the scene of reality were, indeed, a projection of the unconscious. A coach appears, heading toward a distant town, where "Mr. Rochester had no connections." Jane lacks the means to reach that negative destination, so, consigning her soul to hazard, she drives as far as her money can take her. Finalizing a series of injurious acts, she forgets her purse, abandoning her last possessions or, perhaps, abandoned by them. With self-destructive brilliance, she arrives nowhere protected by nothing. Her behavior encodes a self-indifferent death wish, or, a cessation of self-responsibility searching for someone to assume that responsibility.

"Whitcross is no town, nor even a hamlet; it is but a stone pillar set up where four roads meet" (28:284). The place-name, Whitcross, outlines a crucifixion in landscape. From a desire for self-punishment or pristine rebirth Jane assures her complete desolation. The outer world reflects her inner state and appears as a sacrificial nature. Jane disappears into an indifferent environment, nearly dying of inanition until she becomes hungry again. The metaphorical cross she carries is the loss of *all* emotional objects, the return to a blank neutered beginning, absolute orphanhood.

The illusion of natural consolation arises: "I have no relative but the universal mother, Nature: I will seek her breast and ask repose." Jane enters a nature with perceived maternal characteristics, yet its nurturing powers refer to human desire rather than earthly provision. Like Wordsworth[31] she takes refuge in a womb-like hollow, but the search for nurture in landscape is disheartening. Dissatisfied by her dependence on nature, she desires the operation of her human powers. But when Jane turns toward the nearby village, an already harrowing chapter becomes almost unbearably raw. We watch, dismayed, as woman after woman turns from Jane's abject need for food and shelter. Culture itself assumes the face of the rejecting Mother. The parallelism of hunger at Lowood and starvation at Whitcross further aligns Mrs. Reed and Bertha Mason: in each case a maternal figure, competitive and hostile, sends Jane into a world of denial. Women will not help her if she is helpless.

Coming to society in a premonetary helplessness of fundamental need, Jane violates the economic order with her incongruous and rudimentary desperation. Yet the Whitcross sequences constitute less a socio-economic critique than a stage in a romantic progression. Thus, as Jane's will-to-live wanes she observes an *ignis fatuus*, a light in the distant marshes. The presence of the firelight prevents Jane's final yielding, interferes with the peace of the engulfing rain, the temptations of the Dickensonian "letting go":

> And I sank down where I stood, and hid my face against the ground. I lay still a while . . . the rain fell fast, wetting me afresh to the skin. Could I but have stiffened to the still frost—the friendly numbness of death—it might have pelted on . . . but my yet living flesh shuddered to its chilling influence. I rose ere long. The light was yet there. (28:291)

Following its shadowy luster, Jane finds a house whose gleaming candles illumine cleanliness and white furniture, a glowing "peat-fire" and a clock. Standing outside and looking through the window, Jane is precisely in the position of Frankenstein's Creature looking at the cottagers. Like the creature, she is born and raised in alienation from her cultural environment, her circumstances leading to fundamental estrangement. But unlike the monster, Jane is not an irredeemable pariah. (Hence, where *Jane Eyre* is finally a romance realized, *Frankenstein* remains a romance manqué, a fantasy in search of a reality.) In the style of novelistic romance (more fluid and open than the stylistically restricted fairy tale), Jane needs to pass through a stage of primal social displacement before experiencing a near-magical transformation of identity.

Excluded by a close-minded servant-woman, Jane looks surreptitiously through the window, registering

> Two young, graceful women—ladies in every point. . . . I had nowhere seen such faces as theirs: and yet, as I gazed on them, I seemed intimate with every lineament. . . . they each bent over a book, they looked thoughtful almost to severity. A stand between them supported a second candle and two great volumes. . . . in a low voice [Mary] read something, of which not one word was intelligible to me; for it was in an unknown tongue. (28:202)

The words, read by Diana and Mary Rivers, are in the mellifluous German of a high romantic text. The first line Jane hears, "*Da trat hervor Einer, anzusehen wie die Sternen Nacht*" [Then there stepped forth one, in appearance like the starry sky], describes St. John Rivers, Jane's own Savior. (St. John will emerge as a knight of romance in the form of an Evangelical minister.) The poetry is read by women who reflect values different from romantic splendor, for the Rivers sisters project self-possessed and communicative openness.

Viewing a scene of learning, Jane, like Frankenstein's Creature, observes the enabling powers of language. Words empower knowledge of cultural and individual otherness. If its shelves hold dictionaries and grammars of arcane tongues, the domestic interior of Moor House is expressive in itself. The observed scene combines learning and hominess; combining scholarship and domesticity creates a sort of cozy enlightenment. The juxtaposition of intellectual effort and household grace suggests a turn toward *domestic romance.*[32] More House presents the security of the starting point, its inner glow a kind of self-acceptance; the shared scholarly effort is itself a communion, a less egocentric way-of-being that grows into language acquisition and the capacity to enter into the otherness of separate cultures. The good, safe place allows exploration of the world beyond its borders.

Yet for Jane, such domestic romance exists across an unbridgeable chasm. In another echo of the Creature and the cottagers, the attractiveness of the scene develops in direct ratio to the observer's exclusion from it. The offer of entrance occurs as St. John saves Jane from death by exposure, bringing her forward to hearth and home. (Ironically, he himself constitutes the *unheimlich* element within the *heimlich* scene.)[33] Like Lockwood, Jane enters a house-as-alternative-world, but the imaginative defamiliarization of *Wuthering Heights* is reversed in *Jane Eyre* to restorative homecoming.

St. John saves her life out of duty, curiosity, and, finally, spiritual ambition, but Diana and Mary respond to her with all the intelligence of empathy. St. John makes the moral decision to nourish Jane, although the grace of the saving derives from the sister with the Grecian name:

> Diana (I knew her by the long curls which I saw drooping between me and the fire . . .) broke some bread, dipped it in milk, and put it to my lips. Her face was near mine: I saw there was pity in it, and I felt sympathy in her hurried breathing. In her simple words, too, the same balmlike emotions spoke: "Try to eat." (28:296)

Diana offers maternal sympathy and provision, but her long curls also communicate silent rebellion against patriarchal restriction; for her locks recall the unfettered tresses of Eve in paradise. Subsequently, living with the different members of the Rivers family Jane Eyre (Elliott) experiences directly the difference between St. John's Patriarchal-Christian piety and Diana's sisterly-Hellenist love.

In St. John, Brontë introduces a spiritual imperialist who serves a transcendent cause, the missionary as divinely-inspired romantic. St. John is also an intimidatingly beautiful youth, an *Imaginary Christian Lover* who brings out Jane's female masochism. Once again, she encounters relentless masculine ambition. Rochester and St. John are parallel yet contrasting figures: if the former outrages her with illicit sensuality, the latter violates her by willful spirituality. Rochester threatens to repeat the fiery destruction of the red room, while St. John drives her toward the forlorn isolation of Bewick's illustrations. Each recalls an annihilating process.

The conflicts in the relationship between St. John and Jane reach a dramatic climax in relation to language. Jane pursues humanist learning by studying German. St. John prepares himself simultaneously for a missionary vocation on the dusky plains of India. While barely cordial to a guest he continues to judge, St. John faces her with an unbending imperative. She must give up German and learn "Hindostanee," the language necessary for his self-abnegating yet self-glorifying missionary goals. If Rochester takes her as a sensual object in a *failure* of recognition, St. John takes her as a spiritual object in a *refusal* of recognition. Rochester is importunate and heated in his denial of her *moral self*, St. John is superior and disdainful in denial of her *physical self*. Each opposes her independence. A man of the cloth, white and shining where Brocklehurst is black and gloomy, St. John shares the personal insensitivity of his fellow cleric; both are too blinded by ideology to see something as frail and specific as an individual human (particularly feminine) personality. The male gaze that looks to God sees only a grandiose version of Self. If Helen Burns goes back to her Father in the sympathetic regression of a spiritually gifted child, St. John sees the Father, "the All-perfect," as both the reflection and the goal of his own splendid narcissism.

Thus, serious misreadings of Jane mar the superficial persuasiveness of his moralistic rhetoric:

> In the resolute readiness with which you cut your wealth into four shares . . . I recognised a soul that reveled in the flame and excitement of sacrifice. (34:355)

The statement is obtuse because completely self-reflexive: Jane gives the money in the pleasure of acquiring a family after life-long deprivation; her gifts are generated not by a rigor of discipline, but by an intensity of relationship. St. John is one who projects rather than perceives. Nevertheless, the inexorable quality of St. John's being arouses a cold excitement in Jane. The power of his absolutely convinced personality causes her abject bowing to his authority. The need to please him gradually erodes her own insistent will. Spiritual demand is far more corrosive to her feminine self than sensual need. Rochester appears as a naïve libertine alongside St. John's doctrinal urgency. She agrees to accompany St. John to India, where she will surely die, sharing a glorious end. Indeed, St. John will return at the very end of the novel, for *Jane Eyre* ends in a dualistic closure presenting two types of romance. After the resolutions of Ferndean, the achievement of life-romance between Jane and Rochester, we have a kind of romance of the sacrificed ego in the story of St. John, a figure presented as heroically Christ-like in the end. There he will remind us that the Jesus-ideal can be taken as the ultimate anti-self, the obliteration of the human desiring self as a triumph of the God-serving death-ego.

Returning to Jane's debate with St. John and struggle with herself: she resents the falseness of his love, a love he would fulfill according to the obligations of sacramental marriage, obeying the obligations of matrimony as a biblical commandment. She nevertheless

> was tempted to cease struggling with him—to rush down the torrent of his will into the gulf of his existence, and there lose my own. . . . I contended with my inward dimness of vision, before which clouds yet rolled. I sincerely, deeply, fervently longed to do what was right. . . . The one candle was dying out: the room was full of moonlight. . . . "Jane! Jane! Jane!" nothing more. (35:368–69)[34]

In a significant reversal, the pervasive moonlight that had commanded her separation from physical love now decrees its return. The clear suggestion is that feminine self-possession will be granted *with* Rochester rather than *apart* from him. In comparison to St. John's "torrent of will," overwhelming her like a drowning wave, Rochester makes a pure call in the moonlight, a recognition of being in the expression of a name. Rather than the tide of will, Rochester brings her to an interactive field of desire.

The first re-encounter with Rochester sets the terms for their continuing relationship. The burning of Thornfield is a gothic metonymy for the overthrowing of its master's presumptions; his physical injury represents a curtailment of the will and results in equality with Jane. We need here to reconsider the critical claim that Rochester's injuries, blindness, and loss of a hand, suggest Brontë's castration of her hero.[35] Seeing Rochester again, Jane hardly observes a destroyed man:

> His form was of the same strong and stalwart contour as ever: his port was still erect, his hair was still raven-black. . . . his countenance . . . reminded me of some wronged and fettered wild beast or bird, dangerous to approach in his sullen woe. (37:379)

She imagines kissing him on "his blind ferocity"; his animal corporeality appears strengthened by injuries diminishing pretensions rather than power. The wild, damaged creature seems the more sexualized for being made accessible, brought into the approachable realm. If before he was enraged and engorged, his desire is now stilled in quiescent potentiality. Continuing from that first ankle injury near Thornfield, his body now contains further wounds, openings for the entrance of the other. Unable to see, he meets her in other forms of perception. Injury grants intimacy.

Their being together in the green shade, buried deep in the wood, frames the generativity of their connection. Their house, Ferndean, resembling Tintern Abbey, is "scarce . . . distinguishable from the trees; so dank and green were its decaying walls" (27:379). The "space of enclosed ground" presents a feminine nature, the female landscape of romance, but includes the masculine scene of "interwoven stem, columnar trunk, dense, summer foliage." Its damp earthiness leads to organic growth: first Jane's pregnancy, then Rochester's recovered sight.

Thus each character attains the emotional maturity that allows oneness—he recognizes the limits of domination, while she understand the dangers of separation. They will now become merged partner, two-in-one. The parallels with Freud's interpretation of Plato in *Beyond the Pleasure Principle* are striking. In Freud's reading, the life-drive struggles to unify the sundered parts of an original oneness (*BPP*, 6:58). The self-transcending drive toward the other fractures the isolate ego to find fruition in the greater wholeness. Freud's biological metaphor for human love refers to a union beyond sex while centered in sex. Between Jane and Rochester the partiality is of the spirit—neither is complete without the other—and of the body—Jane always felt physically insignificant, Rochester is now injured. The result of damage and partiality is an intimacy in a searing of injury, a healing in a fusion of wounds. Rather than remaining within the enclosed self to die, Rochester and Jane will remain together always in an experiential eternity. In a mystery understood by Plato and Freud the being-together-in-separateness includes the recognition of ego-transcending death in a *mort-a-deux*. Jane and Rochester, set for a long and peaceful dying-together, discover the power of life.

The final balance of *Jane Eyre*, its romance-of-life, advances through the Lacanian orders. Jane, her self having been nearly destroyed by the Imaginary, recuperates herself in the Symbolic, yet fulfills herself in the Real. Jane and Rochester transcend the Imaginary in blindness, and avoid entrance into a marriage based on mutual imposition of false visual images. Imaginary relationships refer to the transferential dynamics of the visual, with each lover superimposing onto the other that which is wanted or feared, that which is idealized or detested. The sensory intimacies of Rochester and Jane are deeply erotic, composed of touch and hearing rather than sight; Eros echoes in their speech: "We talk, I believe, all day long: to talk to each other is but a more animated and an audible thinking." Yet the Symbolic opens to an intimacy of the inner body, a *searing of soul through bodies*: "No woman was ever nearer to her mate than I am; ever more absolutely bone of his bone and flesh of his flesh." The quotation foregrounds the primitive biblical injunction, recalling the corporeal fusion that Slavoj Žižek identifies with the Real.[36]

Indeed, the ending of *Jane Eyre* relinquishes the forms that turn men and women into Imaginary or Symbolic constructs. Tracing her history in the novel, Jane's discounted status in the Imaginary as a physically plain, hence insignificant, woman may be the secret of her achievements. Rochester, moreover, is connected to the transfigurative power of the *hideous*, for the destruction of the Imaginary releases uncanny sexuality. Brontë arrives through a strange deformation at an eerily beautiful description:

> I see you are being metamorphosed into a lion, or something of that sort. You have 'a faux air' of Nebuchadnezzar in the fields about you. . . . I thought you would be revolted, Jane, when you saw my arm and cicatrised visage. (37:384)

The breaking down of recognizable image into unrecognizable form is the achievement of monstrosity. The reference to the Nebuchadnezzar image is a foray into the unimaginable; beyond remoteness, such an image removes us to the Real by a subversion of

Imaginary power. Brontë moves her hero into a monstrosity that defaces the Imaginary to repudiate it. The monstrous transcends the Imaginary in the visual to do away with the narcissistic pull of the beautiful. Jane's intimacy with monstrosity paradoxically enables a nonthreatening sexuality. The sexual Rochester, Rochester as Phallus, is not damaged at all. Rather, injury has turned *the* male body into *her* male body. All the incursions into his integrity allow him to emulate feminine containing, to be able to hold her as well as to be held by her.

The Real breaks down facades to find what is Really there in that which language cannot express. The Real needs to be understood as a reflection of unconscious material beyond words (it poses a challenge in Lacan's own terms to his monolithic insistence that the unconscious is structured like a language). Arguably, that which is deepest within us is the parental image, *the Imago of the Imaginary*. This unconscious power seems to me simultaneously the greatest threat to and the greatest promise of autonomy. It would appear to be the foundation or lodestone of love. To face it directly is to face the power of the Real, blinding as the Sun (who can see the Sun?), yet to lose it is to lose love. In a stroke of genius, Charlotte Brontë addresses the problem. The Father has to be altered from the sun by the sun, fire is the Father element that can alter the Father, that can give Power new social forms (in modern history it has taken shape as industry, electricity, computers). The damaged Rochester is the Father remade as the lover, made out of fire into the monstrous or absolutely human. He is the lover as Prometheus, or, finally, as Nebuchadnezzar, outcast of the ordinary gods. This is the way death becomes life in the new promise of the Real. The rare realization of the-romance-of-life requires combustion.

7

Space, the Imaginary, and the Death-of-the-Mother: *Sons and Lovers*

Space and the Imaginary

A spatial frame surrounds both the young boy, the central figure in the games of Freud's *Beyond the Pleasure Principle,* and Paul Morel, the protagonist of Lawrence's *Sons and Lovers*. In each text the foregrounding of space places the meaning of narrative action within its encircling context—narrative action *spatializes character* as it *characterizes space.*

The boy's isolated gestures in *Beyond the Pleasure Principle* find neither a receiver nor an interlocutor. He throws objects and projects sounds into surrounding space, playing into an emptiness that thereby acquires figurative meaning. The significance of the spatial frame applies to all four of the games that he plays.[1] In the toy-game, that initial activity where he loses his playthings haphazardly, and in the famous *fort/da!,* the reel-game where he loses his single spinning toy in his crib, the thrown objects intersect with the surrounding environment. In such games space becomes its own metaphor, for its perceptible surface leads to its hidden depths. (Invisible space can be perceived indirectly by that which encloses it and that which it contains.) The objects the boy throws trace encircling space to the place where it disappears: surface space becomes hidden space.

Theoretical Forenote: There are uncanny connections between Ernst, the boy in Beyond the Pleasure Principle, *and Paul Morel, the protagonist of* Sons and Lovers. *Each character loses himself in the limitless spatiality of a maternal surround. The energy of both their narratives concerns itself with Symbolic change, the transformation of the space-of-the-Mother to a place-for-the-self. Ernst achieves this through word and gesture, Paul Morel through art and sexuality and, at the end of the novel, an act of will and a power of thought that lead to being.* Sons and Lovers *provides a full literary elaboration of the-game-of-disappearance.*

The actions of the earlier games are followed by the mirror-game, the play in a glass that reflects first the boy and then nothingness. He disappears from the mirror to leave behind the reflected image of empty space. At this point, the sounds he makes appear more Imaginary than Symbolic, utterances rather than words. They engender no further signification and indicate the end of signifying.

The boy completes his Imaginary series with the rifle-game. Here he throws the Symbolic rifle with a dismissive command: "go to the fwont." The power of the Father is thereby repudiated in a Symbolic action that paradoxically renounces the Symbolic. It demonstrates a desire to return to the Imaginary world shared with the Mother. The boy resigns the rifle's Symbolic firepower, its ability to ignite new powers of speech, and throws away a figure of energy that represents the Father. The toy gun is thrown into the proximate area representing the distant battle, the place where rivals and their symbols magically disappear. Space is presented again as both signifier and signified. Immediate space is the representation of distant space, the visible, transparent surround is exchanged for an invisible area, the faraway battle with the Father.

Relatedly, many of the intimate scenes in *Sons and Lovers* occur within an active spatial surround. The novel's poetics of spatiality are introduced by the moonlit garden scene. The highly symbolized moment occurs after the Father in the text, Walter Morel, violently expels the Mother, Gertrude, from their fractious enclosure to a peaceful expanse. There, in the wider circumambience, she is allowed a freeplay of the soul, and she feels redeemed amid the beauties of nature and the night. Critical readings of the occurrence focus on her feelings of unity with the radiant evening, her experience of self-loss-in-nature.[2]

In earlier interpretations I supplemented the classic view by placing Gertrude at the center of a *feminized* cosmos signified by the mythic moon, the archetypal symbol of the mysterious integrity of woman.[3] I would now stress the *maternal* aspect of the feminine, noting that the powerful otherness of woman begins with the overwhelming sameness of the Mother. I would focus, furthermore, on Lawrence's figurative presentation of circular worlds within worlds where the woman conducts moonlight to make space itself a moonlit womb.

This occurs as Gertrude meditatively walks through the moonlit garden. Showered by the light and immersed into it, she experiences a merger with both the moonlight outside her and the child within her. Mother and child fuse in whiteness, as if disappearing together into a greater maternal source. Their union in body and soul recalls various concepts in poststructuralist psychoanalysis. For Julia Kristeva, the Greek word for space, the *Chora,* refers to our earliest being, a physical and psychical prelingual state, mobile and beset with drive-energies. By means of a brilliant reference to the *Timaeus*,[4] the Platonic dialogue on the creation of the cosmos, she connects space and our earliest being-in-the-world. Platonic speculation inspires metaphorical connection between the *Chora*, the space of geophysical generation, and the body of the mother, the place of biological generation.

The *Chora* begins a larger category of self-expression, the activity Kristeva calls the semiotic.[5] The semiotic subsumes all signifying processes and is not restricted to the communications of language. The *Chora* initiates the semiotic, while the semiotic encompasses the advent of language. Kristeva, like Lacan, describes the accession of the linguistic mode as the Symbolic. In the semiotic order, the child or fetus experiences drive-energies that are articulated by physical rather than linguistic capacities. Including the *Chora,* her theory moves backward to a rudimentary being that precedes both verbal *and* visual apprehension.

The scene of the moonlit garden depicts a wordless state of being that emphasizes both the body and a spirituality experienced in the body. Lawrence's scene also evokes the concept of the *Chorion*, the Greek term for the uterine enclosure that both begins the maternal and ends the fetal body.[6] The *Chorion* is the *Chora* in miniature, the space of our first being. Kristeva locates in the semiotic *Chora*, furthermore, an explanation for texts that resist full explication in language. The Semiotic *Chora* is the background for writing that is characterized by a rhythm that underlies language, that emulates the silent significance that transpires beneath words.

The *Chora* shows many parallels with the Lacanian Imaginary, although the Chora refers to a still earlier stage of being.[7] The *Chora*, which refers to the mode of nondifferentiation between the embryo and its maternal-spatial surround recalls the Lacanian order that arises with the erasure of the boundaries between self and other. Gertrude's experience in the moonlit garden thus presents *the genesis of the Imaginary*,[8] for it points toward an unbounded future relationship between mother and unborn child.

Gertrude's mystical experience, where all spatial and temporal boundaries dissolve, introduces the pre-oedipal into the narrative of *Sons and Lovers*. In relation to Lawrence, the pre-oedipal becomes most illuminating in postmodern elaborations such as those of Kristeva and Lacan, which foreground nonverbal modes of perception and expression. The Kristevan *Chora* and the Lacanian

Imaginary refer to modes of being where the fetus and, later, the child, exists in the wordless experience of the Mother. Scenes showing the unity of the subject with his engendering surround evoke the relationship between space and the earliest self.

Symbolic Mother, Imaginary Father

The genetic merger between Paul and Gertrude is recapitulated during the boy's later life-endangering illness. His sickness, following the mother's self-absenting despair at the death of an older son, appears as a ghostly disintegration of personality (6:171). Now grieving for neglect of the younger son, Gertrude alters the focus of her love with a confession expressed in visual terms: "I should have watched the living, not the dead." Restored by tidal forces within that respond to her attention, Paul, resuscitated, turns from death to life.

He rises "white and fragile" from his sickbed, as if maternal rebinding were his only protection against complete self-dissolution. Lawrence presents the borders between mother and son as abstract energies that deconstruct or reconstruct the physical body. The psychically fragile Paul reverts to states where emotional/visual affirmation by a (M)other inseparable from the self determines the existence of the self.

The dissolution-of-the-body points to the connection between the semiotic *Chora* and the Imaginary: the fetus unified with the mother becomes the boy connected to her in specular/psychic oneness. In Lawrentian narrative, the semiotic and the Imaginary appear as different-but-related conceptions. The *Chora* allows us to read the semiotics of movement communicated silently by the nonverbal body. The silence may be read through Kristeva's own interpretive term, *signifiance*, defined as the "unceasing operation of the drives toward, in, and through language." Reading the silent drives, we reach "a structuring and destructuring *practice*, a passage to the outer *boundaries* of the subject."[9] My point is that the *signifiance* of motion underlies the games and actions of *Sons and Lovers*, especially its artistic and sexual dynamics, as well as my attempts to write about them.

In my view, Lacan's Imaginary has special relevance to Lawrence's cosmic images, where abstract figures of vision or sound pervade and dematerialize the great natural world. I have in mind the "white light" or "white shadow" that characterizes, for example, his soulful encounters with Miriam Leivers. The waves of imagery coalesce to deconstruct the reality of the physical world.

In spiritual scenes with Miriam or passionate scenes with Clara Dawes Lawrence's words transcend their existence in language. That is, Lawrence's waves of images made from words simultaneously exist as if fashioned without words, for they evoke the memory of a more fundamental—affective, kinetic, sensuous—perception. The passages combine sensory impressions of the surrounding world with sensory expressions of psychic states. Similarly, the Lacanian Imaginary refers to more than an image in the mirror, for it entails a process of perception and a struggle for identity. Lawrence's presentation of fields of images complements Lacan's description of fields of energy.[10] Thus, we see that Lawrence, in a pattern recalling both Kristeva and Lacan, presents space as the location of a conflict created by the simultaneous desire for and resistance to merger with the (M)other.

That conflict can be traced back to parental influence. Each of Paul's parents effects him in a way that is both constructive and destructive. The mother's creative fusion with the son becomes deathly when possessive, while the father's creative separateness becomes destructive when hostile. A pictorial indication of the relative influences of mother and father is suggested when, to celebrate the boy's recovery, Walter buys Paul: "a pot of scarlet and gold tulips. They used to flame in the window, in the March sunshine, as [Paul] sat on the sofa chattering to his mother" (6:171). The silent power of the father's gift, which stands apart in chromatic intensity reflected from the sun, contrasts with the humanly supportive yet sometimes shallow—"chattering"—speech shared with the mother.

The relationship between mother and son will remain based on spoken intimacy, sustained and ramified conversation, and this shared speech suggests the way Lawrence alters, or supplements, Lacan's "orders" of perception and expression. Lacan generally identifies the Imaginary with the maternal and the feminine, and the Symbolic with the paternal and the masculine.[11] The Symbolic begins with the-name-of-the-Father, the demanding negative of the *Non/Nom-du-Père*. The father's *No!* expresses the prohibition against the son's Imaginary fusion with the mother. Accepting the "*No!*" of the Father, the child receives his name, a name that releases the power of language and the inscription of values.

Yet it is clear that in Lawrence's *Sons and Lovers*, the empowering *Non/Nom-du-Père* cannot be inscribed in language per se. The father in *Sons and Lovers* is excluded from innovative language by his own sensuous nature, which generally finds modes of expression other than the verbal, and the mother's effective denial of his authority-in-language.[12] The inherent paradoxes here are legion, for the arts of language in this work reside with a dominant and possessive mother. Thus, the articulate Mother subordinates language to the demands of an Imaginary relationship. While language is for Lacan the medium of generative, open signification, the means for psychic advance and liberation, in Lawrence words are more often the medium for psychic merger. Thus, in Paul's relationships with Gertrude and later with Miriam *the Symbolic network fulfills an Imaginary function*. To be sure, the Imaginary and the Symbolic are never entirely separable, and Gertrude's supportive love for Paul unquestionably supplies the roots of his powers. Nevertheless, in a conceptual supplement to Lacanian theory, *Sons and Lovers* presents us with the paradox of a mother-son relationship based in a *verbal-Imaginary order,* a speech that binds rather than separates.

As a completing counter-phenomenon, which supplements Lacanian categories by challenging them, the Father in *Sons and Lovers*, Walter Morel, introduces the paradox of a *visual-Symbolic order*. Thus, the atmosphere in the Morel home denies the force of the father's words, yet tacitly affirms the force of his *work*. Walter's male authority is achieved by a subterfuge against civilizing language. His practical skills, manual abilities that can rise to the level of creative artisanry, achieve the Lacanian "play of signifiers" but without words. The "play of signifiers" refers, after all, to representational fertility and contains, therefore, concurrent suggestions of sexuality.

Hence his threatening force of energy shows an attractive and vital side; in, for example, the way he fashions the straw fuses that illuminate the mine and explode its coal. The image adds, to the destructive power that characterizes him, an unexpected luminosity. Moreover, the careless spirit that animates the active work brings a joy to the children that the mother represses. During such moments the father uses an earthy, affectionate language and is "peculiarly lavish of endearments to his second son." He reveals a talent for narratives of character and image as he tells amusing stories of living creatures.

Thus, for Paul to pass to the independence of the Symbolic order, with its "play of signifiers," its tropes that reveal an independent, creative personality, he needs to find another kind of language, a language that uses an Imaginary means (a visual vocabulary) toward a Symbolic end (free proliferating creation). It is by making things rather than by language that Walter gives Paul a signifying series to serve him as entrance to the Symbolic order. Paul the character and his autobiographical double, Lawrence the artist, accomplish this in an Imaginary language that operates in combined Imaginary/Symbolic tropes.[13]

The resulting creativity is dualistic, creation within creation: Lawrence describes the paintings and objets d'art that Paul makes, framing images by words. Moreover, Lawrence's art is an art of image, evocation, and action that rarely foregrounds language as such. The verbal facility that Paul-the-character and Lawrence-the-artist share with the Mother as a medium of creation borrows from the visual powers of the Father to find the form for creation. In Lawrence's writing or Paul's sketching we may say, with a trace of humor, that the-Name-of-the-Father is replaced by the *Made-of-the-Father* (as in "Made in England").

Language in Lawrence always moves toward the imagistic, the painterly; his Symbolic is woven out of the Imaginary. Thus, for instance, the Lawrentian moon often projects a white net of light around highly imagined or fantasized scenes. It may be reread in the Lacanian context as an Imaginary/Symbolic trope or Symbol for the Imaginary. Lunar scenes are evoked in passages where language dissolves like clouds to reveal a luminous reality. Remembering that Lacan uses "stage" in the double sense of physical place, a dramatic platform, and psychic time, a developmental period (*É*, 5), the moon, in Lawrence, illuminates the "stage" of the Imaginary.

If Lawrence invokes the *moon* as the representation of fusionary experience between mother and son, Lawrence also, like Freud and Lacan, brings forward the *sun* to describe dynamic experience between father and son. Paul's father, a miner who brings out the coal, the fire-fuel, is linked to the Symbolic fire that illuminates and transforms and destructively recreates the world. The affinity between coal-fire and the sun is striking.

Hence it is relevant to *Sons and Lovers* when Freud sees the sun-fantasies of the psychotic judge Schreber as externalizations of the uninternalized father. For psychic emptiness occurs when a son successfully detaches all feeling and desire from the Father. In his reading of the Schreber case, Freud describes the process by which a father becomes unreachably distant as occurring because the Father is *expelled* by rather than *buried in* the unconscious of the son. In Freud's reading, the father returns "from without" in the form of the symbolized sun (*SE*, 12:81–82). Failure of internalization for Freud is creatively reconceived by Lacan as a failure of

Symbolization, the non-inscription of the-Name-of-the-Father. In either case the receiving of the father's powers is necessary for both the generation of an attachment to the world and the formation of a capacity for language.

To move toward creative autonomy, Paul needs the influence of the Father, an influence represented by fire and sun. The Mother is herself divided between the fusionary and the autonomous, and seems at once to want to possess Paul and to encourage him toward independence (her urge for an independent and erotic life originally attracted her to Walter). Hence the psychoanalytic symbolism in an early encounter between Gertrude and the sun *reverses* her urge to absorb her son: "She thrust the infant forward to the crimson, throbbing sun, almost with relief." The mother holds her child up to the sun in a gesture drawing on its energy, for the sun is the source of creative generativity, proliferating in a strength and purity of color. The entire passage (2:50–51) is a psychic parable that refers to the vital energy of the father, reflected in receptive space going red, as if recreated in fire. The sun-energy goes from space to nature and, finally, with the cooperation of the Mother who partially welcomes such vitalization, the fiery power bestows its signifying strength on the child. In this positive transfer, *the sun engenders a son*.[14] Lawrence shows that in the creative transfer from father to son there is a receiving of the *benefit* of paternal power. The key phrase, "the Western space went red," shows the energy of the paternal sun filling maternal space.

The moment of landscape painting anticipates the transfiguring attention paid to nature in Lawrence's own writing. Symbolic landscape painting is intrinsic to Lawrence's art. He accomplishes in his writing what he describes, in a kind of illumination of objects, as a bringing forth of the world into fiery reality. The sun illuminates nature and the soul of the child, allowing him to grow also into an illuminator, a maker. Delineating the opposite of the disturbed process suffered by Schreber, the foreclosure from which he suffers, the action in the horizon in Lawrence indicates the creativity of paternal internalization, a process of *foreopening*.

In the passage I am addressing, the sun (the Phallus) supersedes the moon (the womb) as the alternate source of creativity. The sun refers to the source that Lawrence, like Freud and Lacan, associates with maleness and the father. In an anticlimax, Gertrude returns the child to her "bosom," closing him into the smaller compass of her being and secluding him from the "crimson, throbbing sun." The transformations of the sun, its dynamic and signifying changes, evoke the proliferation force of the Lacanian Phallus, a concept related to Lawrence's celebration of the phallic metaphor. The opposition of moon and sun, depicting the fundamental dualism in Lawrence's writing, refers as well to psychoanalytic dualism, to both the struggle of life against death in Freud and the alternation of the Imaginary and the Symbolic in Lacan.

The Poetics of Space

Paul, like the boy in *Beyond the Pleasure Principle*, explores the inner space of self-discovery through the outer space of play. Lawrence's protagonist, Paul, begins *his* game-series with an assertion in space. Bound to his mother, his "soul always attentive to her," and subordinate to his older sister, Annie, one of Paul's early games starts with his jumping, in demonstrative flight, from the living-room sofa. Ascending from the domestic furnishings associated with mother and big sister, he rebels against household authority. Landing on Annie's "big doll," Arabella, he enacts his opposition to feminine figures. Having smashed Arabella's face, he burns and demolishes her in ritual sacrifice by fire and stone: "He seemed to hate the doll so intensely, because he had broken it" (4:82–83).[15] In the violent aggression of a spatial game Paul separates himself from the maternal.

The depth of Paul's hostility to the doll looks ahead to the euthanasia that ends his relationship with Gertrude, and the painful endings he creates when he rejects his lovers, Miriam Leivers and Clara Dawes. The desired obliteration of Arabella from reality and memory initiates what I call the-romance-of-death, that narrative pattern where aggression is projected outward in dramatic action, and emotional dependency *on* a loved object is transformed to injury *of* that object.

If the violence within Paul finds expression in a destructive game, the conflict between the parents finds representation in a dynamic image. I refer to the scene of cosmic enactment, or action within a greater natural expanse. The cosmic enactment focuses on space as a factor in a figurative interplay. Such scenes project human conflict into natural images, and operate in metaphors where psychic energy takes elemental form. In one relevant sequence, the Morel family moves to a house at the juncture between the town and open nature. The children are awed by the great expanse. During the night they fear its looming ash-tree, which screams in the winter storm as if echoing parental strife. The "shrieking" tree echoes both "the booming shouts of his father . . .

[and] the sharp replies of his mother." The children are left with "a feeling of horror . . . and a sense of blood" (4:84).

The scene is about abuse (verbal and physical), with the tree translating the father's attack and the mother's protest into fierce sonorities of natural anguish. The screams of the tree and the vastness of the night adumbrate the terror the children feel with the attack on the mother. The ferocious wind empties space of Maternal presence. The children in bed are terrified by reality-symbols more potent than dreams. The howling tree refers ironically to the white-blanched flowers of the moonlit garden, for the moon is down in a night of darkness and blood, filled with the fury of the father.

The violence of Lawrence's description recalls the style of writing Kristeva describes as a *genotext*.[16] The genotext may be understood as an expression of drive-energy into language, referring to the kind of writing that moves below the verbal to articulations of sound by repetition and rhythm. In its expression of preverbal drive and feeling the genotext is a transcription of the Semiotic Chora. In the ash-tree vignette, the genotextual elements are strongest in its mounting pace and onomatopoetic language, its pointing to sounds-before-language, as in its "shouts" and "cries," its variants on the key-word, or sound, "shriek." The piercing medley of "shrieking" nature parallels the Kristevan conception of a "text" (opposed to the more conscious and worked through "narrative") as a pastiche of linguistic traces in sound-fragments not words. Lawrence's textual fragment begins an exploding of the scene, and accords with Kristeva's notion that the true text *tears at* the "univocal" narrative. (As *Sons and Lovers* is a stylistically unstable work, in which a play of voices and tones occurs, it contains only *fragments* of "text" in the Kristevan sense).

The later Scargill Street sequence returns to the open space of the town, and adumbrates a different psychic situation. The game takes place on a universal background where the children play near infinite blackness. In its vastness gender roles dissolve and a larger imagination prevails, "the girls joining in the fights and the games, the boys taking part in the dancing games and rings and make belief of the girls" (4:101). Illuminated points from industrial hollows provide relief from the unbordered night. For nature becomes a regressive power threatening children who wish to find their own way. The "great scoop of darkness" suggests the Mother at an unbridgeable distance, but also the necessity for something more, for a light of creation and play. The darkness of the expanse projects an isolating Chora, the swallowing night suggesting a fall into endlessness. The children are strengthened in the unnatural light of industrialized energy, associated with the Father. Their psychical development is reified by attraction to the fabricated light beamed from the working world. This reclaimed light of the Father inspires imaginative play, with the games showing a fluidity of social roles and inscribing a place for furious activity. Hence the single light of the lamppost is a harnessing of power.

Above the play around the lamppost a brooding image suggests a goal of Lawrentian art:

> Paul never forgot . . . seeing a big red moon lift itself up, slowly . . . steadily, like a great bird. And he thought of the bible, that the moon should be turned to blood. (4:101)

Both the vitality and the violence of the Father are captured by Lawrence through his metaphor of the blood, the life-sustaining current of the body.[17] (We recall here the mythological connection between fire and blood.) The blood refigures the looming moon, a circle of wholeness now vitalized. Lawrence marries the masculine and the feminine when blood on the moon combines the fierce energy of the Father with the full stability of the Mother. The Imaginary moon and the Symbolic blood-fire become inseparable in a composite trope.

In the Magic Forest

Lawrence introduces Miriam Leivers as a Pre-Raphaelite figure in prose, a narrative portrait of a spiritual image. He explores the dream within the dreamer, for Miriam inspires the reader's fantasy by looking like "King Cophetua's beggar maid."[18] The maiden in the Burne-Jones painting is notable for her tragic gaze, and Miriam, in her "romantic rags," presents an *Imaginary image* of the visionary and unreal. Within her fantasizing mind she imagines herself among figures who reflect an idealized self. She synthesizes religious and artistic characters into a glorified spectacle: "Christ and God made one great figure . . . when a tremendous sunset burned out the western sky; and . . . Rob Roys and Guy Mannerings rustled the sunny leaves" (7:173). Illuminated by Miriam's imagined sun, the entire panorama burns into oneness. Her quality of "a maiden . . . dreaming" refers to both the way she impresses her readers, becoming part of our dream, and her seeing herself as a character in her own dream.

Lawrence places Miriam in a Pre-Raphaelite context then abandons a compelling framework. We know that Lawrence despised the Rossettian circle, "as far as I am concerned, the Pre-Raphaelites don't exist,"[19] yet the early presentations of Miriam show the vivid dreaminess of their style. Subsequently, Miriam loses her radiance and becomes a less clarified character. Lawrence abandons the most interesting dimension of a character for no very clear reason—unless he wants to show Paul denying, and thus robbing her of, her dreaming self. (Despite his dismissal of the pre-Raphaelites, there is a Burne-Jones element in Lawrence's art.)

Only Miriam's deep gaze is sustained from her Pre-Raphaelite introduction. Desiring appropriation of his spirit, her love for Paul becomes part of a devouring dream. Her eyes long to draw Paul in, to bring images into her fantasy, while his hands work to bring things out, to draw images into realization. Miriam's gaze takes the fiery as a special object; her love for Paul always quickens in relation to scenes of burning light. She frames images of desire from masculine tropes: "Beyond, one rift of rich gold . . . seemed to make him stand out in dark relief. She saw him slender and firm, as if the setting sun had given him to her" (7:201). Miriam's attraction to fire indicates both her desire to appropriate the masculine force, her wanting spiritual possession, and her opposed desire *to be possessed by* its vitality. For Miriam's possessiveness protects her against desire, her longing for an eroticism of feeling. A series of painful encounters show her secret attraction to his male beauty. Paul refuses her tremulous desire; he withholds himself from her, defended against unfaithfulness to his original object of desire.

In the swinging scene, Paul dispenses with the transitional objects of the boy in the *fort/da* game (objects that, as I argued earlier, represent not the mother but the boy himself). Paul throws himself into a flux of movement directly, abandoned to a pulsating rhythm: "He was swinging through the air, every bit of him swinging, like a bird that swoops for joy of movement." His game supplements the boy's fort/da game because one object of his Symbolic play, the woman who would share his driving movement, directly participates in the scene. A further dimension of meaning emerges when he escapes the total isolation of the child's game. Watching him has an empowering effect, he "rouses a warmth" in her. She later attempts to swing, although restricted by the physical inhibitions of a Puritanical upbringing. His proximity initiates a lessening of restrictions in her. "Her crimson cap hung over her dark curls, her beautiful warm face, so still in a kind of brooding, was lifted towards him" (7:181). The joyous momentum of his own swinging alters as he observes her. Just as he perceives her beauty, her watching, a swallow flies from the scene: "I didn't know a bird was watching." The two observing presences, girl and the swallow, the one associated with the other, interrupt his rhythm, for at precisely this point

> He swung negligently. She could feel him falling and lifting through the air, *as if he were lying on some force*.
> "Now I'll die," he said in a detached, dreamy voice, as though he were the dying motion of the swing. (7:181, italics mine)

He falls in a cessation of lifting and drifts down to an intrinsic power in the invisible air. The underlying power draws away his energy, for Paul vacillates between life and death, discovering pleasure in both the *release of* and *relief from* energy. The swinging clearly projects the polarity of its meaning. The intensifying energy of the swing establishes a unifying rhythm, an atmosphere suggesting the pleasure of *being together with a visible presence*, the fading energy of the swing suggests the pleasure of *being alone with an invisible presence*.

Paul soon swings wildly again until "he was nothing but a piece of swinging stuff, not a particle of him that did not swing." The shifting alterations of the activity itself encompasses the polarities of life and death. Paul's "detached, dreamy voice" suggests a tentative exploration of death that parallels the boy's "loud, long, drawn-out 'o-o-o-o', accompanied by an expression of interest and satisfaction" (2:14). These actions cannot be worked-through within the life of experience. Paul and the boy play games that never resolve themselves or solidify into a single meaning. Their games adumbrate semiotic play without a Symbolic solution, a kind of pendulum swing ad infinitum.

The indeterminable state reified in activity is subsequently expressed in an aesthetic theory. Paul's ideas about painting, somewhere between the optical focus of impressionism and the natural design of art nouveau, value the play of light and shape between colors and forms. The play never focalizes on a completed structure. Paul's interest is in "the shimmering protoplasm in the leaves . . . and not the stiffness of the shape. Only the shimmeriness is the real living. The shape is a dead crust" (7:183). This energetic quality finds dramatic incarnation in a pine tree cluster: "Now look at them and tell me, are they pine trunks or are they red coals, standing up pieces of fire in that darkness. There's God's burning bush . . . that burned not away" (7:183). Besides grounding the aesthetic that rejects a pre-Raphaelite visual finish, Lawrence provides a rationale for the vacillations that take place within the beings of his character. The vacillations between life and death, Symbolic and Imaginary, simultaneously express Lawrentian ideas about the continuing dynamic of being. The alterations that occur within Paul anticipate the carbon-of-character idea employed in the composition of *The Rainbow*.

The fiery energies of the pine trees find a counterpart in an equal dynamic outpouring of white. At the entrance to the wood, sky, trees, and flowers frame the conflicting passions of the characters. Miriam brings Paul to share her discovery of a wildly fecund rose-bush. They discover, in late evening under a "mother-of-pearl" sky, its profusion of white flowers: the rose-bush "had thrown its briars over a hawthorn bush and its long streamers trailed thick, right down to the grass, splashing the darkness everywhere with great spilt stars, pure white. In bosses of ivory and large splashed stars the roses gleamed on the darkness of foliage and stems and grass" (7:195). The dark suggestion of the scene "kindle[d] something in their souls." The narrator, often identifying with Paul, interprets Miriam's longing as a "communion" of the spirit. Yet the dynamic interplay of scene and character moves in an opposed direction. The scene paints a state of receptivity as the path of Miriam's "dark eyes" lies open and her lips are "parted." The brilliant "great spilt stars" splashing the landscape attests to Lawrence's unconscious identification with the feminine. In the shadows of the wood, the star-flowers are the feminine parallel to his flame of pine. First transformed to stars in a counterpart rather than a reflection of the vital sun, the moon (in another Symbolic transformation) comes down to earth.

But Paul, framed by the maternal sky, feels imprisoned by the generosity of the outpour. Abandoning Miriam in her approachableness, he returns home to Gertrude in a "delicious delirium" of freedom. Having escaped the reality of female desire, he accepts his mother's destructive perception of its subject. Gertrude turns Miriam into a devouring figure: "She is one of those who will want to suck a man's soul out till he has none of his own left . . . and he [will] . . . let himself be absorbed." The mother both projects and discovers the negation of desire in the beloved.

Aside from her corrosive antagonism to Miriam, Gertrude emerges as a sympathetic figure, a richer character than either Miriam or Clara. Her complex being emerges in the juxtaposition of inward and outward realities. We can distinguish the *mother*-in-the-present from the *Mother*-in-the-past. Gertrude in the actual world is sensible, wholesome, humorous. Her level-headed sanity contrasts with the Imaginary Mother whose traces appear indirectly. Indeed, the direct appearance of the Imaginary Mother is rare in life or literature. In *Sons and Lovers*, the Mother manifests herself in the illusion and actuality of death.

More commonly, the Imaginary Mother appears in figures that manifest, or displace, the Imaginary dimension. We may add to the psychoanalytic notion of *deferred action*, of *Nachträglichkeit*, the equally significant concept of a *deferred image* (displaced in time as well as space). The *Mother-in-the-Mind* imposes herself on the *Lover-in-the-World*. The imposition constructs the process Freud describes as a "stereotype plate," a template of the beloved continually repeating itself in transferential love.[20] In *Sons and Lovers*, Gertrude displaces her unconscious fusionary desires to Miriam (less to the more physical figure of Clara), and thus can be whole and spontaneous with Paul.

Hence the relationship between mother and son becomes many-sided, romantic, while the relationship with the beloved remains one-dimensional mythic. Pale Miriam of the deep eyes (and full-bodied Clara) yield in Paul's affections to the individualized woman whose forehead Paul knows "so well: the deep marks between the brows, the rising of the fine hair, greying now, and the proud setting of the temples" (7:197). The Mother is the more romantic figure, in the sense of being more evolved, plastic, realistic. It is the beloved who takes mythic form, subordinate to an image in the mind. The mythic Mother is realized while the real Lover is mythicized.

Two sequences express the vexation of relations between Paul, Gertrude, and Miriam, to demonstrate the way Lawrence forges a cosmic scene into a signifying composition. The first passage occurs after Paul contrasts the Norman Arch, going onward in "the dogged leaping forward of the persistent human soul, on and on, nobody knows where," with the gothic arch, which "leapt up at Heaven and touched the ecstasy and lost itself in the divine. Himself, he said, was Norman, Miriam was Gothic" (7:215). The Norman impulse, repeating itself and moored in the earth, gives architectural form to the principle of the Symbolic, while the gothic self-loss in a higher principle sacralizes the Imaginary.

When Paul places Miriam within the Imaginary-gothic she bows in humble consent, yet both are thrilled by a fiery moon that arouses bodily correspondence in each of the lovers. "The immense and ruddy moon" recalls the crimson-capped Miriam of the swinging-scene, the light of the sun refracts to the woman in red-tinted shadows. Yet Paul's "blood . . . concentrated like flame" remains entrapped in his chest, for he places Miriam beyond its reach. Her womanhood begins to unfold, but it has only potential existence, and her hesitations turn to irreparable blocks when reinforced by his inhibitions. Her resulting helplessness remains painful to watch, but his sufferings are caused not by the woman without but the woman within:

> And he, coming home from his walks with Miriam, was wild with torture. . . . Then, brought up against a stile, he stood for some minutes and did not move. There was a great hollow of darkness fronting him, and on the black upslopes, patches of tiny lights, and in the lowest trough of the night, a flare of the pit. It was all weird and dreadful. Why was he torn so, almost bewildered and unable to move? . . . Why did [Miriam] make him feel as if he were uncertain of himself, insecure, an indefinite thing, as if he had not sufficient sheathing to prevent the night and the space breaking into him? How he hated her! (8:231)

The great hollow of darkness returns to the great emptiness of night; death and the maternal unite in his mind to isolate him from women. He separates himself from women by displacing to them his fear of fusion; the lover-he-is-with becomes the beloved-in-the-mind who repeats the threatening face of the Mother. Thus, the beloved reinforces the absorbing maternal surround with which she is identified. The paradox inheres in the way the woman-he-is-with both removes and duplicates the Mother. If she interferes with the maternal bond, she lacks within herself the strength to replace it; she rather arouses the self-disintegrating dimension of the maternal, recreating the Mother-in-the-past successfully masked by the mother-in-the-present. The manifest hostility to the signifying figure allows denial of the latent hostility to the signified figure.

At the same time the reinforcement of troubled feminine relations takes him further from the paternal force; the father is represented by the industrial flares distanced in the deepest reaches of the night. Here the strangely haunting interpolation of the *stile*, a physical block to the great night and its contained energies, can reveal its significance by a homophonic relation to *style*, the power of writing that can possess and reforge those energies. The maternal will break through his sheathing, the oppositional force of his being, until he reaches the Father by recreating him.

Paul's repeated rejections of Miriam return to another text where a beloved is injured in the midst of a wood. We recall the Freudian romance composed in a few spellbinding lines, a reading—or misreading—of Tasso's *Gerusalemme Liberata*. Therein "Tancred . . . unwittingly kills his beloved Clorinda in a duel while she is disguised in the armour of an enemy knight. After her burial he makes his way into a strange magic forest which strikes the Crusaders' army with terror" (*SE*, 18:22). Indeed, Miriam becomes an enemy, certainly of Gertrude and perhaps of Paul: "If Miriam caused his mother suffering then he hated her." The enemy knight emerges in the form of the beloved who conceals the Mother; but the enemy-beloved, *merely disguised as someone different from the Mother*, dissolves. After injuring the Beloved/Mother the young knight goes deeper into the forest, until he encounters them both murderously once again.

The Psychoanalysis of Fire

Fire is the reachable but still unknowable sun; domestic fire interacts with culture as a humanized spark of the cosmic fire. Comparable appearances of fire in Freud, Lawrence, and Lacan, create an intertextual image. In all three writers burning connotes psychic change, and shows a progression or regression that reconfigures the inner world. Fire emerges not only as an image, but as a trope, an elaborate figurative device; its function is to transform previously established meaning and the transformations of fire deny stability in interpretation.

Conflict in *Sons and Lovers* is dramatized by fire. The process of disappearance and return expresses itself in two sequences of burning. The first concerns the scorching of Gertrude's loaves of bread, while the second shows the incineration of Gertrude's present to Paul, another form of nouriture, a "pork-pie." Each sequence shows the burning of nourishment as a sacrifice of food. The sacrifice motifs dominate passages concerning psychic—nearly physical—incest; the scenes communicate sacrificial punishments of prohibited sexuality. If the earlier scene describes a sacrifice of the Mother in a refusal to yield to her, the later scene ends with a sacrifice of the Father and a reinstatement of her. The earlier scene shows Paul's disappearance *from* the Mother, the second shows his return *to* her.

In the first sequence Paul guards the bread baking in the oven, maintaining productivity in an environment controlled by the Mother.[21] Indeed, the Ceres-like suggestions of bread place Gertrude as a life-sustaining figure—hence Weiss's association of the bread with Gertrude's "heart" (42). But the significance of the narrative alters with its progress. The dramatization as a whole contains three similar but different encounters between Paul and

Miriam. The three brief scenes clarify one another, for each focuses on unfulfilled desire. In the first Paul, the visual artist representing Lawrence the verbal artist[22] shows Miriam a rose he has prepared as a fashion prototype:

> The spread cloth with its wonderful reddish roses and dark green stems, all so simple, and somehow so wicked looking, lay at her feet. She went on her knees before it, her dark curls dropping. He saw her crouched voluptuously before his work, and his heart beat quickly. (8:241)

Lawrence the writer paints with words while Paul the painter creates a metaphorical image in the language of color and design. Paul's rose exemplifies art nouveau, the style that begins modernism in architecture and the applied arts. Its stylistic newness antiquates the nineteenth-century reliance on the past for aesthetic approaches and ideological convictions. Art nouveau, its name denoting the new (a visual way of presenting the Symbolic), forswears the influence of domineering priority, that which we already know and which undercuts our creativity (a visual way of understanding the Imaginary). Paul's particular design, a classic art nouveau rose pattern, intertwines male and female representations in a decorative eroticism. The "wickedness" of Paul's pattern suggests its erotic quality; Symbolic in the Lacanian sense it suggests creative originality.

Miriam responds to the design with devotion disguising sexuality, her genuflection both a tribute to Paul's spirit and a submission to his body. The atmosphere becomes suggestive of a mutual erotic quest. But as Miriam remains bent over the painted cloth, Paul abandons their tension in deference to a prior responsibility: "'By Jove, the bread!' he cried. He took the top loaves out, tapped them vigorously. They were done" (8:241).

Miriam remains on her knees, in sacrifice or communion, and talks about the "cruelty" of the rose, yet despite the arousal inspired by his own design Paul remains loyal to filial obligation. Retreating from Eros, he converses with Miriam in an emotional intimacy that recalls his childhood sickbed connection to Gertrude. He finds "the most intense pleasure in talking about his work to Miriam. All his passion, all his wild blood went into this intercourse with her, when he talked and conceived his work" (8:241).

The movement from the design to the discussion of it is devitalizing, as if something dissolves in the movement from visual realization to verbal abstraction. (Once again there is a kind of reversal of

Lacanian categories: the images are freer than the words.) With Miriam, Paul recapitulates the dissolutional position, the original unbordered relationship with the Mother, reversed in power but perpetuated in essence. Miriam duplicates Gertrude's dominating will in her own possessive spirit. Yet it is Paul who dominates their communication, his strength restricted to the Imaginary mode in a verbal egocentricity that banishes the relations of desire. He closes the woman into the secondariness of undesiring and perceives her as a blank vessel of reception, "She did not understand, any more than a woman understands when she conceives a child in her womb." Miriam's substitutive role occurs in the regressive area where aesthetic experience retreats from the Symbolic back to the Imaginary, a withdrawal from the desire of the other.

The denial of the other replaces the Symbolism-of-Eros by the Imagination-of-Thanatos. Thus Paul's language produces an unhealthy psychic intimacy. In an earlier discussion the bright fusion between Paul and Miriam operates like light that pervades their separate beings, the language a kind of transfusion of the non-self:

> She wanted to draw all of him into her. It urged him to an intensity like madness. . . . He was discussing Michael Angelo. . . . there he lay in the white intensity of his search . . . almost inhuman as if in a trance. (8:232)

The scenes, abstract and rarefied into the area of psychic sublimation, fulfill the desire for a mentalized relationship in both characters. Miriam is the woman who dissolves the very body of desire, leaving the man "ghostish, disembodied" (8:232). As the atmosphere between Paul and Miriam becomes increasingly morbid, Beatrice enters the room. In her provocative spontaneity, she relieves a psychically charged atmosphere: "Paul bent forward to her to light his cigarette at hers. . . . Miriam saw his . . . full, almost sensual mouth quivering. *He was not himself*, and she could not bear it. . . . she had no connection with him, she might as well not have existed. She hated his thick hair for being tumbled loose on his forehead" (8:244, italics mine). With abstract words (it is ironic that Paul abstracts Michaelangelo) replaced by bodily signifiers, the scene alters from mentalized fusion, the Lawrentian Imaginary, to physical individuation, the Lawrentian Symbolic. The action, presented from Miriam's point of view, apprehends a different mode of perception. Paul's not being "himself" indicates his separation from the Imaginary self diffused in the fantasy world with Miriam. The cigarette lights up the Symbolic in a point of masculine fire.

Miriam gazes at Paul and Beatrice, the observed moment affording insight into the observer. Miriam watches implied erotic contact distanced in the visual field of a crossover between the Imaginary and Symbolic modes. In Lacanian language Beatrice and Paul are now traversed—pervaded—by the Symbolic. In Lawrentian language they are independent selves, no longer fused in oneness. Miriam feels alienated strangeness from the empowering autonomy of Eros.

As an image before her eyes, Paul and Beatrice represent the form Miriam *desires but cannot possess*. Paul becomes the desired object who waits at an uncrossable distance, the beloved object who performs a desired-prohibited action, and Beatrice becomes Miriam's *alienated self-other in action*.[23] Miriam looks into *an experience that in its visuality is itself like a mirror*, and finds the Other she both embraces and rejects.

Beatrice appears as perhaps the other-in-the-mirror, she plays a mediating role as, almost, the little object a′ (*petit objet a′*) that both is and is not the self.[24] The other woman is the duplicate of Miriam's desire, the object that desires as Miriam cannot desire defines *her own passionate unconscious*. The inspired Miriam now turns to the Phallic element in Paul: "Why might she not press his body with her two hands. It looked so firm and every whit living. And he would let other girls why not her" (8:246).

Yet Miriam also appears as a censuring presence placing the Symbolic under limitation. She is nonparticipating, a necessary third figure in the sexual game between Paul and Beatrice. Their erotic play is predicated on the silent presence (both disapproving and desirous) toward which it feigns indifference, for the triangulated event is conditioned on its witness. When Paul forgets prior obligation, Miriam wears her restrictive maternal guise to remind him of the bread, now emitting a "bluish smoke" from the oven door (8:244). Paradoxically, Beatrice transfers responsibility for the burnt bread to Miriam, correctly predicting that Gertrude will come to a corresponding conclusion. The complete confidence with which she shifts blame derives from *unconscious knowledge*, a certitude based on silent transmission.

In the third scene between Miriam and Paul, she reads him her intimate diary, written in French. Miriam allows erotic play in the unfamiliar speech of a foreign language: defamiliarization releases the unconscious:

> *Ce matin les oiseaux m'ont éveillé. . . . Il faisait encore un crépuscule. Mais la petite fenêtre de ma chambre était blême, et puis, jaûne* [sic] *et*

> *tous les oiseaux du bois éclatèrent dans un chanson vif et résonnant. Toute l'aûbe tressaillit. J'avais rêve de vous. Est-ce que vous voyez aussi l'aûbe? Les oiseaux m'éveillent presque tous les matins, et toujours il y a quelque chose de terreur dans le cri des grives. Il est si clair—. . . .* (8:246–47)
>
> [This morning the birds awakened me. . . . It was still dawn. But the little window in my chamber was pale, and then, yellow, and all the birds in the woods burst into vivid and resonant song. The dawn itself resounded. I dreamt of you. Did you see the dawn as well? The birds awaken me almost every morning, and there is always terror in the cry of the thrushes. It is so clear. . . . — author's translation.]

Miriam's composition traces the ascension of erotic feeling in metaphor: sunlight replaces the drained morning before sunrise, its transfiguration communicated by the bedroom window going from *blême* to *jaune*. The whole creation affirms an erotic wish, or dreamlike wish-fulfillment, with the sunrise describing the accession of male presence, now reified in the sun/son. Miriam's feeling of *terreur* recalls the beautiful opening of Rilke's *First Duino Elegy*, its claim that "Beauty's nothing but the beginning of Terror we're still just able to bear" (21). In its Lawrentian variation this appears as: terror is the beginning of Eros we cannot endure but creatively-destructively embrace. In Lacanian language, the passage suggests that the acquiring of the Symbolic freeplay of erotic and intellectual pleasure (*jouissance*) entails a dreadful beginning.

Paul cannot respond to the Eros both expressed and hidden by its French articulation. Miriam remains distant from Eros not because she lacks desire, but because her desire is conditional, experienced as a tremulous and reflective passion-in-the-mirror requiring affirmation from the Other. In the relationship between Paul and Miriam, the stammering of conscious speech yields to the fierce language of the unconscious. Thus Paul responds to Miriam's tentative Eros with a cruel refusal. His unconscious discourse expresses itself in action, in a kind of No-of-the-Lover. The *no* reveals itself in "the flinging down of the pencil," an expression of male withholding. The pencil is handled similarly in an earlier scene, a moment of satanic acting-out: "Once he threw the pencil in her face" (7:189). Later, incensed at her inability to master algebraic abstraction, Paul barely controls his rekindled fury: "And still, when he saw her eager, silent, as it were blind face, he felt he wanted to throw the pencil in it" (7:189). In a kind of fury of the Symbolic, we have a struggle of its different forms. Paul's sublimation of Eros, represented by the abstracting pencil, expresses its anger in relation to Miriam's reification of Eros, her sensuous Symbolic dawn.

With the return of the Mother we enter the next major scene. She arrives in a doubled image, her matronly disapproval, with its hint of domestic sexuality, repeated in the appearance of Paul's sister: "Annie, her blouse unfastened, her long ropes of hair twisted into a plait, went up to bed, bidding him a very curt goodnight" (8:250). Annie reinforces the mother's silent withdrawal. Yet soon after, Paul and Gertrude, beginning with a conventional goodnight embrace, enter into "a long fervent kiss." During their incestuous action Gertrude explicitly discards the father, "And I've never—you know, Paul —I've never had a husband—not really" (8:252). Her rhythmic words are separated by deep pauses, her breaths verbal spaces inviting Paul to enter.

The father's arrival interrupts their forbidden contact; in a stark confrontation the characters return to a rudimentary conflict of Mother, Father, and Son. Morel walks in on them, condemns their "mischief," then returns:

> . . . with a piece of pork-pie in his fist. It was what Mrs Morel had bought for her son.
>
> "Nor was that bought for you. . . ."
>
> "Wha-at—wha-at!" snarled Morel, toppling his balance. "Wha-at—not for me?" He looked at the piece of meat and crust, and suddenly, in a vicious spurt of temper, flung it into the fire. Paul started to his feet. . . . He would at that moment dearly have loved to have a smack at something. Morel was half crouching, fists up, ready to spring. . . . "Right!" said Paul, his eyes upon the side of his father's mouth, where in another instant his fist would have hit. He ached for that stroke. (8:252–53)

The father annihilates a central symbol. Indeed, the climactic sequence engages two signifiers, the one devouring the other. The pork-pie serves as ritualized object conferring masculine supremacy. The wife/mother's choice between father and son, the power confirmed through ritual consumption, recalls the rivalry of *Totem and Taboo*. Paul, like the sons in Freud's essay on anthropology and incest, assumes power by consuming that which belongs to the father. The ritual use of food allows an act of representative incorporation. By a rudimentary oneness of signifier and signified, in Freud's essay the aboriginal sons consume the father himself, usurping not only his position but his body in an act of cannibalism (*SE* 13:140–46).

Yet in *Sons and Lovers* the father avoids overthrowal by the son.

The reassertion of paternal supremacy occurs through the domestic fire, the family hearth burning Walter's coal. Morel takes the symbol of masculine victory, the pork-pie that the mother confers on her dominant male and sacrifices it to the fire. The blaze of primal fire asserts Morel's dominance and reminds Gertrude that only he can pass on its power, for the *Non/Nom du Père* cannot be transmitted by the mother.

Following the same sequence as *Totem and Taboo,* the assertion of primal supremacy incites the violent resistance of the son. Strangely, Paul targets the erogenous (also verbal) zone of his father's mouth. The language of destructive desire, the "stroke" for which Paul "aches," conflates the blow to the Father with the harm suffered by the Mother. It is the mother who appears to receive a "stroke," its terrible evidence appearing mutely at her mouth. For the marked feature of the father inscribes itself in blood on the mother's drained face:

> . . . he heard a faint moan from behind. His mother was deadly pale, and dark at the mouth. . . . She began to struggle with herself. Her open eyes watched him, although she could not move. (253)

The forbidden attack on the father is eerily mirrored in the near-death of the mother: what Paul fails to do to one parent he nearly does to the second, and the transformation reflects an unsettling bond. Desiring to avenge himself Paul discovers *that to injure the father is to injure the mother* (after an extended deferral Oedipus makes the same discovery.)

Under the deep shadow of paternal resentment and reflected through parents whose indivisibility remains inexplicable, we approach the atmosphere of the third Lacanian order, the inarticulable *Real*. Real/ity extends to two key areas. There is the sexuality of the mouth, the father's aggression against a masculine trope overshadowed by the stronger feminine trope. For the mouth is dark not pale, *alive in its deathliness*, and projecting a female sexuality that extends to death and something unspeakable, a blurring of life-identity by maternal blood. The maternal power continues still further with the unbearable *gaze from the depths of death*. The erotic gaze, we realize, is indisseverable from the body, for the gaze is the body-animating window and mirror of desire. The death gaze reflects the separation of the psyche from the body, propelling the reader into mysticism or terror. (Such a gaze dominates the penultimate sequence of *Wuthering Heights*.)

Parental bonding shows a Real finality shattering the subject's narcissistic illusions. Neither the Imaginary nor the Symbolic grants full unification with the mother or full replacement of the father. The fantasy of omnipotence, of possessing the body of the mother by usurping the authority of the father, is destroyed in this scene by paternal *power* and maternal *mortality*. Paul has been doubly assaulted, facing the father's hostility, and the mother's collapse, itself aggressive toward both father and son. The scene consumes not only Imaginary and Symbolic representations, but the process of representation itself, and leaves its characters vulnerable before the abyss of the Real.

In a moving passage of the *Four Fundamental Concepts*, Lacan explores the disturbing reverberations of fire as the Symbol that removes the screen of the Symbolic. He analyzes the important "dream of the burning child," from Freud's *The Interpretation of Dreams* (*SE*, 5:509). The dream concerns a bereaved father whose dead son appears before him to say: "Father can't you see I'm burning?" The father then awakens to find that the watchman had fallen asleep and that the boy's body had been burned by a fallen candle. Freud reads the dream as an interchange of dream and reality, with the reality of the fire disrupting the dream, and the dream itself the fulfillment of the father's understandable wish for his to son be alive a little longer.

In his *Four Fundamental Concepts*, Lacan takes this further. Like Freud he sees the dream as an entrance to death, but adds that the fire signals the boy's return from the Freudian Beyond, for unbearable and unformed fire suggests an "underlying" Real/ity.

> But the terrible vision of the dead son taking the father by the arm designates a beyond that makes itself heard in the dream. Desire manifests itself in the dream by the loss expressed in an image at the most cruel point of the object. . . . *Father, can't you see I'm burning*? This sentence is itself a firebrand—of itself it brings fire where it falls—and one cannot see what is burning, for the flames blind us to the fact that the fire bears on the *Unterlegt*, on the *Untertragen*, on the real. (*Concepts*, 59)

Bowie connects these passages to the traumatic dreams of *Beyond the Pleasure Principle* with their introduction of traumas-beyond-integration, to which the subject helplessly returns, and the traces of which are found in the Real that exists beyond the pleasure principle (105). His point is that the child's statement in the dream is a repetition of the important reality preceding the dream, that the death of the child is repeated in the verbal fragment, and the unfathomable Real evokes death itself.

The relevance of this to the food-burning scenes, which are about loss and rejection, is that the mother momentarily dead in the world of life contrasts and parallels the child in Freud momentarily alive in the world of death. This is an uncanny border-crossing, strengthened by the gaze of the dead mother, the stare from eyes of death in a paralyzed body; for if the boy in the dream defies death to live a moment longer with the father, the mother in Lawrence defies life to bind her son to her dying body. She unifies with him in the impossible Real, which can only mean, *she wants him to die with her*. Such death describes the dying of the sexual self in its fullness, a sacrifice for the Mother.

Therefore, Paul remains desperately weak (in the next chapter "The Defeat of Miriam" he relinquishes the erotic) until he takes his mother's life to return life to himself, while from the moment of fiery confrontation Walter is broken, for Gertrude will reside elsewhere beyond him. The scene beginning with the father's defeat of the son, incinerating his connection to the mother in an Imaginary blaze, ends with both men helpless before the mother's projection of the Real, or, more precisely, her stripping away of projections to reveal the Real.

It is notable that the earlier or more accessible orders begin with *the maternal image*, with the Imaginary going toward her in fusion and the Symbolic going away from her in translation. The Real emerges in a stark and original oedipal context, revealing itself when the original object of desire appears to *defeat her Imaginary representation*. In a work like *Sons and Lovers*, analogous with creations of legendary power like *Oedipus Rex* and *Hamlet*, the Real is the Mother as she exists separated, vulnerable, but unsusceptible to connection. In *Oedipus Rex* and *Hamlet*, the death of the mother marks the end of the main action, with maternal death decreeing the closure of the play at the point when the condensation of imaginative meaning, the literary, comes to the end of its play. The Real appears at the end of language, coming to its end before the mother in her dying, which is another way of saying *the unImaginable mother*. The body of the mother in its dying expresses the ultimate unreachableness of the psyche/soul of the mother. In *Sons and Lovers*, the Death-of-the-Mother erases the-Name-of-the-Father.

Three Faces of Clorinda

Paul first sees Clara Dawes in juxtaposition with Miriam. The "defiant carriage" of the older woman dominates the "meditative bearing" of the younger (8:222), for Clara is perceived as a presence while Miriam is intuited as an image. Paul takes pleasure in describing Clara's physical superiority to Miriam, while Miriam's sexuality becomes actual in a dialogue with Clara: " [Miriam] doesn't want your soul communion. . . . she wants you" (10:321). Each woman becomes more real for Paul as she is described to the other. Perceived in relation to one another they combine in a *composite image of desire*.

Thus Paul approaches Clara only after the failed passion with Miriam. Before their affair he scatters flowers over Clara's kneeling body in an act of premonitory grimness. Uprooting the flowers, integral centers of color, he exchanges natural context for dark cultural significance: "I thought you wanted a funeral." Clara prefers blossoms rooted in the earth, while Paul's metonymical gesture surrounds life-desire with death.

Such deathliness pervades his passionate encounter with Miriam. The poignant scene occurs in a wooded landscape, a cherry orchard whose fruits are devoured by ravens. An invisible power underlies the fading scene of cherry-picking at dusk. In a proleptic passage, Miriam watches "the gold clouds fall to pieces, and go in immense, rose coloured ruin towards the darkness" (11:330). The passage describes a play of *cosmic correlativity* where the dissipation of human energy parallels the dispersal of natural light. The attenuating radiance of nature predicts the approaching dissolution of love. In such passages the writing in the firmament—the active sky where Wordsworth finds the "Characters of the Great Apocalypse"— refers to the vicissitudes of the desiring body. The tumultuous horizon predicts the fate of passion: "He stood against a pine-tree trunk and took her in his arms. She relinquished herself to him—but, it was a sacrifice, in which she felt something of horror. This thick-voiced, oblivious man was a stranger to her."

While he feels disheartened because "her soul had stood apart from him, in a sort of horror," she stands apart not from him, but from the dark oblivion which prevents his realization of her. She appears to abandon him because he disappears into a darkness of sexuality-in-isolation. It is Paul who vanishes into a passional self as he leans against a pine tree and enfolds her; he as if dissolves into his own separate desire that excludes the other. The vanishing into isolated passion denies emotional and sexual fulfillment, while the "stranger" Miriam faces is an absence in the space of a lover.

Thus she loses Paul first in his sexual assertion, then in his psychic regression, feeling "afraid before of the brute in him: now of the mystic." The mystical quality signals the transition from the universal Imaginary to the deathly Real. For in the aftermath of a failed erotic experience, Paul transcends the Imaginary. He enters the dismalness of the Real as reified in nonvisual apprehensions: he smells the distanced pine trees, listens to the hiss of the rain, and touches Miriam with fingers that "wandered over her face pitifully."

Isolation leads to a feeling of disintegration as, passively, he feels the rain soak through him. Simulating the dissolution of body into earth, his feeling of liquefaction identifies orgasm and death. He becomes despondent in a depression that follows, apparently, contact without intimacy. When he lies listlessly on the wet ground, covered by the metaphorical rain, he is dismayed by an unfulfilling arousal. Unreciprocated passion occurs in a landscape pervaded by invisible forces:

> To him now life seemed a shadow, day *a white shadow, night, and death*, and stillness, and inaction, this seemed like *being*. To be alive to be urgent, and insistent, that was *not-to-be*. The highest of all was, to melt out into the darkness and sway there, identified with the great Being. (11:331—italics Lawrence's and mine)

Passion dissipates with the actual woman, yet the dispersal of surface intensity reverses the relationship of reality and shadow. Surface reality becomes the "white shadow" of nonreality, an illusion, while the "grey shadow" of the foreshadowing sky becomes a living darkness, an invisible "being" with an infinite depth of presence. A disappearance occurs into a darkness of isolation that introduces the figure behind nature, the maternal image of the hidden beloved. With the appearance of "the Great Being" we return to the moonlit garden, and the cherry-picking scene bears all the unconscious meaning of the semiotic Chora. Paul rejects the beloved-in-the-world for an immersion in another beloved figure, the one held deep in circumambient spheres. He turns from the image of the manifest lover because his loyalties are with a latent force.

Thus, Lawrentian Being appears after the disappearance of the lover, occurring between the isolated self and an invisible presence. One critic argues that it "is Being, not the Nothingness of Night, that calls to Paul Morel, and Lawrentian Being will never be imagined as a mystical fusion of Self and Other."[25] Yet when Paul disappears from the embrace of the beloved, he achieves being in a "mystical fusion" with the maternal presence in nature. Being is achieved in a nonbeing that diffuses into a larger existence.

Through Miriam, Paul discovers the force embodied by surrounding "darkness," for being is a state where the body dissolves to reveal the larger psyche/soul, and peace is achieved in the darkness of a Night that goes from the Imaginary to the Real.

Losing himself in the "Great Being" behind the forest-curtain of nature, Paul plays the-game-of-disappearance. The disappearance game leads seamlessly to the-romance-of-death, for the woman who would come with him into the darkness is abandoned. He sees her as one who resists his passion, when she is actually ambivalent, desiring and resistant in an altering way. He transforms the beloved from one who would take him in passion to one who would prevent passionate encounter. By an aural pun, and considering the meaning of Tancred/Clorinda, she is the Enemy (K)night, the one he injures as he searches for the truer object. For when the Lover places the beloved in the armor of a rival, the enemy *night* becomes the enemy *knight*. It is this denying and injuring of the beloved that is symbolized by the loss of the evening's "crimson" light. Finally, a gray frame encompasses the desolate scene with Miriam.

Contrarily, in the "Passion" chapter Paul turns to Clara amid a landscape of intensity. They descend a "cliff of red earth [that] sloped swiftly down . . . to the river that glimmered and was dark between the foliage" (12:353). Thus, they climb down—with a touch of vertigo—to the glimmering river, approaching a feminine life-force. The reddish color of the natural surroundings connects Clara to the earth as Mother and vital matrix, and to the generative Father, to Walter Morel whose face had been like "the flower of his body, ruddy" (1:18). The felt physicality of Clara is the gift of the afternoon; in a formal reorganization, like a Cubist painting, her "mouth was offered him, and her throat, her eyes were half shut, her breast was tilted as if it asked for him" (12:353). Her face and figure are dismantled and reconstructed, a collage of sensual offerings around an unfocused gaze. Thereupon her feminine body expands to a female principle, with sexual tropes projected by the scenery of earth and river.

The discovery of the body continues in a place of seclusion. On the side of the red slope: "Two beech trees side by side on the hill held a little level on the upper face, between their roots" (12:355). In the rooted alcove in the earth, Paul and Clara find a place of timelessness, the secluded space of romance, and discover one another in the connection that obliterates the world: "there was nothing in the afternoon but themselves" (12:355). The generative waters around Clara contrast with the "black water" Paul associates, earlier, with Miriam. There the black water, like the "pale blotch" of Miriam's face (11:328), expresses the irresolution of her physical image, the absence of the Symbolic Body between Paul and Miriam. The contrasts in the land- and waterscapes surrounding the women refer to contrasts in Paul's ambivalent perceptions of feminine sexuality. The differing qualities in nature refer to altering male responses to the female, to life and death in the body of woman.

Miriam's paleness merges, moreover, with the "ivory pallor" of the real mother, of Gertrude. Paul returns to whiteness indirectly as he witnesses the disintegration of Clara's red flowers. The union of Paul and Clara comes apart in the act of fulfillment: "When she arose, he . . . saw suddenly sprinkled on the black wet beech roots many scarlet carnation petals, like splashed drops of blood" (12:355). The torn carnations signal threats to Eros, for the sanguinary image predicts later injuries. The petals are scattered on the roots and across her breast; in the falling they coalesce in foreboding prophesy: "red, small splashes fell from her bosom *streaming down her dress to her feet*" (my emphasis). The embrace with Paul dissolves a natural image which streams from her in blood. The connection to Tancred/Clorinda is startling: "[Tancred] slashes with his sword at a tall tree; *but blood streams from the cut* and the voice of Clorinda, whose soul is imprisoned in the tree, is heard complaining that he has wounded his beloved once again" (*SE*, 3:22, my italics).

Paul will destroy and reject both Miriam (the enemy knight) and Clara (the forest tree), disguises for the presence he must engage ultimately. The deeper maternal source is the true face of Clorinda, the love-object to love and destroy. Paul injures Gertrude literally by *being with* his (other) lovers, but injures her Symbolically when he *rejects* the younger women. Their Symbolic significance in the substitution play is more significant than their actual—historical—roles in his life. The knight who penetrates the beloved in her disguises aims at a hidden image.

If Tancred wounds Clorinda in her forms, Paul injures the disguised women until the time comes to hurt the Real object. We hear the voice of Gertrude, the Mother as eternal confidante, interspersed amidst his relationships. She appears at crucial junctures in his love-affairs, intervening in relationships to dismantle them. After Paul's fistfight with Dawes she expresses a confident relief: "'And now I should have done with them all,' she said quietly" (13:412). Yet after leaving her replacements he will destroy the Mother in the world, if not in the mind.

Indeed, when Paul (like Tancred) injures his objects, he wounds nature itself. He injures not only the hidden signified, Clorinda, the beloved object, but expresses hostility to the forest of signifiers, the tropes that stand between the self and its final goal. The scenes with his love-objects-in-the-world occur in enchanted forests, contexts for the violation of natural elements. His unconscious desire is to cut down the field of signifiers and return to the signified. Clara is a deferring object, one who delays the reaching of the final object, the Mother of nondesiring desire. As part of a chain of energy-releasing deferrals, Clara represents the Lacanian Symbolic. Destroying the Symbols that distract him, *the knight with his sword, Paul, Tancred, attempts the murder of the Symbolic order.*

Paul will reject Clara in the end despite their shared experiences of physical communion in the cosmic surround. The first such description is tidal, empowered by "the tremendous living flood," the biblical sweep of waters. The generative force underlying living things suggests both Lawrence's mystic vitalism and Freud's biological Eros. The flood is fertilizing, transformed to the oceanic wind, "the tremendous heave that lifted every glass blade its little height, and every tree, and every living thing" (13:398). The waves of wind are like a maternal encircling, though at times the elements of nature remain animatedly discrete while the oceanic force is replete with the vitalized objects of the world, "the thrust of the manifold grass stems, the cry of the peewit, the wheel of the stars." We are told also that the "magnificent power could overwhelm them, identify them altogether with itself." The bond between them prevents reversion to the tidal force, but reversion to the oceanic arouses Clara's dissatisfaction: "She had been there, but she had not gripped the . . . something . . . she was mad to have." She feels his connection to a force beyond, but desires to possess him herself as he is already possessed by something else. She repeats the force that defeats her.

The subsequent passion scene adduces a fiery cosmos: "It was as if he and the stars and the dark herbage and Clara were licked up in an immense tongue of flame" (13:408). More biblical than romantic, the passage recalls the burning bush that illuminates and intensifies, the paradox of conflagration without destruction. This is the masculine trope-energy of fire; the language or tongue of the Father is expressed in manual images, a kinetic energy that suggests a making of art, object, or text: "His hands were like creatures, living; his limbs, his body were all life and consciousness, subject to no will of his, but living in themselves." Finding a creative seam between Lawrence and Lacan, we find that the hands and the body produce Symbolic objects, while the will and the psyche (spirit) return to Imaginary objects.

In the flood-sequence, there is a sexualization of the feminine force, the moon of the feminine psyche transformed to the water of the feminine body. In the fire-sequence the universe of things remains deeply integral: the psyche encounters its perceptions in a way that protects the integrity of itself and what it perceives. "Everything rushed along in living beside him, everything was still, perfect in itself, along with him." The masculine principle fires subject and object into singleness, the Symbolic as creative perception.

But such grand scenes of *romantic Eros* entail the threat of regression, the possibility of the subject's collapse into the psychic forces that find analogies in the living universe. Tracing the connection between the cosmic and the psychic, the self-integrity that coincides with the perception of an integral universe of things implies a resolution of the oedipal dynamic, a progressive rather than a regressive state of being. Passages describing the disintegration of self in both of them (Paul dissolving into Clara at the theatre, Clara dissolving into the ocean at the shore) suggest, however, the return to retrogressive states.[26]

Accordingly, the scenes of fulfillment occur in the chapter called "Baxter Dawes." The necessary encounter with the Father, or Father figure, is dramatized therein. Paul is psychically obligated (owes an unconscious debt) to the substitute Father because of the maternal quality in Clara: Paul feels enclosed in an illicit structure because he perceives her as secretly possessed by Baxter. The relationship between Paul and Dawes, with its "peculiar feeling of intimacy," shows the uncanny motif of the Doppelgänger.[27] Dawes mediates between Paul and Walter as the simultaneous double of Son and Father, creating a bridge between alienated characters. The disturbing connection between Paul and Dawes culminates in murderous violence. Their struggle appears as final, an Agon or death-battle Paul nearly consummates: "He was quite unconscious, only his body had taken upon itself to kill this other man. . . . Then, suddenly, he relaxed full of wonder and misgiving"(13:410). The relenting has disastrous consequences, for Dawes subjects Paul to a merciless battering.

The relaxing of the deathly hold occurs in a complex recognition. The unconscious taboo against the murder of the Father is invoked. Moreover, the need to punish the other yields to the deeper need for self-punishment, the sudden relenting combines a fear of parricide and a *desire for self-injury, or death*. The punishment ritual, like the mercy killing, contributes to the transformations of the text, the deep changes that add a romantic element to sequences that remain, nevertheless, psychologically realistic. The relenting of the strangle-hold is a yielding of transferential projection; Paul realizes that Baxter is not an image from the mind, but a man on the verge of death. Nor will Baxter continue to see Paul as the enemy after the beating. Violence disperses transferential fantasy to break the paranoid lock. Relaxing his hold, Paul realizes, in a passage from unconscious to conscious perception, that *Baxter is not his father*.[28] Baxter is the last enemy Paul confronts in the forest of his own "magic"—unreal because projected from the psyche—projections.

After being mauled by Dawes, Paul returns to Gertrude, stumbling toward her as victim and invalid. Their final period together, dominated by physical suffering, begins with the injury to Paul. Gertrude communicates her own grievous illness after his catastrophe. The text implies self-destruction as an unconscious motivation for her sickness. For she listens with grim forbearance to his pessimistic utterances about his erotic life: "'I feel sometimes as if I wronged my women, mother'. . . . And I never shall meet the right woman while you live,' he said. She was very quiet. Now she began to feel again tired, as if she were done. . . . The feeling that things were going in a circle made him mad" (13:394).

The plot of circular injuries repeats itself. In the complexity of her character, she grieves for what she cannot prevent. She is prepared to sacrifice herself, knowing he will never flourish while she is alive. Her troubled silence suggests her division between her feelings and her needs. He will live as she dies.

Once he enters into the process of her dying, there is a renewal of intimacy; death permits the expression of feelings that always implied deathliness. The scenes of her dying are like extended love-poetry, with her death releasing buried passion: "Her blue eyes smiled straight into his, like a girl's, warm, laughing with tender love. It made him pant with terror, agony, and love" (14:429). The oedipal bond is inevitably a death-bond, not to be expressed or fulfilled. In her literal dying, she realizes a metaphor, for she always pulls him toward dissolution.

Now he spurns Miriam, who turns to him with the love of the body, giving what he needs selflessly, or offering what he cannot accept: "she kissed him and kissed him," but there is no vital man to respond to her, "she could not kiss the agony." Similarly, when he turns to Clara from emotionless need, "she began to have a kind of horror of him. . . . it made her feel as if death itself had her in its grip" (14:431). He arranges the reconciliation of Clara and Baxter as he leads his mother through her dying. Clara makes self-submissive restitution to her husband, while Gertrude utters inexorable words of condemnation for an unfulfilled life: "She did not forgive [her husband]. . . . And a few things, the things that had been most bitter to her, came up so strongly, that they broke from her, and she told her son" (14:429). By the psychic economy of the final section, the substitutive release of Clara allows Paul's fearful closeness to Gertrude. Similarly, the closeness with Baxter permits indifference to Walter, the image of the Father demolished by the Mother's words.

As the cancer proliferates, Paul summons the anarchic courage to take her life. In an overwrought atmosphere recalling the ritual destruction of the doll, Paul administers an overdose of morphine. If the mercy killing is a moral necessity, ending her suffering is but one reason for ending her life. Her death empowers his love. Over her body he expresses the passionate recognition he withholds from other women. His embrace of the dead mother is the Oedipal *Liebestod* of a bereaved Son: "He kneeled down and put his face to hers and his arms around her. 'My love, my love, oh my love . . .'" (14:443). After her death she is reborn to her youth. To Morel she resembles his "young wife again," but for Paul she is the reproduction of deepest memory. The young Mother of childhood, the image of earliest attachment, reappears:

> She lay like a girl asleep and dreaming of her love. The mouth was a little open, as if wondering from the suffering, but her face was young, her brow clear and white as if life had never touched it. He looked again at the eyebrows, at the small winsome nose, a bit on one side. She was young again. Only the hair as it arched so beautifully from her temples was mixed with silver, and the two simple plaits that lay on her shoulders were filigree of silver and brown. (14:445)

The recognition of Gertrude in her individuality distinguishes the passage, for its clarity and specificity of description is unmatched in *Sons and Lovers*. Yet the portrait has a double meaning. We have a face that exists in the outer world, suddenly young and fresh, delivered from the burden of life and suffering. At the same time the purity and perfection of the face suggests its existence as an internal image. The actual Mother in her dying releases the Imaginary mother in her beauty. This dual image holds his loyalty and draws his passion. Utmost outer reality returns to utmost inner love.

The Mother in her dying is Gertrude, but also Clorinda, the last lover, object of driven malice, whom he takes as his own in the infliction of injury. Her duality is gracefully captured in the silver and brown plaits of hair, entwining the idealized image in the mind and the actual image in the world. The two colors are also the going inward and the going outward, life and death. We realize something not apparent from *Beyond the Pleasure Principle*, but emerging from our reading of *Sons and Lovers*. Tancred runs through his objects-of-injury because the deeper object can be loved only in death. The aim of injury is not to destroy, but to release, hold, take and destroy the last love-object.

The much-debated close of *Sons and Lovers* shows Paul entering the love-death merger, accepting absolute threat, finding life-energy not against but through that entrance. A disintegration of being occurs with the death of his mother, with its dissolution of subject/object barriers, the whirl of being and non-being that distinguishes "Derelict," the disintegrative last chapter of *Sons and Lovers*. The beautiful ending of the novel has been analyzed ad infinitum, as affirmative or destructive, toward the Mother or the Father, toward life or death. Yet such a stark alternative reduces the complexity of the novel's final sequences; just as metapsychology always traces the dualist interplay of the drives, so we are never faced with life *or* death in absolute form in writing as intricate as the close of *Sons and Lovers*:

> On every side the immense dark silence seemed pressing him, so tiny a speck, into extinction, and yet, almost nothing, he could not be extinct. Night, in which everything was lost, went reaching out, beyond stars and sun. Stars and sun, a few bright grains, went spinning round for terror and holding each other in embrace, there in a darkness that outpassed them all and left them tiny and daunted. So much, and himself, infinitesimal, at the core a nothingness, and yet not nothing. . . . no, he would not give in. Turning sharply, he walked toward the city's gold phosphorescence. . . . He would not take that direction, to the darkness, to follow her. He walked towards the faintly humming, glowing town, quickly. (15:464).

The "gold phosphorescence" of the city transmutes the gold pollen of the moonlit flowers, recuperating the sought power faded in mother-child fusion. The transformation of a rural to an urban scene implies the incorporation of the working world, the father's spurned strength gathered by the son. Advancing toward the father the son also finds a life-force in the very union with the mother that threatened a fade into annihilation. The combining of space and suns/sons is a last act of homage to both parents, to the lost vitality that had once bound Mother and Father.[29] Having released himself in an art of annulment and achievement, disappearance and return, the artist finds his own life in the disappearing Mother, and alters the deathly fusion of the moonlit garden. With the play of death continuing in the life of art, endlessness comes to an ending and back again.

8

Afterword: The Listening Other and the Turn to Speech

I CONCLUDE BY EXAMINING THE ROLE OF THE LISTENING OTHER AND the subject's turn to speech in the formation of categories of romance. My claim is that the difference between the deathly Imaginary and vital Symbolic realms depends on a relationship between speaker and listener. Furthermore, this relationship resides at the heart of romance. The listener determines the *world* in which the speaker eventually finds himself. The listening other/speaking subject connection strengthens the parallels between psychoanalysis (the psychoanalytic microtext) and literature (the literary macrotext) traced in this study. Many similarities of mood and tone—related atmospheres—bridge the narrative fragments in *Beyond the Pleasure Principle* and the novelistic romances, *Frankenstein, Wuthering Heights, Jane Eyre,* and *Sons and Lovers.*

Most crucially, however, both the psychoanalytic fragments, which reveal the origins of romance, and the literary texts, which render elaborations of romance, respond to the narrative situation where a speaker turns to a listener in an urgent appeal. He desires (and it is a desire) an empathic *reading* of his speech. In his need to be sympathetically heard the Ancient Mariner is the voice-behind-the-voices, and *The Rime of the Ancient Mariner* the text-behind-the-texts, of English novelistic romance. The sensitive response of the listener *in* language can free the speaker *for* language.

The speaking subject/listening other configuration underlies the psychoanalytic transference. The analyst in the transference serves as the belated prototype of the listening other. Psychoanalysis, as a quest through figurative obstacles toward an ambivalent goal, is belated romance. In Freudian-Lacanian terms, we can place the analyst as at once the Imaginary image from the past and the Symbolic interlocutor in the present. His responsiveness as listener determines the fate of a speaker who exists between two ways of being. Whether the subject will move toward the Imaginary, back to an entrapping image, or the Symbolic, forward to a release from that image, depends largely on the response of the listening other.

The way of the Symbolic is the way of desire. In Freud's preferred metaphor, desire refers to energy, the figure of the bio-electrical spark, activated between two separate beings. Lacan applies the desiring spark to activity beyond reproduction, to the ongoing never-to-be-satisfied imperatives of creativity and language; Lacan denies that reproductive process, or any discernible expression of being, fulfills desire. Desire remains after bodily drives are satisfied, yet the continuing quest for unfulfillable desire brings the vital-quality into life. The literary elaboration of desire is the bright face of romance. (By *literary* I refer to the conscious exploration of the expressive possibilities afforded by the use of *letters*.)

My reading of the connection between the Freudian death-drive and the Lacanian Imaginary discovers a backward movement of being. This entails a return to early relationships with unconscious figures. The experience of return involves merger with such figures. To repeat nonautonomous states-of-being is to move away from desire toward fusionary figures who restrict desire even as they are themselves its strongest sources. This paradox alienates the subject from desire. In another paradox, the motion (psychic tendency) away from desire is a dark (negative yet not based on negation) category of desire, the strong and independent force of anti-desire. The literary elaboration of anti-desire is the dark face of romance.

Anti-desire opposes desire, tending to rise from unconscious sources where desire operates closer to consciousness. Similarly, anti-desire enlists an unconscious will where desire tends to operate with the conscious will. Above all, anti-desire valorizes a past that acquires the power to *displace* the present. The subject subjected to the past feels usurped by negative states of being: paralysis, terror, blankness, violence. A significant strategy for resisting the regression inherent in the Imaginary is the address to the listening other rather than Other. The question of the capitalization of the "O" in other seems to me not an incidental issue. I take the other with the small "o" as the one who grants autonomy to the subject by being autonomous himself, by remaining *apart from* the subject, and the Other with the capital "O" as one who remains *a part of* the subject, dominating or dominated. Thus, within the five paradigmatic fragments of romance traced in this study (fragments of narrative, paradigms of meaning), we can discover a paradigm-of-paradigms in the relation of speaker and listener. That relation bears on the progress and meaning of the various works, microtexts and macrotexts, that engage us.

I begin with the absent narrative, the elusive metaphor pervading all the death fragments, the return to the wound in a dream. (All four of the death-fragments—the-romance-of-life is in a separate category—can be described by this title, all the titles being suitable to all the fragments, so that it is with some arbitrariness that I have foregrounded one element in each case.) To finalize a reading of the return to the wound we need to look at the most difficult chapter in *Beyond the Pleasure Principle*, the fourth, an abstruse neurobiological study of binding and unbinding, *Bindung und Entbindung*. We can take binding and unbinding as a dynamic way of describing the transformation of id into ego. This is an internal acquiring of culture, the development of a civilization of the self. Binding is achieving a certain internal form, putting drives into coherent patterns, making them accessible and controllable. Fastening the neurobiological to the psychological and, ultimately, to the ethical dimension of existence, Freud addresses himself to dreams and says that *we return to the unbound in order to bind*; it is for this purpose that we obsessively, fanatically return to the area of the unbound:

> . . . dreams endeavour[ing] to master the stimulus retrospectively. . . . they afford us a view of a function of the mental apparatus which, though it does not contradict the pleasure principle, seems to be more primitive than the purpose of gaining pleasure and avoiding unpleasure.
>
> . . . . If there is a 'beyond the pleasure principle', it is only consistent to grant that there was also a time before the purpose of dreams was the fulfillment of wishes. . . . May not dreams which, with a view to the psychical binding of traumatic impression, obey the compulsion to repeat—may not such dreams occur *outside* analysis as well? (*SE*, 18:32–33)

This explains the-dream-of-the-wound as the belated effort to fill the gap in the psyche left by the trauma, to reweave the tear in the fabric of being; we return to the wound to heal it. Thus, Freud discusses the rehabilitation of damaged selves. His belated reading of the dreams of wounded veterans can be applied to the dreams of spiritually wounded fictional protagonists. We can understand Jane Eyre's dreams as a return to the scene of abandonment; being left behind inside the dream, she is enabled to leave Rochester behind outside the dream, her dream allowing the escape of injury. Combining the-dream-of-the-wound and the-game-of-disappearance, she disappears from injury in a self-strengthening. The restorative return to the wound applies in a different way to Paul Morel. Paul has visionary experiences rather than dreams, but his erotic experiences with Miriam and Clara are dreamlike, and he returns to them in a reparative manner until he discovers a deeper dream in his final object. Combining the-dream-of-the-wound and the-romance-of-death Paul's visionary experiences bring him toward the Real/ity of the dying Mother. He approaches the death-in-love union, the liberating injury to the beloved, essential to Paul's independence and the novel's resolution.

In one of his last works, *An Outline of Psycho-Analysis,* Freud returns to the question of binding and unbinding on a metapsychological scale. Therein he finds desire to be the final binding force, the aim of Eros "to establish ever greater unities and to preserve them . . . to bind together." The same essay finds that "the destructive instincts" work "to undo connections and so to destroy things" (*SE*, 23:148). The unbinding of the death drive is the disheveled return to anarchy, to the period before the law-underlying-love is conferred through the Name-of-the-Father. All our ego-directed life, however successful and triumphant, is a dying. We die in our fashion by intimations and anticipations of death experienced as an unraveling; instances of unbinding keep the ego bound in life while preventing the higher binding of self and other in Eros.

The ego holds us to the protracted death-process by transfixion and paralysis. It turns time backward like a director of experimental cinema, freezing, dismantling or inverting temporality. The techniques of the ego for projecting the death-process are varied, traceable through the four death paradigms (the ego has no dominion over the-romance-of-life). The-dream-of-the-wound brings the dreamer back to the helplessness of injury: in the poetics of the death-ego, trauma is continually reinstituted and, thus, continually defamiliarized. The recreation of the trauma in the unfamiliar dream (un/familiar being a privileged example of negation) holds the wound in front of the dreamer to renew its fatality. This is precisely the function of Victor's graveyard dream in *Frankenstein*.

But the dreamer is divided between observer and actor. The actor, the-self-in-the-dream, returns to the injury; the observer, the self-watching-the-dream can understand the injury. Bringing together the Freudian dream-of-the-wound with Catherine's dream in *Wuthering Heights*, we are aware of another variable in the reading of dreams: *the role of the second observer*. The dream-observer speaks to the second observer, his interlocutor, in a search for the interpreter of dreams. In *Beyond the Pleasure Principle*, Freud holds back from a reading of the trauma dream, resists the specific details of a trauma which sublates the wish-fulfillment theory, to move the notion of wish to a greater complexity. Yet the reparation of the trauma depends on the language of the interpreter. Freud resists the turn to language, or provides no evidence of such a turn, in front of the wounded dreamer. Nelly Dean refuses to hear Catherine's transformative dream, which goes through the young woman's mind like "wine through water." Catherine's transcendental "I *am* Heathcliff" speech suggests that her untold dream was about merger-in-death, like the rocks beneath living nature. The dream may have held the beginnings of a romantic transubstantiation, a lost Symbol. Catherine's unrecited dream narrative, like her incompleted diary, begins the Symbolic transformation of the Imaginary, the replacing of Heathcliff as fusionary Other with Heathcliff as living other. But in the lack of a sympathetic listener the transforming speech is never completed.

In the-game-of-disappearance, the observing other is passive, yet what we know of the game is his recording of it. He records the boy who becomes the object of his speculative examination. The boy turns himself into the object of a search, thus making the game into a *quest-within-a-quest,* perhaps a negative quest if the boy wants the other to look but not to find. Does he not throw himself, as he throws his toys, in order to be found? Not when he brings the other to the space that swallows him as though to open an abyss, *as though he were an abyss*. The boy uses the poetics of the death-play to remain within the death-play. This despite Lacan's persuasive reading of the boy's verbal expressions as the discovery of the Symbolic in language. Lacan takes the game further than Freud does but not far enough when, in the boy's game, Symbolic systems serve the Imaginary by returning to it, by holding both the player and the observer within it. The boy creates an art of the Imaginary, Imaginary games with Symbolic images in them. Lacan's mistake is not to notice that the boy accesses language in order to facilitate the Symbolism of return. There is no active other in the isolation of the boy's game. He disappears into himself in silent play. Disappearance is the eliding of the other in the universe of self.

The-game-of-disappearance is indigenous to romance, the romance-protagonist will disappear from the scene of reality, slide down the side of the world like the Ancient Mariner. But disappearance is behind the principle of transformation, the disappearance into the self precedes change, seen as a visible alteration in the Creature, Jane Eyre, and Paul Morel, yet perhaps most evocative when invisible, as in relation to Heathcliff, a character never revealed by interior narrative. I have argued that the boy plays disappearance, not disappearance and return. Which is the form found in the novelistic romances? The same as in the game: disappearance with no real discovery—at best, a false discovery, which is the most that can be said for Freud's optimistic misreading of the boy's continuing disappearance. The disappearance of the character is a plea for discovery, a wanting to be found, but the disappearing self remains undiscoverable. Walton and Victor and the Creature each disappear not to be found. Victor avoids a Creature who demonstrates a capacity to find him (indeed, to *find him out*). *Disappearance is inspired by the retreat from the non-listening Other*, the object that rejects us to introduce into us internal processes of disintegration.

Recuperation occurs within us after we disappear, alone. The Creature is corrupted but then self-rehabilitated in unutterable isolation. Jane Eyre disappears into Whitcross and Moor House and her cottage in Morton to come back as someone else. Catherine disappears into herself while she is being abandoned by others, left to go mad. Paul Morel disappears in and reappears from erotic relationships, his deepest encounters—and this is characteristic of Lawrentian characters—are intrapsychic, even as his greatest desire is to find the way out of the depths of self. *Disappearance is the despair of desire,* involution into self. Hence the boy goes toward the cot, discovers language, but only on the journey homeward.

The transference itself, the-play-of-substitution, occurs by definition in front of a listening other. Yet the compulsion to repeat remains mystifying. Why go back to the destructive dimension of primary relations? Why expose oneself again to original prohibition and punishment? I would reassert in this connection the specific interests of the ego, and describe the repetition-compulsion as the most efficient device the ego has devised for holding the self within the category of intrapsychic desire that I have named anti-desire. The images of primary desire, the Mother and Father of passions and interdictions are leading figures (not characters) in the kingdom of the ego. As part of the intrapsyche of the subject himself the leading figures within him come under the jurisdiction of the ego, preserver and destroyer of the encompassing organism. The kingdom of the ego is the intrapsychic realm and to establish its supremacy it brings the subject back to his romance Imaginary with inner figures.

The ego that functions in this manner is the mythic-ego, another face of the more familiar reality-ego. (The reality-ego, paradoxically, is more *familiar* because *de/familiarized*, because resisting the *familial*). The reality-ego locates the subject firmly in his surroundings, surviving to die, and resists the powers of desire. The mythic-ego submerges the subject in his past desires to resist present desires. The reality-ego and mythic-ego share a purpose: the holding of the living-dying subject separate on his isolated trajectory. The return of the subject to his inner world engenders the repetitive-satanic quality, or style, of transferential experience.

The holding to primal figures serves the ego by closing out *the other of desire*, the other drive toward the other kingdom. *Functioning in its intrapsychic realm the mythic ego develops its astonishing artistic powers*. These powers, which Freud understands as the demonic, relate to *the atemporality of the mythic-ego* (the reality-ego functions in ultra-temporality, using means that oppose the romantic-ego, it achieves a similar desire-opposing end). The temporality of repetition functions by superimposition, the condensation of past and present establishing the time-frame of romance. Widening to depth rather than narrowing to linearity, repetition is the depth-metaphor of romance, the fourth dimension of narrative. Freud takes the compulsion to repeat as death, but, as with many Freudian concepts, the idea contains its own antithesis. The experience of the repetition-compulsion, Heathcliff seeing Catherine in Cathy, Jane Eyre re-experiencing Mrs. Reed in Bertha Mason, Paul unable to deliver a mortal blow to Baxter Dawes, suggests that repetition *immemorializes* events and images. The compulsion to repeat can project a terrible eternity.

The task of the analyst in the transference is to *temporalize* the past, to romantic/ize (Freud would say real/ize) the mythic image. (This also suggests that there is a romantic ego struggling to get out of itself, trying to transcend the mythic ego by making contact with another.) The analyst needs to modify the past by the present, preventing the patient from modifying the antithetical process. The analysand stops time by doubling the referential meaning of temporal events. The worst-case scenario is Oedipus finding the present shattered by the past. The detective work of Oedipus follows the ironic plot of a tragic ego, representing that within us which overwhelms present characters by past figures. The superimposition of past and present modes of being leads to the catastrophes of the transference, reversing time to break its flow. The ego's capacity to invert or freeze temporal movement leads to aesthetic enormity, sublime perceptions of death-in-being. A poem like Keats's "Sonnet to The Elgin Marbles," is a contemplation of nature by the death-ego, "the aim of all life is death" presented on the geocultural level, cross-sections of time disposed on cloudy mountains, gives us the beautiful poetry of the death-ego. (The death-ego appears at the point where the ego takes pleasure in its deathly triumph.)

In every romance there is a key moment when a figure at the heart of the transference has the power to move backward or forward according to the speech of an other. Perhaps the prototype here is Teiresius, who *does not* speak. Had he found a way to speak, to conciliate, to replace, to lead away, without actual deceit that would, of course, be unthinkable, he might have taken Oedipus from the Imaginary to the Symbolic instead of sending him to the deepest hell of the Real. Victor or Delacey in *Frankenstein*, Nelly Dean in *Wuthering Heights,* Mrs. Reed in *Jane Eyre,* Mrs. Morel in *Sons and Lovers,* are the others called upon not only to listen but to speak.

Lack of speech precedes the violence of the-romance-of-death. It begins in that infrequent part of the-game-of-disappearance when the boy brings the toy back. If he brings it back to throw it away we have the beginning of the-romance-of-death. Instead of losing ourselves in the primary process of the-play-of-substitution we take control and inflict injury on the objects to which we return. Yet I read this oppositely from Freud, for he sees it as an example of the passivity of fate and I see it as absolutely active; perhaps we can combine these and talk about an activity that culminates in passivity. (In the-romance-of-death we change signifiers but we are powerless to change the signified—to alter the signified is to enter into the-romance-of-life.) We keep destroying objects, enemies, until we discover, as our fate, that it is the beloved we wish to destroy. This is what happens when we fail to receive the benefits of listening; unlistened to we are undeveloped and uncultivated. We remain locked in fundamental connections; we displace them to threatening objects which we shatter. The non-listening other is projected to the victims of the death-romance. Heathcliff tries to destroy Isabella and Cathy because Catherine never listens fully and allows herself to be divided from him. The Creature becomes a murderer because of his unreceived speech.

The struggle in the death-romance is toward the image waiting at the end. We fight to find the one who should have listened and refused, the one who holds us in the Imaginary forest. We find her and destroy her because as long as she refuses to listen the forest will hold us. To "destroy" her is to free the mind from her dominion—once she has gone we may look for other voices in representations of the lover without or the vital self within. This is precisely the story of *Sons and Lovers.* Paul finds the objects that lead to desire, parental images of energy translated into the living universe and burgeoning town, after he takes Gertrude's life.

Lawrence thereafter seeks the vital romance-of-life through much of his prose and poetry. Yet the-romance-of-life remains paradoxical. Despite their existence within time, as part of reproductive process, romances of life, like the ending of *Jane Eyre,* an ending which finds its further development in such Lawrentian works as *Women in Love* and *Lady Chatterley's Lover*, are experienced as timeless. What is the eternity of life-romance? Perhaps the timelessness of such romance relates to union beyond the temporal limitations of the single self. The idea of listening as erotic communion is strengthened when we recall that *Jane Eyre, Women in Love*, and *Lady Chatterley's Lover* are speaking texts, full of intimacies of voice. To identify love with speaking is to understand the old romance dichotomy of Eros and agapé, physical and spiritual love, anew. The lover in body and voice, sexual and Symbolic, with traces of the Imaginary in her gaze, combines time and timelessness in the being-together of life-romance. The listening other gives us to the contours of the passing time; releasing us from the static internal figures of the mythic world, the beloved awaits in the other eternity.

Notes

Chapter 1. Introduction: The Romance of Desire, or the Unattainable in Twenty-Nine Takes

1. Northrop Frye, *Anatomy of Criticism: Four Essays* (New York: Atheneum, 1968), 186. Fryean romance describes the travails of erotic quest, the gallant libido battling in the forest of projected restrictions: "the quest-romance is the search of the libido or desiring self for a fulfillment that will deliver it from the anxieties of reality but will still contain that reality," (193). Frye's psychoanalytic metaphor is compelling, but remains of limited usefulness when his notion of "reality" is so one-sided. While acknowledging the role of demonic romance, Frye diminishes the significance of the dark experience presented as a transitional stage, rather than an alternative goal, of the romantic journey: "most romances exhibit a cyclical structure of a descent into a night world and a return to the idyllic world." *The Secular Scripture: A Study of the Structure of Romance* (Cambridge: Harvard University Press, 1976), 54.

In a more recent study, influenced by Frye, Ann Dobyns argues that romance follows the contours of abstraction rather than the demands of verisimilitude; romance reveals itself as the illustration of an idea rather than the imitation of a[n] action." *The Voices of Romance* [Newark: University of Delaware Press, 1989], 18. Dobyns notes that Frye's stress on the themes of romance (as opposed to the plot-based aesthetic of "mimetic fiction") subordinates action to "mood" and that "like . . . works of abstract art, romances make prominent the spatial rather than the psychological structure of the stories they tell" (10). Her questionable distinction between the "spatial" and the "psychological" indicates a narrow approach to the psyche (an implicit identification of psychology and realism). Perceiving the psyche in broader—or deeper—terms, I would argue that the predominance of "theme" may be reconceived as a pervasive state-of-being that influences setting as well as character, background as well as foreground. *The space in romance is psychological space*, for it equates cosmic vision with a psychic dream.

2. Sigmund Freud's *The Interpretation of Dreams*, in *The Standard Edition of The Complete Psychological Works of Sigmund Freud*, trans. and ed. James Strachey, et al., 24 vols. (London: Hogarth Press, 1953–74), vols. 4–5. *The Interpretation of Dreams* is cited hereafter in the text as *IOD*. "Creative Writers and Daydreaming," *SE*, 9:142–53. *The Standard Edition* is cited hereafter in the text as *SE*.

3. The unlovely Anglo-Saxon "want," a word that unites absence and hunger, remains the foundation of the Gallic-Latin abstraction "desire."

4. If references to death are rare, references to the death-drive are nonexistent in Freud's writings on literature and the arts. (As an exploration of metapsychological principles rather than an aesthetic application of those principles, "The Uncanny" belongs in a separate category.) In the essay on Dostoevsky, Freud re-

fers to death in relation to Dostoevsky's epilepsy and takes note of Dostoevsky's wish for the death of his father. Neither instance involves consideration of death as a principle or motive. While *The Interpretation of Dreams* is distinguished by evocative discussions of death and the dreamer, Freud writes his *magnum opus* before he begins to consider death as a drive or desire.

5. Lacan's elusive descriptions (hardly definitions) foreground the transformations of desire, an elusive motivating power "eternally stretching forth towards the *desire for something else*—of metonymy" (emphasis Lacan's). *Écrits: A Selection,* trans. Alan Sheridan (New York: Norton, 1977), 167. *Écrits* (in English) cited hereafter in the text as *É*. Lacan centralizes metonymy in the narrativizing of psychic life partly in response to Roman Jacobson's influential article on the two axes of language (including figurative or literary language): the metaphorical, based on the axis of similarity, and the metonymical, based on the axis of contiguity. "Two Aspects of Language and Two Types of Aphasic Disturbances," in Roman Jakobson and Morris Halle, *Fundamentals of Language* (The Hague: Mouton, 1956), 55–82.

Peter Brooks applies the energy of desire, as it drives through a metonymic chain of objects in the narrative, to a reading of plot. Thus, desire yields a "textual erotics," a reading of narrative simultaneously about the desire of the protagonist *in* the narrative and the desire of the reader to find the comprehensive significance *of* the narrative. Brooks's provocative examination recovers Freudian and Lacanian forces for literary study in an authentically original manner. Yet he is not at his most persuasive when he identifies desire with the ambition of the nineteenth century novelistic hero (for example, Julien Sorel in *The Red and the Black*). Admitting that desire is a worrisomely general term, his own overly general application of the concept fails to make an essential distinction between egoistic and erotic desire. Brooks, *Reading for the Plot: Design and Intention in Narrative* (New York: Random House, 1984).

Lacan himself characteristically covers the imprints of desire, denying a clear equation between desire and another abstraction, always giving the screw of *désir* another turn: "Desire is neither the appetite for satisfaction, nor the demand for love, but the difference which results from the subtraction of the first from the second, the very phenomenon of their splitting." From Jacques Lacan, *Écrits* (Paris: Seuil, 1966), 691 (in French). Quoted and translated in Patrick Colm Hogan and Lalita Pandit, eds., *Criticism and Lacan: Essays and Dialogue on Language, Structure, and the Unconscious* (Athens: University of Georgia Press, 1990), xvii. Hogan and Pandit provide a comparatively clear definition of Lacan's generative concept: "Following common economic usage, Lacan carefully distinguishes need from *demand*. The latter, for Lacan, always exceeds the former—we demand more than we need. The objects of demand which exceed need are, then, the objects of our *desire*. . . . *Need* aims at satisfaction. *Desire* aims at *jouissance*" (xvii). In Ellie Ragland-Sullivan's useful gloss: "*Jouissance* means sexual pleasure, but at an abstract level it could be described as the temporary pleasure afforded by substitute objects or by others' recognition (substitutes for the original other). At this juncture *jouissance* and Desire meet in the concept of the *plus-de-jouir*." Ellie Ragland-Sullivan, *Jacques Lacan and the Philosophy of Psychoanalysis* (Urbana: University of Illinois Press, 1987), 271.

6. Freud does a clear analysis of the elements of the drive, divided between *Drang* (pressure), *Ziel* (aim), *Objekt* (object), and *Quelle* (source). Yet each element opens questions as to the precise meaning of its content and all are subsumed under the overarching metaphor, *Trieb*. See "Instincts and Their Vicissitudes," *SE*, 14:122. The four structures request deconstruction.

7. Frye notes that "the romancer does not attempt to create 'real people' so much as stylized figures which expand into psychological archetypes" (*Anatomy of Criticism*, 304). In a closely related point, although Freudian where Frye is Jungian, Baruch Hochman claims "the romance is closer [than the novel] to the unconscious life, radiating from and cleaving more closely to the world of dreams. . . . In romance, people are driven, rather than conscious; coerced, rather than struggling volitionally to achieve ends that their conscious selves affirm" Hochman, *Character in Literature* (Ithaca: Cornell University Press, 1985), 77.

8. Patricia A. Parker, *Inescapable Romance: Studies in the Poetics of a Mode* (Princeton: Princeton University Press, 1979), 4.

9. Malcolm Bowie captures this "quicksilver" quality of Lacan's *désir:* "desire is the moving mover of all signifying processes, the insinuating genie that runs through the endless concatenations of language." *Lacan*(London: Fontana, 1991), 131. Bowie's reading identifies *désir* with the Symbolic order.

10. John P. Muller and William J. Richardson observe that the *manque à être* may refer to " 'lack of being,' or 'deficiency in regard to being,' or 'the state of being in 'want of' being.' . . . It is precisely this 'want-to-be' that we take to be the key to Lacan's understanding of desire: the radical and humanly unsatisfiable yearning of the infant for the lost paradise of complete fusion with its All—a wanting born of want." *Lacan and Language: A Reader's Guide to* Écrits (New York: International Universities Press, 1982), 22. The authors take the wanting of original fusion as the origin of desire. Yet the original point is not so much a wanting as a having; there is some proto-memory of oneness, the point *before* the advent of desire, to which we wish to return. Brooks puts this clearly when he argues: "Desire is inherently unsatisfied and unsatisfiable since it is linked to memory traces and seeks its realization in the hallucinatory reproduction of indestructible signs of infantile satisfaction: it reposes on phantasmatic scenarios of satisfaction" (*Reading for the Plot*, 55).

11. Hence I cannot agree with Linda Williams's conclusion that death is the other desire, equivalent to, perhaps even privileged above, the desire for love: "Desire is, then, not necessarily the agent of life instincts; it also, or perhaps fundamentally, serves the death drive—desire culminates in the extinction of the subject." *Critical Desire: Psychoanalysis and the Literary Subject* (London: Arnold, 1995), 156.

12. For a discussion of the spellbinding power of depictions of the Imaginary see my essay "Woman as Fatal Other: A Reading in Revisionary Romanticism," *Etudes Lawrenciennes* 20 (1999): 59–88.

13. Mieke Bal, skeptical about the critical usefulness of the category, "myth," insists that the mythic signified cannot be separated from its individual signifier and that a total reliance on the universality of myth is a kind of desire for the obliteration of individuality. "Myth à la lettre: Freud, Mann, Genesis and Rembrandt, and the story of the son," in Shlomit Rimmon-Kenan, ed. *Discourse in Psychoanalysis and Literature* (London: Methuen, 1987), 57–89. Hence my own quest for the mythic (a repertoire of thought- and feeling-tendencies culturally determined yet existing beyond the borders of culture) focuses on its inscription in a specific psyche, text, or inherited legend. In a classic study, (which goes back to 1972, but certain critics seem to me to transcend the historical dialectic of criticism and achieve permanent usefulness) René Girard adds a significant element to our understanding of the mythic in psyche and text. Recalling that the legend of Oedipus begins in the mythology of the scapegoat, Girard reads Oedipus as one sacrificed by his culture in the maintenance of its integrity and purity. This im-

plies that the self-destructive tendencies of the son in the oedipal struggle, also when that struggle is renewed in the compulsion to repeat, entails self-sacrifice; hence the son can reverse the murder of the father described in *Totem and Taboo* (*SE*, 13:1–162) and submit to his fate. Such universal psychic traces are part of the "mythic." Girard, *Violence and the Sacred*, trans. Patrick Gregory (1972; Rpt., Baltimore: Johns Hopkins University Press, 1979). For a discussion of how Girard's striking notion pertains to Kafka's "Metamorphosis," the reader is directed to my essay: "The Anxiety of History: Kafka's Allegory of the Oedipal Scapegoat." *Journal of the Kakfa Society of America* 16,2 (June 1992): 4–19.

14. In another important study, Girard shows that a number of major novels of the Western tradition, *Don Quixote*, *Madame Bovary*, and *The Red and the Black*, integrate into their narrative structures a self-conscious critique of the genesis and operation of desire. This for Girard is the very fissure between the novel and the romance. *Deceit, Desire & the Novel: Self and Other in Literary Structure*, trans. Yvonne Freccero (1961; Rpt. Baltimore: Johns Hopkins University Press, 1976).

15. Among the essays that contain considered examinations of the drives are *Civilization and Its Discontents*, *The Ego and the Id*, and *An Outline of Psychoanalysis*.

Chapter 2. Desire and Anti-Desire in *Beyond the Pleasure Principle*

1. Parker, *Inescapable Romance*, 3–15.

2. The nature or meaning of the Freudian "beyond" remains notoriously elusive, despite the fact that its discovery is the informing project of *Beyond the Pleasure Principle*. The issue continues to arouse perplexity, and sometimes impatience, among commentators who suggest, ultimately, that *nothing* is beyond the pleasure principle. Thus, in a provocative denial of Freud's thesis, Leo Bersani argues that far "from proposing an instinct which would supersede or somehow have priority over the pleasure principle, Freud's book is actually his most revealing and most disguised exploration of the nature of pleasure." *The Freudian Body: Psychoanalysis and Art* (New York: Columbia University Press, 1986). All references to *Beyond the Pleasure Principle* cite the *Standard Edition*. Subsequent citations, abbreviated initially as *BPP*, appear in my text according to chapter and page.

3. For a discussion of the history and meaning of metapsychology, see my ensuing chapter on "Negation and Negative Capability."

4. Ricoeur claims that "only Eros is beyond the pleasure principle," expressing his skepticism in a paradoxical statement. If we take Eros as the height of pleasure, we are left with the problem that the rhythmic tensions of sexuality place the erotic outside the boundaries of the Nirvana and constancy principles—the laws which according to Freud govern pleasure. Ricouer can thus conclude convincingly that: "the reason we do not know what is beyond the pleasure principle is that we do not know what pleasure is." *Freud and Philosophy: An Essay on Interpretation*, trans. Denis Savage (New Haven: Yale University Press, 1970), 320, 322. Ricoeur's paradox is pointed out elegantly in Derrida's assertion "that the pleasure *principle* makes war on pleasure." Derrida suggests pleasure would be beyond the pleasure principle were it not for the mastering power of a principle

which is in itself "the prince *of* pleasure, the prince whose pleasure is the conquered, chained, bound, restricted, tired subject." This leads, in an arresting circumlocution, to a reaching of the beyond by way of Nietzsche: "Beyond the pleasure principle—power," yet—characteristically—Derrida withdraws the apparent resolution in a return to *différance*: "the death drive [a return to the pleasure principle] . . . no less overflows power." Derrida, *The Post Card: From Socrates to Freud and Beyond*, trans. and intro. Alan Bass (Chicago: University of Chicago Press, 1987), 399, 400, 405.

5. Cf. Richard Boothby, "Metapsychology . . . was Freud's answer to metaphysics." *Death and Desire: Psychoanalytic Theory in Lacan's Return to Freud* (New York: Routledge, 1991), 4.

6. Responding to its bold figurative dimension (its rhetorical *risks*), Harold Bloom describes *Beyond the Pleasure Principle* as both a "High Romantic crisis-poem" and "a post-Romantic crisis-lyric." "Freud's Concepts of Defense and the Poetic Will," in *The Literary Freud: Mechanisms of Defense and the Poetic Will*, ed. Joseph H. Smith (New Haven: Yale University Press, 1980), 9, 11. Yet *Beyond the Pleasure Principle* (1920) is not a unique example of psychoanalytic romance; the almost contemporary *Uncanny* (1919), provides another instance of the genre: written the one after the other the two essays provide our fullest introduction to both psychoanalytic romance and romantic psychoanalysis.

7. Freud, *Civilization and Its Discontents*, in *SE*, 21:117.

8. I am being controversial here, because many commentators would say that self-preservation leads, naturally, to life. But I make the connection, germane to my entire argument, on the basis of the role of the ego.

9. Bloom discusses the catastrophic in Freud in "Freud and the Poetic Sublime: A Catastrophe Theory of Creativity," *Antaeus*, no. 30/31 (Spring 1978): 355–77. One problem with Bloom's reading of the issue is his taking the death-drive literally, so to speak, accepting it in the speculative form Freud gives it in his surface presentation. Not seeing the way death is woven into the narratives of *Beyond the Pleasure Principle* (and elsewhere) Bloom can claim, quite erroneously, that the figurative elements in the essay express themselves only in relation to Eros (368).

Interested in narrativity and plot where Bloom's concerns are figurativity and image, Peter Brooks reads the relationship between drive-energy and literary expression with a similar one-sidedness. Brooks concludes a reading of the "dynamic model" of *Beyond the Pleasure Principle* with a dichotomy that "structures ends (death, quiescence, nonnarratability) against beginnings (Eros, stimulation into tension, the desire of narrative)." (Brooks, *Reading for the Plot*, 107). To restrict the creativity of instinctual force to the proliferations of desire is to overlook the content of the thanatotic narratives informing Freud's essay.

10. Geoffrey Hartman has written about this in his discussion of the "middle" in literature, the sometimes elided middle being equivalent to cosmic emptiness, and the full middle, as created in the poetic structure of "tmesis," providing richness in literature or, for that matter, experience. Hartman takes—perhaps inevitably—*Oedipus Rex* as his exemplary text:

> we can say that Oedipus, killing his father and marrying his mother, simply elides individual identity and is allowed no being properly his own. . . . Oedipus is redundant: he is his father and as his father he is nothing, for he returns to the womb that bore him. His life-line does not exist. . . . Human life, like a poetical figure, is an indeterminate middle between over overspecified poles always threatening to collapse it. The poles may be birth and death, father and mother, mother and wife, love and judgment, heaven and earth,

> first things and last things. Art narrates that middle region and charts it like a purgatory, for only if it exists can life exist. . . . The excluded middle is a tragedy also for the imagination.

Geoffrey Hartman, "The Voice of the Shuttle: Language from the Point of View of Literature," in *Beyond Formalism: Literary Essays 1958–70* (New Haven: Yale University Press, 1970), 348.

11. There is a consensus among critics who write from both a feminist and a psychoanalytic point of view that Freud minimizes many issues crucial to feminism in his writing; such issues include the role of the Mother, the place of woman, and the centrality of the mother-infant relation (the pre-oedipal). Among the many studies that engage these issues in an illuminating way I would mention Madelon Sprengnether, *The Spectral Mother: Freud, Feminism, and Psychoanalysis* (Ithaca: Cornell University Press, 1990); Sarah Kofman, *The Enigma of Woman: Woman in Freud's Writings*, trans. Catherine Porter (Ithaca: Cornell University Press, 1985); and Christiane Oliver, *Jocasta's Children: The Imprint of the Mother*, trans. George Craig (London: Routledge, 1989).

12. There are subjective reasons for Freud's resistance to reading some of the elements in the Oedipus legend. One such element is adduced by Peter Rudnytsky, who records that at the same time that Freud uncovered the universal significance of the *Oedipus Rex*, he performed a significant "bungled action," recorded in the *Psychopathology of Everyday Life*:

> [While] engaged in his most intensive self-analysis, Freud regularly visited an elderly lady . . . for the purposes of giving her a morphine injection and eye lotion into her eye. On one occasion . . . he confused his two normally routine duties, and realized to his horror that he had put a few drops of morphine into her eye

Peter Rudnytsky, *Freud and Oedipus* (New York, Columbia University Press, 1987), 62.

The critic sees the action as both "a symbolic act of incest" and an "expression of unconscious hostility to women" (63–64). The second point interests me particularly because this comparatively minor yet vivid mistake reinforces what Freud's slightly remote and dismissive attitude toward woman implies most tellingly that there is a partial blindness in his own reading of the Oedipus tale.

13. At this point in *Beyond the Pleasure Principle* there is a kind of return to the *On Narcissism* position. In the 1914 essay, each of the dualistic drives is sexual, but they are divided between the familiar sexual drives, aimed at an object, and the narcissistic drives aimed at the ego. Narcissistic love can go two ways; some narcissistic energy can achieve a positive equilibrium between self-affirmation and movement outward toward the other, but if the energy-of-self-love remains trapped altogether within the ego we will "fall ill" ("On Narcissisms," *SE*, 14:85); a dominating secondary narcissism is one of the death-detours (*SE*, 14:69–102).

14. In a famous statement, Freud affirms that "the theory of the instincts is our mythology. Instincts are mythical entities, magnificent in their indefiniteness." "Anxiety and Instinctual Life," *SE*, 22:95.

15. Ernst Jones notes the history of a significant and misattributed term:

> "It is a little odd that Freud himself never, except in conversation, used for the death instinct the term *Thanatos*, one which has become so popular since. At first he used the terms 'death instinct' and 'destructive instinct' indiscriminately, alternating between them, but in his discussion with Einstein about war he made the distinction that the for-

mer is directed against the self and the latter, derived from it, is directed outwards. Stekely had in 1909 used the word *Thanatos* to signify a death-wish, but it was Federn who introduced it in the present context."

Ernst Jones, *The Life and Work of Sigmund Freud*, 3 vols, eds. Lionel Trilling and Stephen Marcus (New York: Basic Books, 1961), 3:295.

16. Among critics who have noted Freud's use of literary techniques in his creative work are Patrick J. Mahony, *Freud as a Writer*, expanded ed., (New Haven: Yale University Press, 1987); and Stephen Marcus, "Freud and Dora: Story, History, Case History," *In Dora's Case: Freud-Hysteria-Feminism*, eds. Charles Bernheimer and Claire Kahane (New York: Columbia University Press, 1985), 56–91.

17. Freud's major point in the essay is straightforward: "the death instinct which is operative in the organism—primal sadism—is identical with masochism" (*SE,* 19:164).

18. Most critics restrict their analyses to the *fort/da* game. See Mahony, *Freud as a Writer*, 39; Peter Gay, *Freud: A Life for Our Time* (New York: Norton, 1988), 399–400; and Leo Bersani, *The Freudian Body: Psychoanalysis and Art* (New York: Columbia University Press, 1986), 57–58.

19. Derrida emphasizes the autobiographical element, the familial interplay between Freud and his grandson, in both "Coming Into One's Own" (*Psychoanalysis & the Question of the Text*, ed. Geoffrey H. Hartman [Baltimore: Johns Hopkins University Press, 1978], 114–48), and in a later version of the same essay in *The Post Card,* 292–337.

20. Lacan writes of the boy's "games of occultation which Freud, in a flash of genius, revealed to us so that we might recognize in them that the moment in which desire becomes human is also that in which the child is born into language"(*Écrits* 103). Mahony provides us with a most elaborate discussion of the significance of the child's two utterances, e.g.: "The *f* and *t* of *fort*, are unvoiced dental consonants; they contrast with the *d* of *da* the world of presence. The phonation of the phonetically complex marked *d* involves going back and down in the mouth and vibrating the larynx; the resulting sound is thus 'more present' in the body" (40). Such an analysis raises the same questions as attempts to analyze prosody according to quantifiable phonetics.

21. D. W. Winnicott, like Lacan, may help us comprehend some of the ramifications of the game: for the boy seems to be playing variations on such Winnicottian concepts as the transitional object and potential space. See his *Playing and Reality* (Harmondsworth: Penguin, 1980).

22. Freud, "The Uncanny," *SE*, 13:249.

23. Socrates describes the special role of the spirit or "daemon" as "the medium of the prophetic arts" (*Symposium*, 202e, 203a); elsewhere he discusses the daemon as a kind of demigod, the good man who comes back from death with wisdom *(Cratylus*, 398b, c); also in this connection, see his discussion of the poet as inspired and possessed by the gods (*Ion*, 533, 534). All references to *Plato: The Collected Dialogues*, ed. Edith Hamilton and Huntington Cairns (Princeton: Princeton University Press, 1961).

24. *The Norton Anthology of World Masterpieces*, ed. Maynard Mack, et al., (Norton: New York, 1997), 633.

25. Lacanian texts important for the study of the Imaginary, Symbolic, and Real orders include "Function and Field of Speech and Language in Psychoanalysis" (*É*, 30–113) and "The Split Between the Eye and the Gaze," in *The Four Fundamental Concepts of Psycho-Analysis*, ed. Jacques-Alain Miller, trans. Alan Sheridan (New York: Norton, 1981), pp. 67–78.

Secondary sources are useful , perhaps essential, to the study of Lacan. For helpful critiques the reader is referred to Malcolm Bowie, *Lacan* (London: Fontana, 1991); Ellie Ragland-Sullivan, *Jacques Lacan and the Philosophy of Psychoanalysis*; *Speech and Language in Psychoanalysis: Jacques Lacan*, trans. with notes and commentary by Anthony Wilden (Baltimore: Johns Hopkins University Press, 1968); and John P. Muller and William J. Richardson, *Lacan and Language: A Reader's Guide to Écrits* (New York: International Universities Press, 1982).

26. In their indispensable *Language of Psycho-Analysis*, trans. Donald Nicholson-Smith (New York: Norton, 1973), Jean Laplanche and J.-B. Pontalis, provide three meanings for "foreclosure" (166–69), the most relevant of them for our purposes is based on a quotation of Freud: "[In an] energetic and successful . . . defence . . . the ego rejects the incompatible idea together with its affect and behaves as if the idea had never occurred to the ego at all." Freud, "The Neuro-Psychoses of Defence," *SE*, 3:58.

27. A significant discussion of the Real may be found in the "Tuché and Automaton" chapter of Lacan's *Four Fundamental Concepts* (53–64).

28. I. A. Richards, ed., *The Portable Coleridge*, New York: Penguin, 1978, p. 216. All Coleridge citations are to this edition.

Chapter 3. The Secret Affinities of Metapsychology and Romance: Freud's "Negation" and Keats's "Negative Capability"

1. Walter Benjamin, *Illuminations*, ed. Hannah Arendt; trans. Harry Zohn (New York: Schocken, 1969), 202.

2. Critics have discussed this notion in other contexts. For Avital Ronell, the fantasmatic refers to the haunted relationships of literary biography, specifically the way that Goethe, as the Bloomian father-ghost of German letters, disturbs the writing of Freud, Eckermann, and Benjamin. See *Dictations: On Haunted Writing* (Bloomington: Indiana University Press, 1986). The clinical role of the phantom—as a deleterious message from the "crypt," a transposition from the unconscious of the parent to the unconscious of the child—is a theme discussed in Nicolas Abraham, "Notes on the Phantom: A Complement to Freud's Metapsychology," *Critical Inquiry* 13, 2 (Winter 1987): 287–92.

3. Freud, *The Origins of Psychoanalysis: Letters to Wilhelm Fleiss*, trans. Eric Moshacher and James Strachey, intro. Steven Marcus (New York: Basic Books, 1977), 216. Hereafter cited as *OP*.

4. Jean Laplanche and J.-B. Pontalis, *The Language of Psycho-Analysis,* trans. Donald Nicholson-Smith (New York: Norton, 1973), 249, 249–50.

5. Gay, *Freud*, 363. Freud reveals his ambivalence toward both philosophy and literature by dismissing metaphysics as an illusory history of projected wishes, and deprecating fiction as a fantasy-replacement of reality, while still describing "philosophical insight" as his deepest "longing," and envying creative writers their effortless attainment of "secret knowledge" (Gay, *Freud*, 118).

6. Gay, *Freud*, 24.

7. Describing the continuing power of an inspiring predecessor, Ronell recalls the memorable Faustian quotation inscribing Goethe on the frontispiece of *The Psychopathology of Everyday Life*:

> "Now fills the air so many a haunting shape,
> That no one knows how best he may escape"
>
> (*SE*, 6:vii)

Her implication is that the epigraph introduces a scriptive phantom to the company of the psychic spectres behind human error—"haunting shapes" perplex discourse as well as experience (3–5).

8. Laplanche and Pontalis insist on the recognition of "*strictly* metapsychological texts" (*Language of Psycho-Analysis*, 250) that "underpin psycho-analytic psychology," developing fundamental "principles." Willfully disciplining Freud's "problem child," the authors resist metaphysics to impoverish metapsychology. Indeed there are fierce disagreements about the valid definition or interpretation (the choice of word already indicating the epistemic grounds of the argument) of metapsychology.

9. See Steven Reisner, "Reading the Metapsychology: Classical Revisionism, Seduction, and the Self in Freudian Psychoanalysis," *Psychoanalytic Psychology* 8, 4 (1991): 439–62.

10. See Freud, *The Origins of Psychoanalysis: Letters to Wilhelm Fleiss*, 246.

11. Commentators have noted the figurative role of the goddess Psyche within the internalization of natural experience which characterizes Keatsian romance. See James Engell, *The Creative Imagination: Enlightenment to Romanticism* (Cambridge: Harvard University Press, 1981), 291–92; Stanley M. Leavy, "John Keats's Psychology of the Creative Imagination," *The Psychoanalytic Quarterly* 39 (1970): 192–93; Brooke Hopkins, "Keats' *Negative Capability* and Winnicott's Creative Play, "*American Imago* 41 (Spring 1984): 98–99.

12. See "The Question of a *Weltanschauung*," *SE*, 22:159.

13. Gay, *Freud*, 372–73.

14. Freud admits that his comprehension of women is "obscure and full of gaps" ("Dissolution of the Oedipus Complex," *SE*, 19:177). Gay observes the paradox whereby Freud insists that the discovery of "the memory picture of [the] mother as it had dominated . . . since the beginning of childhood" is an overarching clinical imperative, yet, "almost deliberately evading this insight, Freud exile[s] mothers to the margins of his case histories" (Gay, *Freud*, 505).

15. Shoshana Felman, "To Open the Question," *Yale French Studies* 55–56 (1977): 10.

16. For the Hippolyte reference see: "*Commentaire Parle Sur La Verneinung De Freud*." Jacques Lacan, *Écrits*, Paris: Seuil, 1966; 881. Richard Boothby's statement appears in, *Death and Desire: Psychoanalytic Theory in Lacan's Return to Freud* (New York: Routledge, 1991), 189.

17. Leavy, "John Keats's Psychology of the Creative Imagination," 186.

18. The relationship of affect and negation remains problematical when negation reveals prohibited thoughts but not prohibited feelings. Feelings are more successful than ideas in resisting the entrance into consciousness.

19. Laplanche and Pontalis trace the complex (or self-contradictory) qualities associated with fantasy in Freud's writing. Originating in infantile hallucinations that substitute imaginary visions for real objects, psychoanalysis finds our first object of desire in an image from reality. "Fantasy and the Origins of Sexuality." *International Journal of Psychoanalysis* 49, 1 (1968): 15. But, the authors refer also to the contrasting notion of "psychical reality," which claims that the "original fantasy is first and foremost fantasy," (10). The authors make a useful distinction between Freud's preferred term *Phantasie* (translated as phantasy or

fantasy), the "world of the imagination," as opposed to the philosophical *Einbildungskraft*, "the faculty of imagining" (*Language of Psycho-Analysis*, 314).

20. Felman, "To Open the Question," 10; emphasis Felman's.

21. Stuart M. Sperry takes "sensation" as the determining concept of Keatsian poetics. It is of considerable interest that Keats's clearest definition of "sensation" is found among his notes as a medical student at Guy's hospital. Keats's ideas are as influenced by his medical-scientific studies as Freud's ideas are influenced by his literary-philosophical studies. *Keats the Poet* (1973; Princeton: Princeton University Press, 1994).

22. Hyder Edward Rollins, ed., *The Letters of John Keats 1814–21* (Cambridge: Harvard University Press, 1958), 1:185. Hereafter cited as *LJK*.

23. Letters relevant to negative capability include: To Benjamin Bailey, 22 November 1817, ("the authenticity of the imagination") hereafter cited as *L1*; To George and Tom Keats ("negative capability"), 21 or 27 December 1817, hereafter cited as *L2*; To Richard Woodhouse, 27 October 1818 (on the "Poetical Identity"), hereafter cited as *L3*; the complete reference will include the volume and page in Rollins, ed., *The Letters of John Keats*, and the letter number. Citations from other letters will refer to *LJK* only.

24. Walter Jackson Bate describes the informing power in the Keatsian imagination as an "objective idealism" because its visionary flights return to the natural world. *John Keats* (London: Oxford University Press, 1967), 238.

25. Taking "Mourning and Melancholia" as his specimen text, Leon Waldoff analyzes Keats's poetry in terms of the restitution of the lost mother. *Keats and the Silent Work of the Imagination* (Urbana: University of Illinois Press, 1985), 196.

26. "Freud and Literature," in Lionel Trilling, *The Liberal Imagination: Essays on Literature and Society*, ed. Lionel Trilling (New York: Doubleday, 1953), 45.

27. John Keats, *Complete Poems*, ed. Jack Stillinger (Cambridge: Harvard University Press, 1978). References are cited in the text.

28. In Susan Wolfson's reading, "La Belle Dame sans Merci" exemplifies the way romance may become "a field of explicit questions for its teller and its listener—and ultimately for its reader." *The Questioning Presence: Wordsworth, Keats, and the Interrogative Mode in Romantic Poetry* (Ithaca: Cornell University Press, 1986), 296.

Chapter 4. Revenge, Desire, and the Exclusion of Romance: *Frankenstein*

1. Mary Shelley, *Frankenstein, or the Modern Prometheus*, ed. M. K. Joseph (Oxford: Oxford University Press, 1980), "Introduction," 5, italics mine. Subsequent references will refer to section (introduction, chapter, or letter) and page number. Letters to be cited by roman numerals and chapters by arabic numerals. Sequential citings of the same reference to page number only.

2. See, for example, Jane Dunn's biography, *Moon in Eclipse: A Life of Mary Shelley* (New York: St. Martin's 1978), 21, 28.

3. For a reading of the novel that discerns enormous repressed aggression within Shelley toward father and husband see Ulrich Knoepflmacher, "Thoughts on the Aggression of Daughters" in *The Endurance of Frankenstein*, ed. George

Levine and U. C. Knoepflmacher (Berkeley: University of California Press, 1977), 88–122.

4. Ellen Moers is one of many writers, critics, and biographers who refer to the double injury Shelley associated with the experience of birth. Her own mother, the writer and feminist Mary Wollstonecraft, died a few days after giving birth to her, while, at the time of the writing of *Frankenstein*, Shelley had lost a child, an unnamed daughter, a few days after giving birth (she was to lose two more). For Mary Shelley, giving birth and being born were both associated with irreparable trauma.

5. Ann Mellor, *Mary Shelley: Her Life, Her Fiction, Her Monsters* (New York: Routledge, 1989), 59–60.

6. Barbara Johnson, "My Monster/My Self," *Diacritics* 12 (1982): 3–4.

7. See, for example, Beth Newman, "Narratives of Seduction and the Seductions of Narrative: The Frame Structure of *Frankenstein,*" *ELH* 53 (1986): 144, 154, 159.

8. Thus Mary Poovey reads *Frankenstein* as a novel that "calls into question, not the social conventions that inhibit creativity, but rather the egotism that Mary Shelley associates with the artist's monstrous self-assertion." Poovey, *The Proper Lady and the Woman Writer: Ideology as Style in the Works of Mary Wollstonecraft, Mary Shelley, and Jane Austen* (Chicago: University of Chicago Press, 1984), 122. Elsewhere Poovey emphasizes the "fatal kinship of the imagination, nature, and death," in the novel. "My Hideous Progeny: Mary Shelley and the Feminization of Romanticism," *PMLA* 95, 3 (1980): 336. Mellor argues that "Mary Shelley perceived that the Romantic ideology [with its] . . . effort to marry the finite and the infinite . . . too frequently entailed a sublime indifference to the progeny of . . . that marriage" (*Mary Shelley*, 80) . Margaret Homans discusses the "subtlety" of a strategy whereby Shelley "disguise[s] her criticism of [romantic poetry] . . . to appear to be a docile wife and 'devout listener' to the conversations of important men." *Bearing the Word: Language and Female Experience in Nineteenth-Century Women's Writing* (Chicago: Chicago University Press, 1986), 116.

9. The phrase is from Marc Rubinstein, "'My Accursed Origin': The Search for the Mother in Frankenstein," *Studies in Romanticism* 15 (Spring 1976): 172.

10. This aspect of Victor clearly reflects Percy Shelley and has been taken as an aspect of Mary's conscious subversion of Percy. Yet, an earlier study sees Victor's visionary idealism as evidence of Mary's passionate admiration of her husband. See Christopher Small, *Ariel Like a Harpy: Shelley, Mary, and Frankenstein* (London: Gollanz, 1972), 100–21.

11. Mellor demonstrates that the 1818 *Frankenstein* is written in a more specific and compelling style than the 1831 version, and that Percy imposed on the novel elements of repetition and flatness, the empty idealization that one might describe as the *Alastor*-like quality (*Mary Shelley*, 57–68, 170–76, 219–24).

12. Interesting comparisons of *Frankenstein* and Alastor appear in Homans, *Bearing the Word*, 103–9, 113–14; I discuss Alastor in terms relevant to the present examination in "Woman as Fatal Other," 60–68.

13. For two different discussions of the family romance, see Freud's brief article on the subject, *SE*, 9:235–44, and the more compelling remarks in a letter of 1897 (*Origins of Psychoanalysis*, 256–57).

14. "Some Early Unpublished Letters of Freud," *International Journal of Psycho-Analysis* 50 (1969): 424.

15. The reader is referred to Goethe's "Nature," discussed in my chapter on "Negation and Negative Capability," above.

16. According to one philosophical textbook "*Naturphilosophie* saw the whole of reality underpinned by certain basic archetypes. . . . Significant in such areas as the newly developing theory of electricity, *Naturphilosophie* made its greatest impact in the biological sciences." *The Oxford Companion to Philosophy*, ed. Ted Honderich (Oxford: Oxford University Press, 1995), 608. Victor Frankenstein, like Mary Shelley, liberates Promethean electricity in the deformed form of the Creature.

Harold Bloom, in "Frankenstein or The Modern Prometheus," identifies the fiery-electrical element with increased awareness, a romance goal that turns to "dejection" because "all Romantic horrors are diseases of excessive consciousness, of the self unable to bear the self." *The Ringers in the Tower* (Chicago: University of Chicago Press, 1971), 127. If so, the Prometheus figure in the novel reverses itself to take the form of the Creature: Victor suffers from the confusions of the repressed consciousness.

17. Gay, *Freud*, p. 34. This material is taken from the chapter called "The Lure of Research" in Gay's biography (*Freud*, 22–36), itself based on Freud's "Autobiographical Study," (*SE*, 20: 3–76).

18. Cf. Lacan: "The phallus is the privileged signifier of that mark in which the role of the logos is joined with the advent of desire" (*É*, 287). I take this to mean: the phallus unlocks the languages of desire.

19. Percy Shelley's *Mt. Blanc* presents natural devastation as that which inspires an imagination it simultaneously resists. The unresponsive landscape yields poetic benefits in the imaginative demand for response. Shelley explores the mountain's ravaged face, finding compensation for terror in vision. Beyond "Silence and solitude," destruction and ruin elicit "the human mind's imaginings" (ll. 144, 43). From the mount's "hideous[ly] . . . shapes" (ll. 69–70) Shelley meditates on "the old Earthquake-daemon" (l. 72) mother of disintegration. The "silent snow" brings rumination on its preceding "sea of fire," (ll. 74, 73), the metaphor for transforming energy. All references to Shelley's poetry cite *Shelley: Poetical Works*, ed. Thomas Hutchinson, 2nd ed. (Oxford: Oxford University Press, 1970), 532–35.

Victor, however, is disoriented by desolated views; his feeling of futility inspires a return to the composure of the mountain's snowy face. The image pacifying the scene repeats the tropes of *Mt. Blanc*, but now reversed: Victor replaces Percy Shelley's sea of fire with a "sea or . . . vast river of ice, wound among . . . mountains" (*Frankenstein*,10:98). The frozen landscape suggests the limitations of his vision, his incapacity to integrate the disruptive forces in nature. The narrative voices of Victor Frankenstein and Percy Shelley share a sense of awe before monuments of the natural, but diverge in regard to landscapes of destruction. In their approaches to natural ruin, *Mt. Blanc* and *Frankenstein* are dramatically opposed.

20. Jeffrey Berman writes about Victor's many narcissistic traits with almost-clinical persuasiveness. Berman takes the exaggerated size of the creature as a physical expression of Victor's grandiosity, noting that the scientist "remains fixated on the magnitude of his creation," *Narcissism and the Novel* (New York: New York University Press, 1990), 61.

The startling apparition of the Creature on Mt. Blanc suggests another way of looking at his disfigured grandeur. Mary Shelley places a grotesque figure at the center of a romantic landscape. Indeed, the Creature violates a series of vivid romantic scenes that recall Coleridge's glacial seas as well as Wordsworth's snowy mountains. The juxtaposition reveals the hidden intimacy between the sublime and the grotesque: the literalization of enormity has an effect antithetic to the imagination of enormity. Literalization provides a similar key to the distinction between the romantic and the gothic. Romanticism achieves invisible influence within the mind or heart . But gothic effects, as Ellen Moers points out, are physical and address "the body itself" "Female Gothic," in *The Endurance of Frankenstein*, Levine and Knoepflmacher, 77. Arguably, then, sublime is to romantic as grotesque is to gothic. Cf. Aryeh Sachs, "The grotesque is . . . *the inverse of the ideal*", *The English Grotesque: An Anthology from Langland to Joyce* (Jerusalem: Israel University Press, 1969), xxxi–xxxii, italics Sachs.

21. Note Lacan's distinguishing of the full word (*la parole pleine*) from the empty word (*la parole vide*) according to whether the subject is capable of "the assumption of his desire." Jacques Lacan, *Speech and Language in Psychoanalysis*, trans. with notes and commentary Anthony Wilden (Baltimore: Johns Hopkins University Press, 1968), 9–27.

22. Cf. Peter Brooks on the Creature's confrontation with his dread reflection: "This speculary *cogito*, where the Monster witnesses his outward identity as alien to his inner desire, estranged, determined by the view and judgment of the Other, clinches the importance of language as the symbolic order that must compensate for nature." "Godlike Science/Unhallowed Arts: Language, Nature, and Monstrosity," in *Endurance of Frankenstein*, 210.

23. Fire, thus, represents the emotional, instinctual, but above all intellectual forces that take the Creature beyond Victor. Gaston Bachelard connects Promethean fire to the child's ideological rebellion against fathers and teacher to assert that "the Promethean complex is the Oedipus complex of the life of the intellect." *The Psychoanalysis of Fire*, trans. Alan C. M. Ross (London: Routledge, 1964), 12.

24. In one of the few images that successfully bridges the fictional *Frankenstein* with a film version of *Frankenstein*, we may picture Elsa Lancaster in *Bride of Frankenstein* as representing the female monster. (Why does the female image translate more successfully than the male in this case?)

25. Slavoj Žižek, *The Metastases of Enjoyment* (London: Verso, 1994), 116. Žižek's vivid conceptualizations on this subject derive from the Lacanian notion of *le corps morcelé*, the body in bits and pieces. Our physical self-conception is fundamentally fractured; it depends on fleeting mirror-images for an illusory sense of unity (Lacan, *Speech and Language in Psychoanalysis*, 174).

Chapter 5. From Demonic Romance to Satanic Myth: *Wuthering Heights*

1. Two critiques of desire in literature take *Wuthering Heights* as an exemplary text. For Leo Bersani, desire expresses the deconstructive tendency of instincts which shatter the illusion of a coherent identity by the force of perverse and violent demand. His reading of Brontë's novel bases itself on the clash between familial complacency (the novel aims toward the peaceful reconciliation of Earnshaws and Lintons) and the drive of desire toward radical metamorphosis (Heathcliff's disruptive being allows Catherine's entrance into inhuman identities). Bersani, *A Future for Astyanax: Character and Desire in Literature* (Boston: Little, Brown, 1976). Disagreeing with Bersani by making a case for retrieving reason from the ravages of desire, Eugene Goodheart, nevertheless, takes a related position. He argues that the distinguishing element in Brontë is a transcendent, yet incestuous (transcendent *because* incestuous) imagination: "The deepest psy-

chic and cultural prohibition is the incest taboo. . . . With unequalled intensity in modern literature, Emily Brontë imagines desire breaking through the barrier of insatiability to an ultimate satisfaction in death." Goodheart, *Desire and Its Discontents* (New York: Columbia University Press, 1991), 109–10. Bersani and Goodheart each refer to a language of desire which escapes the social restrictions on desire. Nancy Armstrong suggests that Brontë widens the field of expressed desire when she protests against "the main presupposition on which most Brontë criticism rests, namely, the curiously tenacious belief that writing and desire are ontologically different and ideologically opposed." *Desire and Domestic Fiction: A Political History of the Novel* (Oxford: Oxford University Press, 1987), 189. Jay Clayton—more sympathetic to historicist than psychoanalytic approaches—provides an overview of these issues in "Narrative and Theories of Desire," in *Critical Inquiry* 16, 1 (Autumn 1989): 33–53. My own reading of the theme (or power) in Brontë concerns the way her language combines the expression and elusiveness of desire (what is said reveals what cannot be said): *Wuthering Heights* partly captures an uncapturable object in a continuing approach.

2. Emily Brontë, *Wuthering Heights*, 3rd ed., ed. William M. Sale, Jr. and Richard J. Dunn (New York: Norton, 1990), 5. Hereafter cited in the text by chapter and page number.

3. Beth Newman notes that Lockwood is threatened by the reciprocal glance, "Lockwood's account of his abortive flirtation intimates a psychic structure whereby a woman who 'looks a return' at a man threatens to immobilize him." Newman brings in the archetypal Medusa whose paralyzing "evil eye" appropriates the gaze from the (culturally dominant) male. "'The Situation of the Looker-On': Gender, Narration, and Gaze in *Wuthering Heights*," *PMLA* 105, 5 (October 1990): 1030–31. It might be added that the Gorgon's serpentine hair (with its snakes' eyes) contributes to her phallic and scopic power.

4. Steven Vine notes that the etymology of "wuthering" comprises "trembling" as well as "attack," its turmoil originating within as well as without. Finding striking semantic significance in aural repetition he traces "the Wuther of the Other," the strife created in Catherine and Heathcliff when each of the lovers remains punishingly separate from (yet *in*) the other. "The Wuther of the Other in *Wuthering Heights*," *Nineteenth Century Literature* 49, 3 (December 1994): 340.

5. Freud's discussion of the structure of beating-fantasies (and the gender of the one fantasizing) may apply to the relation between Emily Brontë, as implied author, Heathcliff, and Lockwood: "The person beating is never the father, but is either left undetermined . . . or turns . . . into a representative of the father. The figure of the child who is producing the beating-phantasy no longer itself appears in it. . . . Most frequently it is boys who are being beaten (in girls' phantasies), but none of them is personally known to the subject." "A Child is Being Beaten," *SE*, 17:185–86.

6. See Sandra Gilbert and Susan Gubar, *The Madwoman in the Attic: The Woman Writer and the Nineteenth-Century Imagination* (New Haven: Yale University Press, 1979), 248–308. Reading *Wuthering Heights* as a "strong" (showing Bloomian originality) romance reverses the (patronizing) critical tradition that identifies women and romance in their common (social and literary) disenfranchisement. Laurie Langbauer bases her sustained consideration of related issues on the various ways that male novelists and critics negate (in the Freudian sense) women and romance to valorize the novel as the preferred genre of patriarchy. *Women and Romance: The Consolations of Gender in the English Novel* (Ithaca: Cornell University Press, 1990).

7. Brontë's elusive biography reveals a final connection between the narrator at the center of the narrative and the author at its circumference. Catherine Earnshaw specifies a quantity of lost time: "It's twenty years . . . I've been a waif for twenty years" (3:20). Within the narrative twenty years seems arbitrary—no more precise than a rough average of the twenty-four years from Old Earnshaw's death and the seventeen years from Catherine's death. But the twenty year hiatus appears more compelling as Brontëan autobiography. Twenty years after the deaths of her two older sisters, Maria and Elizabeth, Brontë begins writing her single novel: it is as though *Wuthering Heights* were an imaginative struggle to recuperate beloved objects from the space of lost time.

8. Deconstructive readings find neither a unifying interpretation nor an authorial voice in the novel. Such interpretations are provided by J. Hillis Miller ("*Wuthering Heights*: Repetition and the 'Uncanny'," *Fiction and Repetition* [Cambridge: Harvard University Press, 1982], 42–72; and Carol Jacobs, At the Threshold of Interpretation, *Uncontainable Romanticism: Shelley, Brontë, Kleist* (Baltimore: Johns Hopkins University Press, 1989), 61–81. Both critics take *Wuthering Heights* as an examination of the way language negates and inverts ad infinitum its own capacity for meaning. The deconstructive view, "the secret truth about *Wuthering Heights* . . . is that there is no secret truth (Miller, "*Wuthering Heights*," 51) is a presupposition of most contemporary writing on the novel. Still, it remains doubtful that *Wuthering Heights* commits itself only to non-commitment.

9. Daniel Rubey, "The Troubled House of Oedipus and Chrétein's Neo-Tristan: Re-writing the Mythologies of Desire," in *The Persistence of Myth: Psychoanalytic and Structural Perspectives*, ed. Peter L. Rudnytsky (New York: The Guilford Press, 1988), 69. This volume, with the same pagination, appears as an issue of *The Psychoanalytic Review* 75, 1 (Spring 1988).

10. Gilbert and Gubar, *Madwoman in the Attic*, 284.

11. Felman writes that in Western culture literature has given the repressed subjectivity of madness a voice, while madness has given literature the voice of its full subversive power. *Writing and Madness (Literature/ Philosophy/Psychoanalysis)*, trans. Noel Evans (Ithaca: Cornell University Press, 1985).

12. The essay entitled *Le Papillon*, one of several expository pieces Brontë wrote for Ms. Heger at the Pensionne Heger in Brussels, includes statements like: "*La nature est un problème inexplicable, elle existe sur un principle de destruction; il faut que tout être soit l'instrument infatigable de mort aux autres*." Winifred Gérin, *Emily Brontë* (Oxford: Oxford University Press, 1971), 272.

13. See Philip K. Wion, "The Absent Mother in Emily Brontë's *Wuthering Heights*," *American Imago* 42, 2 (1985): 143–64.

14. In a nearly forgotten but important monograph, Joseph C. Rhinegold traces the ways in which the maternal becomes threatening and may be perceived as murderous. *The Mother, Anxiety, and Death: The Catastrophic Death Complex* (Boston: Little, Brown, 1967).

15. Useful discussions of the relationship between repetition and revenge are offered in the chapter entitled "When Words Prevail Not: Grief, Revenge, and Language in Kyd and Shakespeare," in Peter M. Sacks, *The English Elegy: Studies in the Genre from Spenser to Yeats* (Baltimore: Johns Hopkins University Press, 1985), 64–89, and throughout the argument—with its sustained consideration of death and doubling—of John Irwin's *Doubling and Incest, Repetition and Revenge: A Speculative Reading of Faulkner* (Baltimore: Johns Hopkins University Press, 1985).

16. In an application of the Kristevan dialectic between the abject and the sublime to *Wuthering Heights*, Marci Gordon observes that Catherine and Heathcliff are *both* subject to "abjection"; each goes through a process of physical degradation and psychic-spiritual exaltation: "Neither Catherine nor Heathcliff deliberately starves him/herself . . . in an effort to discard the body in favor of a purely spiritual existence. Rather, their longing to breakthrough the impediment of the body leads to devouring of self, and each other as 'other'." Marci M. Gordon, "Kristeva's Abject and Sublime in Brontë's *Wuthering Heights*," *Literature and Psychology* 34, 3 (1988): 47–48.

17. Cf. the reference to Slavoj Žižek in chapter 4, note 25.

18. "Among these imagoes are some that represent the elective vectors of aggressive intentions, which they provide with an efficacity that might be called magical. These are the images of castration, mutilation, dismemberment, dislocation, evisceration, devouring, bursting open of the body" (*É.*, 11).

Chapter 6. From Child of the Imaginary to the Real Life of a Woman: *Jane Eyre*

1. Influenced by Roman Jacobson's division of the two ways in which we make meaning in language, Thomas Weiskel makes a distinction between the Positive Sublime, based on the metaphorical axis, where an absence of meaning in natural grandeur impels us toward *substitution*, or *other meaning*, and the Negative Sublime, where an excess of meaning impels us toward *contiguity*, or *further meaning*. Citing Lacan, Weiskel designates the Positive Sublime as Imaginary and the Negative Sublime as Symbolic. *The Romantic Sublime: Studies in the Structure and Psychology of Transcendence* (1976; Rpt. Baltimore: Johns Hopkins University Press, 1986), 150–51.

2. Charlotte Brontë, *Jane Eyre*, 2nd ed., ed. Richard J. Dunn (New York: Norton, 1987), 5; ch. 1. Hereafter cited in the text by chapter and page numbers.

3. Nature defeating our expectations of nature is one of the themes in Mellor's comprehensive study, *English Romantic Irony* (Cambridge: Harvard University Press, 1980).

4. Charles Rosen and Henri Zenner remind us that Bewick was not just an illustrator but an interpretive artist; thus, Jane views not just a reflection but a conception of the natural. *Romanticism and Realism: The Mythology of Nineteenth-Century Art* (New York: Norton, 1984), 1–7, 71–96. Similarly, Andrew Griffin recognizes that the Bewick text and Jane's rumination on it constitute a response not to just to the phenomenon of ice but "to the idea of ice itself." "Fire and Ice in Frankenstein," *Endurance of Frankenstein*, 52.

5. For John Kucich, repression is a positive Victorian value and the denial of self is a kind of desire. *Repression in Victorian Fiction: Charlotte Brontë, George Eliot, and Charles Dickens* (Berkeley: University of California Press, 1987).

6. In his *Fragment of an Analysis of a Case of Hysteria*, Freud examines in detail the parallels between jewel case and vagina (*SE*, 7:69–70). Elaine Showalter notes that "the red-room has strong associations with the adult female body; Mrs. Reed . . . is a widow in her prime." *A Literature of Their Own: From Charlotte Brontë to Doris Lessing* (London: Virago, 1978), 115.

7. Jenijoy LaBelle traces the series of Jane's "disturbing" confrontations in the mirror (with herself, with Bertha Mason), to conclude, rightly I think, that she can

"triumph over her mirror image, but the man in her life must of necessity perceive and thus conceive of her in nonvisual terms." *Herself Beheld: The Literature of the Looking Glass* (Ithaca: Cornell University Press, 1988), 138–40. (Hence one of the many advantages of Rochester's final but not total blindness.)

8. See Diane Sadoff for a reading of the return of the dead father—the empowering Father as bringer of the Law—in Charlotte Brontë. Influenced by Helene Moglen's study of Brontë, Sadoff makes much of the master-servant element in the relationship between Jane and Rochester; both critics stress the sadomasochistic elements, as they see it, within that pairing. Yet, the dynamic between Jane and Rochester bases itself on a developing exploration of the possibilities of balance between man and woman—a possibility realized at Ferndean. Diane Sadoff, *Monsters of Affection: Dickens, Eliot, and Brontë on Fatherhood* (Baltimore: Johns Hopkins University Press, 1982), 130–42; Helene Moglen, *Charlotte Brontë: The Self Conceived* (Madison: University of Wisconsin Presss, 1984), 105–51.

9. Paula Sullivan isolates such motifs in "Fairy Tale Elements in *Jane Eyre*," *Journal of Popular Culture* 12 (1978): 61–74.

10. David Cowart discusses "Oedipal Dynamics in *Jane Eyre*" in *Literature and Psychology* 31, 1 (1981): 33–38. In a more recent study Judith Mitchell combines a Freudian Lacanian reading of oedipal themes with a focus on feminist issues. *The Stone and the Scorpion: The Female Subject of Desire in the Novels if Charlotte Brontë, George Eliot, and Thomas Hardy* (Westport, CT: Greenwood, 1994).

11. For Lacan's identification of fire and the Real, see *Four Fundamental Concepts of Psycho-Analysis,* ed. Jacques-Alain Miller, trans. Alan Sheridan (New York: Norton, 1981), 59; I discuss this connection in relation to Freud, Lacan, and Lawrence on pp. 212–20 of the present study.

12. *Totem and Taboo* is discussed, also, in greater detail in the chapter on Lawrence on pp. 217–18 of the present critique. To avoid repetition, I refer the reader to the more substantial analysis.

13. The parallels between the Jane–Mrs. Reed relationship and the Catherine–Nelly Dean relationship are striking.

14. This would be a crossover from the Kristevan semiotic (a feminization of the Imaginary, a return-before-the-return to pre-oedipal and pre-visual experience) to the Lacanian Real. See Julia Kristeva, *Revolution in Poetic Language*, trans. Margaret Waller (New York: Columbia University Press, 1984), 25–26. Lori Langbauer, both critiquing and affirming Kristeva, finds an element of the semiotic woven into romance. She brings forward that element by noting that Mary Wollstonecraft, who writes not as a friend of the romance genre, identifies romance with the maternal (*Women and Romance*, 100–101). Diane Sadoff appears to accept this equivalence (*Monsters of Affection*, 124).

15. For a condensed and useful discussion of Jane in relation to archetypal and fictional feminine role-models, see Adrienne Rich, "*Jane Eyre*: The Temptations of a Motherless Woman," in *Jane Eyre*, 462–75.

16. See the references to "breast" and "part-objects" in R. D. Hinshelwood, *A Dictionary of Kleinian Thought* (London: Free Association, 1991), 238, 378–80.

17. The Freudian *locus classicus* on identification is "The Dissolution of the Oedipus Complex," wherein, interestingly, Freud admits his helplessness before the problem of woman, (*SE*, 19:173–82). Nancy Chodorow makes extensive and influential rectifications of Freudian theory in relation to the development of the young girl, one of her major supplements pertaining to the girl's continued connection to the mother as opposed to the boy's sharply differentiated autonomy.

The girl's connection is humanly enhancing because it strengthens her capacity to form and sustain relationships. Chodorow, *The Reproduction of Mothering: Psychoanalysis and the Sociology of Gender* (Berkeley: University of California Press, 1978). In Jane Eyre the need for connection between mother and daughter would work and pertain to Jane's lack of a mother and the need to compensate for that lack.

18. Dickens, *David Copperfield*, ed. Jerome H. Buckley (New York: Norton, 1990), 119.

19. My article on "Woman as Fatal Other" discusses the feminine suggestions of romantic landscape. John Maynard provides a detailed discussion of the landscape of sexuality in relation to Ferndean: "There is a sense of moving ever more deeply into a highly fertile, darkly withdrawn place; male and female symbols of tree and enclosure suggest fulfillment and unification of sexual opposites." *Charlotte Brontë and Sexuality* (Cambridge: Cambridge University Press, 1984), 141. His placing Ferndean as a location of infinite recess, which evokes hints of both feminine sexuality and sexual fulfillment, indirectly evokes Lockwood entering more and more deeply into the recesses of Wuthering Heights. In Lockwood's case the entrance is sublimated into imaginative curiosity—and in a suggestion of Lockwood's failure of nerve he violently opposes imaginative climaxes.

20. See Anne K. Mellor, ed., *Romanticism and Feminism* (Bloomington: Indiana University Press, 1988) for a collection of essays that define the theoretical and practical meeting points between the two movements.

21. Jung writes of theriomorphic (bestial) or semi-theriomorphic (sphinxes, mermaids, etc.) imagery in relation to a repressed animal instinct. He claims that "animals which represent the instincts . . . appear . . . as *attributes* of the parents . . . the father as a bull." *Symbols of Transformation: An Analysis of a Prelude to a Case of Schizophrenia*, trans. R. F. C. Hull, 2nd ed. (Princeton: Princeton University Press, 1967), 179, 181. I think that Jungian ideas reside as an unacknowledged ghostly presence in Lacanian thought. Certainly the Lacanian Imaginary owes a good deal to the Jungian imago.

22. See Bruno Bettelheim on "The Animal-Groom" cycle of fairy-tales. *The Uses of Enchantment: The Meaning and Importance of Fairy Tales* (1975; Rpt. New York: Vintage, 1989), 282–309.

23. Robert Heilman has made related points about the dialectic of the gothic and the anti-gothic in Brontë. "Charlotte Brontë's 'New Gothic,'" *Jane Eyre*, 458–61.

24. Heilman makes interesting observations about Brontë's "moon-magical" motifs in "Charlotte Brontë, Reason, and the Moon," *Nineteenth-Century Fiction* 14, 4 (March 1960): 302. For a full-length discussion of the moon in Lawrence see my study *The Moon's Dominion: Narrative Dichotomy and Female Dominance in Lawrence's Earlier Novels* (Rutherford, NJ: Fairleigh Dickinson University Press, 1981).

25. Providing the political background to the crushing psychological reality of the governess-vocation, Mary Poovey provides a historicist-psychoanalytical reading of Brontë's novel in "The Anathematized Race: The Governess and *Jane Eyre*," in Richard Feldstein and Judith Roof, eds., *Feminism and Psychoanalysis* (Ithaca: Cornell University Press, 1989), 230–54.

26. Lawrence Moser makes some interesting connections between the fantastic, the surreal and psychic self-revelation (the involuntary depiction that is *not* a self-portrait) in "From Portrait to Person: A Note on the Surrealistic in *Jane Eyre*," *Nineteenth-Century Fiction* 20, 3 (December 1965): 275–81.

27. Laplanche and Pontalis define psychic reality as: "whatever in the subject's psyche presents a consistency and resistance comparable to those displayed by material reality; fundamentally, what is involved here is unconscious desire and its associated phantasies" (*Language of Psycho-Analysis*, 363).

28. Coleridge, "Dejection: An Ode" l. 95.

29. Gilbert and Gubar, *Madwoman in the Attic*, 360.

30. In this sense there is a connection between Lacan and the Platonic parable of the cave: to see the sun is to change the world.

31. See William Wordsworth, *The Prelude* (1850), bk. 1, ll. 67–100, *in The Prelude 1799, 1805, 1850,* eds. Jonathan Wordsworth, et al., (New York: Norton 1979), 33, 35.

32. In her new-historical reading of the rise of fiction by and about women, Nancy Armstrong is wary of the view that sees domesticity as feminine self-marginalization. Yet she may underestimate the radicalism that the foregrounding of the domestic as a supreme value had in Brontë's time; for Brontë domesticity entails a conscious rejection of aggressive or sacrificial male ambition (*Desire and Domestic Fiction*, 3–27).

33. Freud's point is that there is no hominess without un/hominess, and that the domestic is the most pregnant residence of the deathly. "The Uncanny" *SE*, 17:219–226.

34. Ruth Yeazell defends the device of the summons against charges of its being "Gothic claptrap," by finding its "truth is the truth of the psyche." "More True than Real: *Jane Eyre*'s 'Mysterious Summons'." *Nineteenth-Century Fiction* 29 (1974–75): 128.

35. Nina Auerbach dismisses the purported balanced resolution of *Jane Eyre*: "Jane's marriage to Rochester at Ferndean and her final home there seem less a synthesis of . . . two worlds than a partial conquest of one by the other. . . . Rochester is 'stone blind,' a 'sightless block.'" *Romantic Imprisonment: Women and Other Glorified Outcasts* (New York: Columbia University Press, 1986), 203. But Auerbach makes her case by very selective quotation. John Maynard's reminder that "Rochester appears, despite the concentration on his debility, as a potent force appropriate to this sexual stage" (*Charlotte Brontë and Sexuality*, 141) seems more congruent with the text. Moglen damns the resolution of the ending with faint praise: "Rochester's mutilation is . . . the necessary counterpart of Jane's independence: the terrible condition of a relationship of equality" (*Charlotte Brontë*, 142). But accusing Jane (or Brontë) of unmanning Rochester has become a critical commonplace, or consensus, found in handbooks like Walter Allen's *The English Novel: A Short Critical History* (New York: Dutton, 1954), 216.

36. See chapter 4, note 25.

Chapter 7. Space, the Imaginary, and the Death-of-the-Mother: *Sons and Lovers*

1. See the division of the child's playing into a series of games in my chapter on "Beyond the Pleasure Principle," above.

2. The traditional reading of this scene describes it as a merger between the self and a vital nature identified with "phallic power," (Dorothy Van Ghent, *The English Novel: Form and Function* [New York: Harper, 1953], 249), or "the dark

forces of life," (Mark Spilka *The Love Ethic of D. H. Lawrence* [Bloomington: Indiana University Press, 1955], 44).

3. Ben-Ephraim, *Moon's Dominion*, 91–92.

4. Julia Kristeva, *Revolution in Poetic Language*, trans. Margaret Waller (New York: Columbia University Press, 1984), 25–26.

5. Kristeva, *Revolution*, 25–30.

6. The concept is not used explicitly by Kristeva but, according to theorist Michael Payne, is implied clearly by her discussion: "The chorion . . . defines the Semiotic space of the other within the mother, and within its double structure the first communication between the fetus and m(other) occurs." Payne, *Reading Theory: An Introduction to Lacan, Derrida, and Kristeva* (Oxford: Blackwell, 1993), 69.

7. The containing emptiness of surrounding space, an invisible yet inescapable container of things, the untraceable element within which everything traceable is traced, recalls the Lacanian notion of "reality." See Samuel Weber, *Return to Freud: Jacques Lacan's Dislocation of Psychoanalysis*, trans. Michael Levine (Cambridge: Cambridge University Press, 1991), 108. This reality (not to be confused with the Real), the background for the Imaginary and the Symbolic, identifies the unconscious itself as a reservoir of potentiality having the relationship to the action and thought of conscious being that Saussure's *langue* has to his *parole*.

8. Malcolm Bowie finds the Imaginary in "the order of mirror-images, identifications, and reciprocities. It is the dimension of experience in which the individual seeks not merely to placate the Other but to dissolve his otherness by becoming his counterpart." *Lacan* (Cambridge: Harvard University Press, 1991), 92.

9. Kristeva, *Revolution*, 9.

10. Wilden provides one way to conceive the energetic field set up between people on the level of the Imaginary. "The Imaginary death struggle between egos is how things are, rather than how they have to be, whereas the subject's profoundest desire to be 'One' again (to control the Other to whom he becomes subjected) is totally and absolutely irreducible. It is this desire for what is really annihilation (non-difference) that makes human beings human" (*Speech and Language in Psychoanalysis*, 190–91). Ragland-Sullivan sees the Imaginary as an ongoing process: "Imaginary processes are among those that structure mind through formalizable laws, such as projection and absorption, introjection and expulsion, substitution and displacement, and so on" (*Jacques Lacan*, 138). In an additional comment pertinent to the reading of Lawrence, Ragland-Sullivan points out that "the Imaginary is not reducible to the *moi*, the libido, or Desire, nor is it limited to the visual or the unconscious. The Imaginary dimension in being announces itself by inferring . . . a lack of individuation in identity" (140).

11. The distinction between Imaginary and Symbolic comes out most clearly in Lacan's reading of the *fort/da* game. The use of the syllables fort! da! to replace the absent mother (absent in body, voice, and gaze) is the passing to the further order, for "the moment in which desire becomes human is also that in which the child is born into language" (*É*, 103). Language is the law of the father: ambivalent, transformative, prohibitive.

12. In his biography of Lawrence John Worthen discusses the conflicts between Lawrence's parents, Lydia and Arthur Lawrence, in relation to language. Lydia proudly spoke "the king's English," a result of her middle-class background, and scorned Arthur's lower-class dialect. Arthur's imitations of standard English were greeted by the "laughter" of his son and wife. *D. H. Lawrence: The Early Years 1885–1912* (Cambridge: Cambridge University Press, 1991), 61.

13. Earl J. Ingersoll traces the Imaginary in Walter and the Symbolic in Gertrude back to the early relationship between the parents. Gertrude is attracted to Walter's face and body, while Walter is attracted to her demeanor and language. See "Gender and Language in *Sons and Lovers,*" *The Midwest Quarterly* 37, 4 (Summer 1996): 434–47.

14. Critics have written on the sun-sequence in terms of masculinity, reminiscent of Lacan for whom the Phallus is the signifier of desire. Thus L. D. Clarke notes that Gertrude wraps "the child in her motherhood" to prevent its belonging to "the sun or the orbit of life." Clarke, *The Minoan Distance: The Symbolism of Travel in D. H. Lawrence* (Tucson: University of Arizona Press, 1980), 58. Jack F. Stewart explores the cultural ramifications of sun and fire in Lawrence, noting their identification with the cultures and peoples of the South, as water and ice reflect the cold North, and the "dialectic of North and South becomes a dialectic of life and death." Stewart "The Vital Art of Lawrence and Van Gogh," *D. H. Lawrence Review* 19 (1987): 135. Wilden points out that the sun/son homophone creates an indistinguishable union in speech if not in writing: "if the schizophrenic says 'I'm the black sun,' the psychiatrist may well catch the significant ambiguity of 'sun,' but how would the literary author spell it?" (*Speech and Language in Psychoanalysis*, 185).

15. Daniel Dervin connects the destruction of Arabella with "primitive, acted-out identifications with the sexual father." *A "Strange Sapience" The Creative Imagination of D. H. Lawrence* (Amherst: University of Massachusetts Press, 1984), 116. Barbara Ann Schapiro adds an interesting variation to the reading of the doll-burning which fits in well with the later taking of Gertrude's life: "The doll episode . . . displays the emotional and psychic consequences of the doll's *failure* to survive. . . . Without the mother's intact externality or otherness, there are then no limits or bounds to the child's own terrifying destructiveness." *D. H. Lawrence and the Paradoxes of Psychic Life* (Albany: State University of New York Press, 1999), 33–34.

16. Kristeva, *Revolution,* 5–6.

17. In the Timaeus (80e) Plato makes the mythological connection between fire and blood. *Plato: The Collected Dialogues*, ed. Edith Hamilton and Huntington Cairns (Princeton: Princeton University Press, 1961), 1202.

18. The reference is to a painting by Burne-Jones, "King Cophetua and the Beggar Maid" (1884), dominated by a maiden's soulful eyes. See *The Pre-Raphaelites* (London: Bloomsbury, 1989), 64.

19. "Introduction to These Paintings," *Phoenix: The Posthumous Papers of D. H. Lawrence*, ed. Edward D. McDonald (1936; New York: Viking, 1964), 560.

20. See "The Dynamics of the Transference," *SE*, 12:100.

21. Seeing the unity between mother and son in positive terms, Cynthia Lewiecki-Wilson takes the mother-son relationship as a mutual "participation in the creative unconscious." Lewiecki-Wilson, *Writing Against the Family: Gender in Lawrence and Joyce*. (Carbondale: University of Illinois Press, 1994), 76. Wary of a certain sexist bias in earlier psychoanalytic Lawrence-criticism, Lewiecki-Wilson underestimates how threatening the Mother-dominated unconscious is for Paul.

22. Placing Paul as an "impressionist," James Cowan cites an interesting quotation from an earlier version of *Sons and Lovers*: "A pine-trunk's not a tree-trunk, it's a bit of fire . . . I can feel it burning just as the sun burns." *D. H. Lawrence and the Trembling Balance* (University Park: Pennsylvania State University Press, 1990), 54.

23. The question of capitalization and Lacanian categories is not simple. In La-

canian thought the Other with the big "O" refers to the unconscious, while the other with the little o refers to the mirror-reflection. Yet for the sake of general comprehensibility—recognizing that the terminology employed refers to Lacanian ideology— I capitalize the terms Mother, Father, and Other when employing the Lacanian mode generally. Hence the direct reference to individual characters, a specific mother or father, would not be capitalized.

24. Lacan organizes being into 1) the speaking subject; 2) the small object, a′ (*petit objet a′* for *autre*), (the little "o") with which it identifies, but which it cannot have; 3) the ego that models itself on the object it cannot have and is divided commensurately; and 4) the unconscious or large other, A′, (the big "O") which speaks through the subject. It is important to remember that the small object a' is first encountered in early childhood in the unified mirror-image as the Imaginary self-other that at once reifies and alienates the ego. (One both is and is not one's image in the mirror, so that, as Wilden puts it, "the moi is an Imaginary construct" [160]). Lacan's *Schéma L*, which lays out this pattern is found in *The Seminar of Jacques Lacan: Book II, The Ego in Freud's Theory and in the Technique of Psychoanalysis 1954–55,* trans. Sylvana Tomaselli (New York: Norton, 1991), 243.

25. T. H. Adamowski, "Sexuality and Orality in Lawrence," *Mosaic* 13,2 (1980): 87.

26. Lacan and Kristeva enrich but do not alter the fundamentally oedipal dynamic in *Sons and Lovers*. Traditional psychoanalytic readings of *Sons and Lovers* begin with Alfred Booth Kuttner, "A Freudian Appreciation," *The Psychoanalytic Review*, 3 (1916): 293–317, and include the important study by Daniel A. Weiss, *Oedipus in Nottingham: D. H. Lawrence* (Seattle: University of Washington Press, 1962). For a discussion of Frieda's transmission of Freud to Lawrence (via the revisionary ideas of the renegade analyst Otto Gross), see Worthen, pp. 443–44. Recent psychoanalytical studies of Lawrence change emphasis together with the revised concerns of psychoanalysis itself. Judith Ruderman's *D. H. Lawrence and the Devouring Mother* (Durham, NC: Duke University Press, 1984); Margaret Storch's *Sons and Adversaries: Women in William Blake and D. H. Lawrence* (Knoxville: University of Tennessee Press, 1990), together with the studies by Daniel Dervin and Jeffrey Berman approach Lawrence through object-relations theory with an emphasis on preoedipal and narcissistic issues. In her recent study, Barbara Ann Schapiro reads Lawrence in the perspective of the relational approach to psychoanalysis (both the analyst and the patient are subjects so the analysis proceeds in the space between two subjectivities) as worked out by theorists like Stephen Mitchell and Jessica Benjamin. Sandra Gilbert analyzes the Jungian-Lawrentian "Great Mother" in a way that goes beyond Freudian analysis and into sexual politics. See "Potent Griselda: 'The Ladybird' and the Great Mother," in Peter Balbert and Phillip L. Marcus, editors. *D. H. Lawrence: A Centenary Consideration* (Ithaca: Cornell University Press, 1985), 130–61.

27. For what remains the most profound treatment of a now-familiar theme, see Freud's discussion of the double in "The Uncanny" (*SE*, 17:234–45).

28. The process recalls Fredric Jameson's discussion of the resolution of romance, the point where the enemy, "hitherto projecting that insolence which marks a fundamental refusal of recognition," suddenly is enabled to say his name. The name recognition, which combines recognition of the other with self-recognition, allows the other to recognize the formerly disdainful self so the enemy knight loses his "sinister unfamiliarity" (*The Political Unconscious: Narrative as a Socially Symbolic Act* (Ithaca: Cornell University Press, 1981), 119.

29. Jack Stewart describes Lawrence's language at the end of *Sons and Lovers*

as "expressionist, with staccato sentence-forms, broken syntax, poetic parallelisms, and monumental abstractions." *The Vital Art of D. H. Lawrence* (Carbondale: Southern Illinois University Press, 1999), 49. Stewart's listing of stylistic characteristics helps us approach a closure that still remains open, all its vital elements exploding, trying to escape the spatial surround.

Bibliography

Abraham, Nicolas. "Notes on the Phantom: A Complement to Freud's Metapsychology." *Critical Inquiry* 13, 2 (Winter 1987): 287–92.

Adamowski, T. H. "Intimacy at a Distance: Sexuality and Orality in Lawrence." *Mosaic* 13, 2 (1980): 71–89.

Armstrong, Nancy. *Desire and Domestic Fiction: A Political History of the Novel.* New York: Oxford University Press, 1987.

Auerbach, Nina. *Romantic Imprisonment: Women and Other Glorified Outcasts* New York: Columbia University Press, 1986.

Bachelard, Gaston. *The Psychoanalysis of Fire.* Translated by Alan C. M. Ross. London: Routledge, 1964.

Bal, Mieke. "Myth à la lettre: Freud, Mann, Genesis and Rembrandt, and the Story of the Son." In *Discourse in Psychoanalysis and Literature*, edited by Shlomith Rimmon-Kenan. London: Methuen, 1987.

Balbert, Peter, and Phillip L. Marcus, eds. *D. H. Lawrence: A Centenary Consideration.* Ithaca: Cornell University Press, 1985.

Barker, Juliet. *The Brontës.* London: Weidenfeld, 1994.

Bate, Walter Jackson. *John Keats.* London: Oxford University Press, 1967.

———. *Negative Capability. The Intuitive Approach to Keats.* 1939; New York: AMS, 1976.

Beer, Gillian. *The Romance.* London: Methuen, 1970.

Behrendt, Stephen C., ed. *Approaches to Teaching Shelley's Frankenstein.* New York: MLA, 1990.

Bellis, Peter J. "In the Window-Seat: Vision and Power in *Jane Eyre.*" *ELH* 54 (1987): 639–52.

Ben-Ephraim, Gavriel. "The Achievement of Balance in *Lady Chatterley's Lover.*" In *D. H. Lawrence's "Lady": A New Look at "Lady Chatterley's Lover,"* edited by Michael Squires and Dennis Jackson, 136–53. Athens: University of Georgia Press, 1985.

———. "The Anxiety of History: Kafka's Allegory of the Oedipal Scapegoat." *Journal of the Kakfa Society of America* 16, 2 (June 1992): 4–19.

———. *The Moon's Dominion: Narrative Dichotomy and Female Dominance in Lawrence's Earlier Novels.* Rutherford, NJ: Fairleigh Dickinson University Press, 1981.

———. "Woman as Fatal Other: Revisionary Romanticism in Shelley, Rossetti, and Lawrence." *Études Lawrenciennes* 20 (1999): 59–88.

Benjamin, Walter. *Illuminations.* Edited by Hannah Arendt. Translated by Harry Zohn. New York: Schocken, 1969.

Berg, Maggie. *Wuthering Heights: The Writing in the Margin*. New York: Twayne, 1996.

Berman, Jeffrey. *Narcissism and the Novel*. New York: New York University Press, 1990.

Bernheimer, Charles and Claire Kahane, eds. *In Dora's Case: Freud-Hysteria-Feminism*. New York: Columbia University Press, 1985.

Bersani, Leo. *The Freudian Body: Psychoanalysis and Art*. New York: Columbia University Press, 1986.

———. *A Future for Astyanax: Character and Desire in Literature*. Boston: Little, Brown, 1976.

Bettelheim, Bruno. *The Uses of Enchantment: The Meaning and Importance of Fairy Tales*. New York: Vintage, 1977.

Bloom, Harold. *The Anxiety of Influence: A Theory of Poetry*. London: Oxford University Press, 1973.

———."Freud's Concepts of Defense and the Poetic Will." In *The Literary Freud: Mechanisms of Defense and the Poetic Will*, edited by Joseph H. Smith, 1–28. New Haven: Yale University Press, 1980.

———. "Freud and the Poetic Sublime: A Catastrophe Theory of Creativity," *Antaeus* no. 30/31 (Spring 1978): 355–77.

———. *The Ringers in the Tower: Studies in Romantic Tradition*. Chicago: University of Chicago Press, 1971.

———, ed. *Romanticism and Consciousness: Essays in Criticism*. New York: Norton, 1970.

Boothby, Richard. *Death and Desire: Psychoanalytic Theory in Lacan's Return to Freud*. New York: Routledge, 1991.

Borch-Jacobsen, Mikkel. *The Freudian Subject*. Translated by Catherine Porter. Stanford, CA: Stanford University Press, 1988.

———. *Lacan the Absolute Master*. Translated by Douglas Bick. Stanford, CA: Stanford University Press, 1991.

Bowie, Malcolm. *Lacan*. Cambridge: Harvard University Press, 1991.

Brontë, Charlotte. *Jane Eyre*. 2nd ed. Edited by Richard J. Dunn. New York: Norton, 1987.

Brontë, Emily. *Wuthering Heights*. 3rd ed. Edited by William Sale and Richard J. Dunn. New York: Norton, 1990.

Brooks, Peter. *Reading for the Plot: Design and Intention in Narrative*. New York: Random House, 1984.

Buckley, Jerome. *Season of Youth: The Bildungsroman from Dickens to Golding*. Cambridge: Harvard University Press, 1974.

Carmichael, Virginia. "In Search of Bein: Nom/Nom du Pere in *David Copperfield*." *ELH* 54, 3 (1987): 653–67.

Cecil, David. *Early Victorian Novelists: Essays in Revaluation*. London: Constable, 1934.

Chitham, Edward. *A Life of Emily Brontë*. Oxford: Blackwell, 1987.

Chodorow, Nancy. *The Reproduction of Mothering: Psychoanalysis and the Sociology of Gender*. Berkeley: University of California Press, 1978.

Clarke, L. D. *The Minoan Distance: The Symbolism of Travel in D. H. Lawrence*. Tucson: University of Arizona Press, 1980.

Clayton, Jay. *Romantic Vision and the Novel*. Cambridge: Cambridge University Press, 1987.

Cowan, James. *D. H. Lawrence and the Trembling Balance*. State College: Pennsylvania State University Press, 1990.

Cowart, David. "Oedipal Dynamics in *Jane Eyre*." *Literature and Psychology* 31, 1 (1981): 33–38.

Crook, Nora. "In Defence of the 1831 *Frankenstein*." In *Mary Shelley's Fictions: From Frankenstein to Falkner*, edited by Michael Eberle-Sinatra. New York: St. Martin's, 2000.

Daleski, H. M. *The Divided Heroine: A Recurrent Pattern in Six English Novels*. New York: Holmes & Meier, 1984.

Davies, Stevie. *Emily Brontë: The Artist as a Free Woman*. Manchester: Carcanet, 1983.

Derrida, Jacques. *The Post Card: From Socrates to Freud and Beyond*. Translated with an introduction by Alan Bass. Chicago: University of Chicago Press, 1987.

Dervin, Daniel. *A "Strange Sapience" The Creative Imagination of D. H. Lawrence*. Amherst: University of Massachusetts Press, 1984.

Dobyns, Anne. *Two Voices of Romance: Studies in Dialogue and Character*. Newark: University of Delaware Presss, 1989. 70–88.

Dunn, Jane. *Moon In Eclipse: A Life of Mary Shelley*. New York: St. Martin's, 1978.

Eagleton, Terry. *Myths of Power: A Marxist's Study of the Brontës*. London: Macmillan, 1975.

Edwards, Mike. *Charlotte Brontë: The Novels*. New York: St. Martin's, 1999.

Engell, James. *The Creative Imagination: Enlightenment to Romanticism*. Cambridge: Harvard University Press, 1981.

Erlich, Victor. *Russian Formalism: History-Doctrine*. 3rd ed. The Hague: Mouton, 1969.

Feldstein, Richard, and Judith Roof, eds. *Feminism and Psychoanalysis*. Ithaca: Cornell University Press, 1989.

Felman, Shoshana. "To Open the Question." *In Literature and Psychoanalysis: The Question of Reading: Otherwise. Yale French Studies* 55/56 (1977): 5–10.

———. *Jacques Lacan and the Adventure of Insight*. Cambridge: Harvard University Press, 1987.

———. *Writing and Madness (Literature/Philosophy/Psychoanalysis)*. Translated by Martha Noel Evans. Ithaca: Cornell University Press, 1985.

Fine, Ronald E. "Lockwood's Dreams and the Key of *Wuthering Heights*." *Nineteenth-Century Fiction* 24 (1969): 16–30.

Freud, S. *Analysis Terminable and Interminable*. In *The Standard Edition of the Complete Psychological Works of Sigmund Freud*. Translated and edited by James Strachey, et al. 24 vols. London: Hogarth Press, 1953–74. 23:209–54. (*Standard Edition* is cited as *SE* in the text).

———. "Anxiety and Instinctual Life." *SE*, 22:81–111.

———. *Beyond the Pleasure Principle*. *SE*, 18:3–66.

———. "A Child is Being Beaten." *SE*, 17:177–204.

———. "Creative Writers and Day-Dreaming." *SE*, 9:142–53.

———. *Civilization and Its Discontents*. *SE*, 21:59–148.

———. "The Dynamics of Transference." *SE*, 12:97–108.

———. "The Dissolution of the Oedipus Complex." *SE*, 19:173–82.

———. *The Ego and the Id. SE*, 19:3–86.

———. "The Family Romance." *SE*, 9:235–44.

———. "Instincts and Their Vicissitudes." *SE*, 14:111–40.

———. *Jenseits des Lustprinzips. Gesammelte Werke*. London: Imago, 1940. 13:3–69.

———. *The Interpretation of Dreams. SE*, vols. 4–5.

———. "Negation." *SE*, 19:235–39.

———. "Observations on Transference-Love." *SE*, 12:157–71.

———. "On Narcissm." *SE*, 14:69–102.

———. *The Origins of Psychoanalysis: Letters to Wilhelm Fleiss*. Translated by Eric Mosbacher and James Strachey. Introduction by Steven Marcus. New York: Basic Books, 1977.

———. "Psycho-Analytic Notes On An Autobiographical Account of a Case of Paranoia (Dementia Paranoides)." *SE*, 12:3–84.

———. "The Question of a *Weltanschauung*." *SE*, 22:158–82.

———. "Remembering, Repeating and Working-Through." *SE*, 12:145–56.

———. *A Seventeenth Century Demonological Neurosis. SE*, 19:73–107.

———. "Some Early Unpublished Letters of Freud." *International Journal of Psycho-Analysis* 50 (1969): 419–27.

———. "The Theme of the Three Caskets." *SE*, 12:289–302.

———. *Totem and Taboo*. SE, 13:1–164.

———. *The "Uncanny." SE*, 17:219–56.

Frye, Northrop. *Anatomy of Criticism: Four Essays*. New York: Atheneum, 1968.

———. *The Secular Scripture: A Study of the Structure of Romance*. Cambridge: Harvard University Press, 1976.

Galef, David. "Keeping One's Distance: Doubling and Irony *in Wuthering Heights." Studies in the Novel* 25, 3 (1992): 242–49.

Garner, Shirley Nelson, et al. eds. *The (M)other Tongue: Essays in Feminist Psychoanalytic Interpretation*. Ithaca: Cornell University Press, 1985.

Gay, Peter. *Freud: A Life for Our Time*. New York: Norton, 1988.

Gerin, Winifred. *Charlotte Brontë: The Evolution of Genius*. Oxford: Oxford University Press, 1969.

———. *Emily Brontë: A Biography*. Oxford: Oxford University Press, 1971.

Gilbert, Sandra M. and Susan Gubar. *The Madwoman in the Attic: The Woman Writer and the Nineteenth-Century Literary Imagination*. New Haven: Yale University Press, 1979.

Girard, René. *Deceit, Desire, and the Novel: Self and Other in Literary Structure*. Translated by Yvonne Freccero. Baltimore: Johns Hopkins University Press, 1976.

———. *Violence and the Sacred*. Translated by Patrick Gregory. Baltimore: Johns Hopkins University Press, 1977.

Goethe, Johann. *Nature*. Edited and translated by Douglas Miller. New York: Suhrkamp, nd.

Goodheart, Eugene. *Desire and Its Discontents*. New York: Columbia University Press, 1991.

Gordon, Marci M. "Kristeva's Abject and Sublime in Brontë's *Wuthering Heights.*" *Literature and Psychology* 34, 3 (1988): 44–56.

Hafley, James. "The Villain in *Wuthering Heights.*" *Nineteenth-Century Fiction* 11 (1965): 199–215.

Hartman, Geoffrey. *Beyond Formalism: Literary Essays 1958–1970.* New Haven: Yale University Press, 1970.

———, ed. *Psychoanalysis and the Question of the Text.* Baltimore: Johns Hopkins University Press, 1978.

Heilman, Robert B. "Charlotte Brontë, Reason, and the Moon." *Nineteenth-Century Fiction* 14, 4 (March 1960): 283–302.

Hill, John Spencer, ed. *Keats: The Narrative Poems: A Casebook.* London: Macmillan, 1983.

Holbrook, David. *Wuthering Heights: A Drama of Being.* Sheffield: Sheffield Academic Press, 1997.

Homans, Margaret. *Bearing the Word: Language and Female Experience in Nineteenth-Century Women's Writing.* Chicago: University of Chicago Press, 1986.

———. "Repression and Sublimation of Nature in *Wuthering Heights.*" *PMLA* 93, 1 (1978): 9–19.

Hopkins, Brooke. "Keats' *Negative Capability* and Winnicott's Creative Play." *American Imago* 41 (Spring 1984): 85–100.

Hippolyte, Jean. "*Commentaire Parle Sur La Verneinung De Freud.*" Jacques Lacan. *Écrits.* Paris: Seuil, 1966.

Irwin, John T. *Doubling and Incest, Repetition and Revenge: A Speculative Reading of Faulkner.* Baltimore: Johns Hopkins University Press, 1985.

Jacobs, Carol. *Uncontainable Romanticism: Shelley, Brontë, Kleist.* Baltimore: Johns Hopkins University Press, 1989.

James, Henry. "Preface." *The American.* 1907; New York: Augustus M. Kelley, 1970.

Jameson, Fredric. "Magical Narratives: Romance as Genre." *New Literary History* 7, 1 (Autumn 1975): 135–63.

———. *The Political Unconscious: Narrative as a Socially Symbolic Act.* Ithaca: Cornell University Press, 1981.

Johnson, Barbara. "My Monster/My Self." *Diacritics* 12 (1982): 2–10.

Jung, C. G. *Symbols of Transformation: An Analysis to a Prelude to a Case of Schizophrenia.* Translated by R. F. C. Hull. 2nd ed. Princeton: Princeton University Press, 1967.

Kavanaugh, James H. *Emily Brontë.* Oxford: Blackwell, 1985.

Keats, John. *Complete Poems.* Edited by Jack Stillinger. Cambridge: Harvard University Press, 1978.

Kincaid, James R. "Coherent Readers, Incoherent Texts." *Critical Inquiry* 3 (1977): 781–802.

Kiely, Robert. *The Romantic Novel in England.* Cambridge: Harvard University Press, 1972.

Knoepflmacher, U. C. *Emily Brontë: Wuthering Heights.* Cambridge: Cambridge University Press, 1989.

———. *Laughter and Despair: Readings in Ten Novels of the Victorian Era.* Berkeley: University of California Press, 1971.

Kofman, Sarah. *The Enigma of Woman: Woman in Freud's Writings*. Translated by Catherine Porter. Ithaca: Cornell University Press, 1985.

Kristeva, Julia. *The Kristeva Reader*. Edited by Toril Moi. Oxford: Blackwell, 1986.

———. *Revolution in Poetic Language*. Translated by Margaret Waller. New York: Columbia University Press, 1984.

Kucich, John. *Repression in Victorian Fiction: Charlotte Brontë, George Eliot, and Charles Dickens*. Berkeley: University of California Press, 1987.

Kuttner, Alfred Booth. "*Sons and Lovers*: A Freudian Appreciation." *The Psychoanalytic Review* 3 (1916): 293–317.

LaBelle, Jenijoy. *Herself Beheld: The Literature of the Looking Glass*. Ithaca: Cornell University Press, 1988.

Lacan, Jacques. *Écrits*. Paris: Seuil, 1966.

———. *Écrits: A Selection*. Translated by Alan Sheridan. New York: Norton, 1977.

———. *The Four Fundamental Concepts of Psycho-Analysis*. Edited by Jacques-Alain Miller. Translated by Alan Sheridan. New York: Norton, 1981.

———. *The Seminar of Jacques Lacan: Book II, The Ego in Freud's Theory and in the Technique of Psychoanalysis 1954–55*. Translated by Sylvana Tomaselli. New York: Norton, 1991.

———. *Speech and Language in Psychoanalysis*. Translated with commentary by Anthony Wilden. Baltimore: Johns Hopkins University Press, 1968.

Langbauer, Laurie. *Women and Romance: The Consolations of Gender in the English Novel*. Ithaca: Cornell University Press, 1990.

Langbaum, Robert, ed. *The Victorian Age: Essays in History and in Social and Literary Criticism*. New York: Fawcett, 1967.

———. *Life and Death in Psychoanalysis*. Translated Jeffrey Mehlman. Baltimore: Johns Hopkins, 1976.

Laplanche, J., and J.-B. Pontalis. *The Language of Psycho-Analysis*. Translated by Donald Nicholson-Smith. New York: Norton, 1973.

———. "Fantasy and the Origins of Sexuality." *International Journal of Psychoanalysis* 49, 1 (1968): 1–18.

Lawrence, D. H. *Phoenix: The Posthumous Papers of D. H. Lawrence*. Edited by Edward D. McDonald. 1936; New York: Viking, 1964.

———. *Sons and Lovers*. Edited by Helen and Carl Baron. Cambridge: Cambridge University Press, 1992.

Layton, Lynn, and Barbara Ann Schapiro, eds. *Narcissism and the Text: Studies in Literature and the Psychology of Self*. New York: New York University Press, 1986.

Leavy, Stanley M. "John Keats's Psychology of the Creative Imagination." *The Psychoanalytic Quarterly* 39 (1970): 173–97.

Leitch, Vincent B. *Deconstructive Criticism: An Advanced Introduction*. New York: Columbia University Press, 1983.

Levine, George. *The Realist Imagination*. Chicago: 1981.

———, and U. C. Knoepflmacher, eds. *The Endurance of Frankenstein*. Berkeley: University of California Press, 1979.

Lewiecki-Wison,Cynthia. *Writing Against the Family: Gender in Lawrence and Joyce*. Carbondale: University of Illinois Press, 1994.

Macovski, Michael S. "*Wuthering Heights* and the Rhetoric of Interpretation." *ELH* 54 (1987): 363–84.

Mahony, Patrick J. *Freud as a Writer*. New Haven: Yale University Press, 1987.

Martin, Philip W. *Mad Women in Romantic Writing*. Sussex: Harvester, 1987.

Massey, Irving. *The Gaping Pig—Literature and Metamorphosis*. Berkeley: University of California Press, 1976.

Mathison, John D. "Nelly Dean and the Power of *Wuthering Heights*." *Nineteenth-Century Fiction* 11 (1956): 106–29.

Maynard, John. *Charlotte Brontë and Sexuality*. Cambridge: Cambridge University Press, 1987.

Mellor, Anne K. *English Romantic Irony*. Cambridge: Harvard University Press, 1980.

———. *Mary Shelley: Her Life, Her Fiction, Her Monsters*. New York: Routledge, 1989.

———, ed. *Romanticism and Feminism*. Bloomington: Indiana University Press, 1988.

Miller, J. Hillis. *The Disappearance of God: Five Nineteenth Century Writers*. Cambridge: Cambridge University Press, 1963.

———. *Fiction and Repetion: Seven English Novels*. Cambridge: Harvard University Press, 1982.

Mitchell, Judith. *The Stone and the Scorpion: The Female Subject of Desire in the Novels of Charlotte Brontë, George Eliot, and Thomas Hardy*. Westport, CT: Greenwood, 1994.

Moglen, Helene. *Charlotte Brontë: The Self Conceived*. Madison: University of Wisconsin Press, 1984.

Moser, Thomas. "Conflicting Impulses in *Wuthering Heights*." *Nineteenth-Century Fiction* 17 (1962): 1–19.

Muller, John P., and William J. Richardson. *Lacan and Language: A Reader's Guide to* Écrits. New York: International University Press, 1982.

Neumann, Ernst. *The Great Mother: An Analysis of the Archetype*. Translated by Ralph Manheim. Princeton: Princeton University Press, 1972.

Newman, Beth. "Narratives of Seduction and the Seduction of Narrative: The Frame Structure of *Frankenstein*. *ELH* 53, 1 (1986): 141–63.

———. " 'The Situation of the Looker-On': Gender, Narration, and Gaze in *Wuthering Heights*." *PMLA* 105, 5 (October 1990): 1029–41.

O'Connor, Wiliam Van, ed. *Forms of Modern Fiction*. Minneapolis: University of Minnesota Press, 1959.

Olivier, Christiane. *Jocasta's Children: The Imprint of the Mother*. Translated by George Craig. London: Routledge, 1989.

Parker, Patricia A. *Inescapable Romance: Studies in the Poetics of a Mode*. Princeton: Princeton University Press, 1979.

Payne, Michael. *Reading Theory: An Introduction to Lacan, Derrida, and Kristeva*. Oxford: Blackwell, 1993.

Plato. *Plato: The Collected Dialogues*. Edited by Edith Hamilton and Huntington Cairns. Princeton: Princeton University Press, 1961.

Poovey, Mary. "My Hideous Progeny: Mary Shelley and the Feminization of Romanticism." *PMLA* 95, 3 (1980): 332–47.

———. *The Proper Lady and the Woman Writer. Ideology as Style in the works of Mary Wollstonecraft, Mary Shelley, and Jane Austen*. Chicago: University of Chicago Press, 1984.

Pratt, Linda Ray. "'I Shall Be Your Father': Heathcliff's Narrative of Paternity." *Victorian Institute Studies* 20 (1992): 13–38.

Punter, David. *The Literature of Terror*. London: Longman's, 1980.

Quilligan, Maureen. *The Language of Allegory: Defining the Genre*. Ithaca: Cornell University Press, 1979.

Ragland-Sullivan, Ellie. *Jacques Lacan and the Philosophy of Psychoanalysis*. Urbana: University of Illinois Press, 1987.

Reisner, Steven. "Reading the Metapsychology: Classical Revisionism, Seduction, and the Self in Freudian Psychoanalysis." *Psychoanalytic Psychology* 8, 4 (1991): 439–62.

Rheingold, Joseph C. *The Mother, Anxiety, and Death: The Catastrophic Death Complex*. Boston: Little, Brown, 1967.

Ricouer, Paul. *Freud and Philosophy: An Essay on Interpretation*. New Haven: Yale University Press, 1970.

Rimmon-Kenan, Shlomit, ed. *Discourse in Psychoanalysis and Literature*. London: Methuen, 1987.

Roland, Alan, ed. *Psychoanalysis, Creativity, and Literature: A French-American Inquiry*. New York: Columbia University Press, 1978.

Rollins, Hyder Edward, ed. *The Letters of John Keats 1814–21*. 2 vols. Cambridge: Harvard University Press, 1958.

Ronell, Avital. *Dictations: On Haunted Writing*. Bloomington: Indiana University Press, 1986.

Rosen, Charles, and Henri Zerner. *Romanticism and Realism: The Mythology of Nineteenth-Century Art*. New York: Norton, 1984.

Ross, Stephen David, ed. *Art and Its Significance: An Anthology of Aesthetic Theory*. 3rd ed. Albany: State University of New York Press, 1994.

Rubinstein, Marc A. "My Accursed Origins: The Search for the Mother in *Frankenstein*." *Studies in Romanticism* 15 (1976): 165–94.

Ruderman, Judith. *D. H. Lawrence and the Devouring Mother*. Durham, NC: Duke University Press, 1984.

Rudnytsky, Peter L. *Freud and Oedipus*. New York, Columbia University Press, 1987.

———. ed. *The Persistence of Myth: Psychoanalytic and Structuralist Perspectives*. New York: Guilford, 1988.

Sacks, Peter M. *The English Elegy: Studies in the Genre from Spenser to Yeats*. Baltimore: Johns Hopkins University Press, 1985.

Sadoff, Diane. *Monsters of Affection: Dickens, Eliot, and Brontë on Fatherhood*. Baltimore: Johns Hopkins University Press, 1982.

Sandler, Joseph, ed. *On Freud's "Analysis Terminable and Interminable."* New Haven: Yale University Press, 1991.

Sartre, Jean Paul. *What Is Literature?* Cambridge: Harvard University Press, 1988.

Sarup, Madan. *Jacques Lacan*. Toronto: University of Toronto Press, 1992.

Schafer, Roy. *The Analytic Attitude*. London: Hogarth, 1983.

Schapiro, Barbara A. *The Romantic Mother: Narcissistic Patterns in Romantic Poetry*. Baltimore: Johns Hopkins University Press, 1983.

———. *D. H. Lawrence and the Paradoxes of Psychic Life*. Albany: State University of New York Press, 1999.

Schorske, Carl E. *Fin-De-Siècle Vienna: Politics and Culture*. New York: Vintage, 1981.

Shelley, Mary. *Frankenstein, or the Modern Prometheus*. Edited by M. K. Joseph. Oxford: Oxford University Press, 1980.

Sherwin, Paul. "*Frankenstein*: Creation as Catastrophe." *PMLA* 96 (1981): 881–903.

Showalter, Elaine. *A Literature of Their Own: From Charlotte Brontë to Doris Lessing*. London: Virago, 1978.

Small, Christopher. *Ariel Like A Harpy: Shelley, Mary, and Frankenstein*. London: Gollancz, 1972.

Smith, Joseph H., ed. *The Literary Freud: Mechanisms of Defense and the Poetic Will*. New Haven: Yale University Press, 1980.

———, and William Kerrigan, eds. *Taking Chances Derrida, Psychoanalysis and Literature*. Baltimore: Johns Hopkins University Press, 1984.

Spilka, Mark. "*David Copperfield* as Psychological Fiction." *Critical Quarterly* (1959): 292–301.

———. *The Love Ethic of D. H. Lawrence* (Bloomington: Indiana University Press, 1955).

Sperry, Stuart M. *Keats the Poet*. 1973; Princeton: Princeton University Press, 1994.

Sprengnether, Madelon. *The Spectral Mother: Freud, Feminism, and Psychoanalysis*. Ithaca: Cornell University Press, 1990.

Steele, Robert S. *Freud and Jung: Conflicts of Interpretation*. London: Routledge and Kegan Paul, 1982.

Stepansky, Paul E., editor. *Freud: Appraisals and Reappraisals*. 3 vols. Hillsdale, NJ: Analytic Press, 1988.

Stewart, Jack F. *The Vital Art of D. H. Lawrence: Vision and Expression*. Carbondale: Southern Illinois University Press, 1999.

———. "The Vital Art of Lawrence and Van Gogh." *D. H. Lawrence Review* 19 (1987): 123–48.

Stillinger, Jack. *The Hoodwinking of Madeline and Other Essays on Keats's Poems*. Urbana: University of Illinois Press, 1971.

Stoneman, Patsy, ed. *Emily Brontë: Wuthering Heights*. New York: Columbia University Press, 1998.

Storch, Margaret. *Sons and Adversaries: Women in William Blake and D. H. Lawrence*. Knoxville: University of Tennessee Press, 1990.

Sullivan, Paula. "Fairy Tale Elements in *Jane Eyre*." *Journal of Popular Culture* 12 (1978): 61–74.

Thomas, Ronald. *Dreams of Authority: Freud and the Fictions of the Unconscious*. Ithaca: Cornell University Press, 1990.

Trilling, Lionel. *The Liberal Imagination: Essays on Literature and Society*. New York: Doubleday, 1953.

Van Ghent, Dorothy. *The English Novel: Form & Function*. New York: Harper, 1953.

Veeder, William. *Mary Shelley & Frankenstein: The Fate of Androgyny*. Chicago: University of Chicago Press, 1986.

Vine, Steven. "The Wuther of the Other in *Wuthering Heights*." *Nineteenth Century Literature* 49,3 (December 1994): 339–59.

Waldoff, Leon. *Keats and the Silent Work of the Imagination*. Urbana: University of Illinois Press, 1985.

Wasserman, Earl. *The Finer Tone: Keats' Major Poems*. Baltimore: Johns Hopkins University Press, 1967.

Weber, Samuel. *The Legend of Freud*. Minneapolis: University of Minnesota Press, 1982.

———. *Return to Freud: Jacques Lacan's Dislocation of Psychoanalysis*. Translated by Michael Levine. Cambridge: Cambridge University Press, 1991.

Weiskel, Thomas. *The Romantic Sublime: Studies in the Structure and Psychology of Transcendence*. 1976; rpt. Baltimore: Johns Hopkins University Press, 1986.

Weiss, Daniel A. *Oedipus in Nottingham: D. H. Lawrence*. Seattle: University of Washington Press, 1962.

Wilden, Anthony, ed. *Speech and Language in Psychoanalysis: Jacques Lacan*. Translated with commentary by Anthony Wilden. Baltimore: Johns Hopkins University Press, 1968.

Williams, Anne. "Natural Supernaturalism in *Wuthering Heights*." *Studies in Philology* 82, 1 (1985): 104–27.

Williams, Linda. *Critical Desire: Psychoanalysis and the Literary Subject*. London: Arnold, 1995.

Winnicott, D. W. *Playing and Reality*. Harmondsworth: Penguin, 1980.

Wion, Philip K. "The Absent Mother in Emily Brontë's *Wuthering Heights*." *American Imago* 42, 2 (1985): 143–64.

Wolfson, Susan J. *The Questioning Presence: Wordsworth, Keats, and the Interrogative Mode in Romantic Poetry*. Ithaca: Cornell University Press, 1986.

Worthen, John. *D. H. Lawrence: The Early Years 1885–1912*. Cambridge: Cambridge University Press, 1991.

Yeazell, Ruth. "More True than Real: *Jane Eyre*'s 'Mysterious Summons.'" *Nineteenth-Century Fiction* 29 (1974–75): 127–43.

Žižek, Slavoj. *The Metastases of Enjoyment: Six Essays on Woman and Causality* (London: Verso, 1994).

Zytaruk, George J. and James T. Boulton, eds. *The Letters of D. H. Lawrence*. vol. 2. Cambridge: Cambridge University Press, 1982.

Index